CAESAR

DE BELLO GALLICO VII

CAESAR

DE BELLO GALLICO VII

Edited with Introduction,
Notes and Vocabulary by
J. L. WHITELEY

Bristol Classical Press

First published by Macmillan Education Ltd in 1956
Reprinted 1981

This edition published in 2001 by
Bristol Classical Press
an imprint of
Gerald Duckworth & Co. Ltd
61 Frith Street
London W1D 3JL
e-mail: inquiries@duckworth-publishers.co.uk
Website: www.ducknet.co.uk

A catalogue record for this book is available
from the British Library

ISBN 1-85399-632-7

CONTENTS

LIST OF MAPS AND ILLUSTRATIONS   vi

INTRODUCTION:

    (i) GAIUS JULIUS CAESAR   vii

    (ii) THE GAULS   xii

    (iii) THE CIVILIZATION OF THE GAULS   xix

    (iv) THE SEVENTH BOOK OF THE GALLIC
       WAR: A SUMMARY   xxii

    (v) NOTE ON ILLUSTRATION   xli

TEXT   1

NOTES   73

APPENDIX A   183

APPENDIX B   185

VOCABULARY   187

LIST OF MAPS AND ILLUSTRATIONS

MAP OF GAUL	viii
PLATE OF COINS	xiii
PLAN OF GERGOVIA	35
LABIENUS'S CAMPAIGN AGAINST CAMULOGENUS	44
PLAN OF ALESIA	54
ROMAN WORKS AT ALESIA	57
CAESAR'S WORK AT ALESIA – RECONSTRUCTION	59
THE ROMAN AGGER AT AVARICUM	97
GALLIC WALL	107
PLAN OF GERGOVIA	184

INTRODUCTION

(i) Gaius Julius Caesar

Every schoolboy and girl has heard of Julius Caesar, the most famous and, in many ways, the greatest of the ancient Romans ; and by the inhabitants of these islands he will always be remembered because of three things : the month of July (named after him), his invasions of Britain in 55 and 54 B.C., and one of the best-known and most popular of Shakespeare's plays, *Julius Caesar*.

Apart from his achievements as soldier and statesman, Caesar wrote two works of history which hold a permanent place in Latin literature, his account of his own campaigns in Gaul in 58–51 B.C., and his story of the Civil War which later broke out between himself and Pompey. The present book is the seventh of the Gallic commentaries. A detailed summary of its contents will be found later in the Introduction, and an attempt will now be made to describe the political events which led up to Caesar's conquests in Gaul.

In the forty years that passed between Caesar's birth in 101 or 100 B.C., and his arrival in Gaul, the

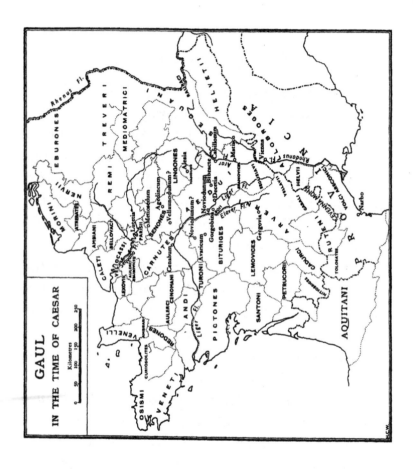

form of government by which Rome had been administered for two and a half centuries was passing through a severe crisis. Theoretically it was democratic in its working, but in practice all the power lay in the hands of the few governing families identified with the senate, whose ambition it was to retain the reins of government to the exclusion of all others. A generation before Caesar's birth, their political supremacy had been temporarily shaken by two ardent reformers, the brothers Tiberius and Gaius Gracchus, who seem to have made an honest attempt to grapple with several serious problems, such as unemployment, the disappearance of the small farmer and the relations between Rome and her allies in Italy. But when the Gracchi lost their lives in faction fights, the senatorial order soon recovered its hold on the government of Rome. In the first century B.C., however, the Senate had to meet further attacks from other reformers and, as both sides were now resorting to force, they each looked for support to the outstanding general of the day who could get bills passed with the aid of his troops. So civil war broke out, and it was characterized by cruelty and massacre on both sides.

In 80 B.C., when Caesar was about twenty, he saw Sulla, the most successful general of that time, lead his troops on behalf of the senate against his political rivals, crush all opposition with a ruthlessness typically Roman, and begin the system of ' proscriptions ' under which all those whose political opinions were regarded as dangerous to the winning side could be outlawed and killed with impunity.

The next twenty years, 80-60 B.C., were momentous in the history of the Roman Republic. Sulla's attempt to buttress the decaying power of the Senate gradually collapsed under attacks from several quarters, including Caesar, who now began to take an active part in politics and held a succession of offices, becoming quaestor in 68 B.C., aedile in 65, praetor in 62, and as propraetor, governor in 61 of Farther Spain, where he gained some minor successes over the natives of what is now Portugal.

On Caesar's return from Spain, the Senate found itself confronted with three ambitious and determined men, Caesar, Pompey and Crassus. Forming a political alliance known in Roman history as the First Triumvirate, (rule of three men), they presented the senate with demands which it was compelled to grant, in Caesar's case a provincial governorship and an opportunity to create an army of soldiers personally devoted to him, without which he realized he could do nothing. He received as his sphere the provinces of Cisalpine Gaul (the Po valley), Illyricum (the N.E. shores of the Adriatic), and

Transalpine Gaul or Gallia Narbonensis (S.E. France).

In 58 B.C. he entered this region with four legions (about 18,000 to 20,000 men), and by 51 B.C. the conquest of all Gaul was complete : he had added a new and rich province to the Roman empire.

During Caesar's absence in Gaul, events had moved rapidly in the political life of Rome. The Triumvirate continued to exist, but very precariously. At one time, in 56 B.C., it almost collapsed, but its three members held a conference, patched up their quarrels and made arrangements for the future ; among these, Caesar's tenure of office was extended for a second period of five years, and Crassus and Pompey also both obtained military commands. But after Crassus was killed fighting in the east, a second and severer crisis arose, in which the Senate, now thoroughly frightened of Caesar, whom they regarded as their principal enemy, contrived gradually to break the alliance between the two surviving triumvirs and to win Pompey over to their side. By the time Caesar had completed the subjugation of Gaul, his most extreme opponents in the Senate were openly clamouring for him to be relieved of his governorship and to return to Rome as a private citizen. Negotiations regarding Caesar's political future dragged on, but in spite of his endeavours to arrive at a compromise, civil war broke out in 49 B.C.

between Caesar and the Senate, now led by Pompey.

This war lasted, with interruptions, from 49 to 45 B.C., when at last Caesar had defeated all the supporters of the Senate and became dictator for life—in effect, sole ruler of the Roman Empire. His activity during these years was remarkable : not only did he move from one part of the Mediterranean to the other in pursuit of his foes, but he found time to administer Rome and the Roman Empire and to introduce some greatly needed reforms.

In 44 B.C., on the 15th of March, he was assassinated. Before his death, however, he had completely destroyed the discredited Roman Republic and laid the foundations of the Roman Empire.

(ii) THE GAULS

The Gauls were Celts, a race that spoke an Aryan language, i.e. a language akin to those spoken by the majority of European peoples, and originally not far removed in relationship from the Romans and other Italian peoples. They appear to have been formed as a nation in the basin of the Upper Danube, and then, after several attempts to move into Central Germany had been repulsed by the Teutonic tribes, to have entered Gaul about 700 B.C. Successive waves of invaders followed and spread into Spain and Britain, and about 400 B.C. reached the Lombardy Plain, which

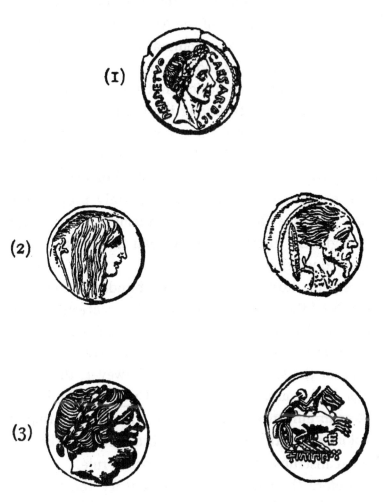

PLATE OF COINS

See pages xli-xlii of the Introduction for notes on these coins.

was called henceforth by the Romans Gallia Cisalpina—Gaul this side of the Alps. In every case the Gauls mingled as the predominating element with the earlier inhabitants of those countries.

It is important to notice that the constant influx of fresh immigrants among the Celtic population of Gaul and Cisalpine Gaul exposed Italy to invasion on the part of individual tribes who were tempted by the prospect of loot and plunder. For example, in 390 B.C. a band of Gauls entered Italy proper and, defeating the Romans and capturing Rome, almost brought the history of this Italian tribe to a premature conclusion.

Again, during the next two hundred years, the Gauls of the Lombardy Plain gave practical aid not only to Rome's enemies in Italy itself, but also to the Carthaginian invader Hannibal. By the beginning of the second century B.C., however, the Romans had completely subdued Cisalpine Gaul, and Roman influence spread rapidly with the planting of colonies and the building of military roads—the two great instruments of Roman imperial rule.

Before the end of the same century the Romans had gained a footing in Gaul proper, and had carved out for themselves enough territory to form a new province, Gallia Transalpina or Gallia Narbonensis. In making this territory a Roman province—

' Provence ' is still its name—they had decisively defeated two Celtic tribes, the Allobroges and the Arverni, and finally had concluded a treaty with the Aedui, the strongest tribe of Central Gaul. This treaty, and the open frontier to the north and north-west of their new province, were destined to give the Romans an opportunity of extending their dominion to the natural boundaries formed by the Atlantic and the Rhine when a suitable occasion offered, as it did in 58 B.C. when Caesar received Cisalpine and Narbonese Gaul as his province.

Two disturbances beyond the then Roman frontier gave Caesar a pretext for carrying Roman arms across it. These were the intended migration into Western Gaul, by way of Roman territory, on the part of the Helvetii, a warlike Celtic tribe living in that part of Switzerland enclosed by the Rhine, the Jura Mountains, the lake of Geneva and the upper Rhone, and the presence in Gaul of a German chieftain Ariovistus, who had originally been invited by the Arverni and Sequani to help them in their struggle with the Aedui, and after fulfilling his mission was outstaying his welcome, and seizing lands belonging to the Sequani. Caesar's subsequent relations with the Gauls and Germans are recounted in the seven books of the ' Gallic War ', which are here briefly summarized.

Book I (58 B.C.). Caesar began by defeating the Helvetii and forced them to return to their native region, and later, at the invitation of the Gallic chieftains, who had been greatly impressed by his vigorous action against the Helvetii, he expelled Ariovistus from Gaul. It is probable that these successes induced Caesar to aim at the total subjugation of Gaul, for he quartered his legions for the winter of 58-57 B.C. among the Sequani, thereby showing that he intended to secure the submission of Central Gaul.

Book II (57 B.C.). The Gauls were not slow to realize that they had merely exchanged Ariovistus for Caesar and in this year the Belgic tribes of N.E. Gaul, with the exception of the Remi, took the field against him. The Nervii offered the fiercest resistance and all but destroyed his army, but eventually both they and the other Belgic tribes were subdued in the course of the same campaign.

Book III (56 B.C.). This year saw an unsuccessful rebellion on the part of the Veneti, leaders of the tribes of the Atlantic or Breton coast, and the Romans marching without much opposition into Aquitania. Towards the end of the year Caesar occupied the northern sea-board between Brittany and Flanders, so that the conquest of Gaul now seemed complete.

Book IV (55 B.C.). Two German tribes, the

Usipetes and the Tencteri, entered northern Belgium with the intention of conquest and settlement. Their arrival aroused hopes of a successful rising in the Gauls of that area, ever ready to seize any opportunity of casting offthe Roman yoke. Caesar, however, after opening negotiations with the invaders, massacred them, not without exposing himself to a charge of treachery. He followed this up by bridging the Rhine in ten days, a remarkable feat, and by a reconnaissance in force on the far side of the river designed to impress and overawe the Germans. The latter half of this year was occupied by the first invasion of Britain, for which the pretext was the assistance given to the Veneti by the Britons during their revolt in the previous year. The real reason was, no doubt, the reputed wealth of the island, which was believed to yield pearls and precious metals.

BOOK V (54 B.C.). In the summer of this year Caesar invaded Britain a second time and succeeded in defeating the tribes of the south-east and marching inland as far as St. Albans, but he did not attempt a permanent occupation. The booty also was disappointingly small.

Caesar's return to Gaul in the early autumn was followed by rumours of restlessness among the Belgic tribes. Shortly after Caesar had stationed his

legions in N.E. Gaul, the Eburones, led by Indutiomarus, attacked one of the Roman camps, and per-
suading the Roman generals to evacuate it under a
guarantee of safe conduct, they treacherously am-
bushed and annihilated the marching column. Encouraged by this success, the Nervii closely besieged
another camp commanded by Q. Cicero, brother of
the famous orator. He managed to pass a message
through to Caesar, who by a forced march arrived in
time to rescue him and his troops. On the death of
Indutiomarus in action against Labienus, another of
Caesar's legati, the tribes of N.E. Gaul abandoned
their plans and the winter passed in comparatively
quiet fashion.

BOOK VI (53 B.C.). During this year there were
further outbreaks among the Gallic tribes, especially
in Belgica. The book also contains Caesar's account
of the Gauls and the Germans.

BOOK VII (52 B.C.). Caesar had now to meet the
most serious revolt of all. Until this year the tribes
of Central Gaul had remained neutral, but now they
organized a formidable rebellion, and gave the leadership to an Arvernian chieftain called Vercingetorix.
But in spite of his resolute generalship and the
national character of the rising, which was joined
even by the Aedui, who had previously been staunch
allies of the Romans, Vercingetorix was eventually

defeated and Gallic resistance was brought to an end.

Leaving the Gallic tribes largely to manage their own affairs and imposing only a nominal tribute, Caesar created conditions favourable to the rapid Romanization of Gaul. The solidity of the foundations thus laid by Caesar can be estimated from the fact that no more than three years later he was able to withdraw most of the legions stationed in Gaul at the outbreak of the Civil War between himself and Pompey.

(iii) THE CIVILIZATION OF THE GAULS

At the beginning of the first century B.C., while the Germans were still completely barbarian, the civilization of the Gauls had reached a comparatively high level. Although the vine was not yet cultivated, corn was grown intensively on a large scale. Walled towns, the strongholds of the various tribes, were springing up and were linked by roads suitable for wheeled traffic. Along these roads and the river valleys passed a considerable volume of trade, including that in tin, which was carried across the Channel from Britain to the ports of the Veneti and thence down to Massilia (Marseilles) for distribution throughout the Mediterranean. Textiles and pottery were chiefly imported, but the Gauls were highly skilled in mining and metal-working. Moreover, coinage was current in every tribe, while the art of writing was probably known to other classes besides the Druids.

The political unit of the Gauls was the tribe (*civitas*), which seems to have consisted of a number of communities united by blood or geographical proximity. Each tribe had a council of elders, and sometimes, especially among the Belgic tribes, a king. In Caesar's time, however, most of the tribes of Central Gaul had abolished monarchy and substituted an elective magistracy, with tenure of office limited to one year.

The chief divisions of the population were : (i) the Druids, a very powerful priestly caste, (ii) the nobles, and (iii) the common people, who had no political rights and for the most part stood in the same relation to their nobles as did later the serfs of England to the Norman barons. It was of course the nobles who filled the tribal councils and magistracies.

These nobles were at once the strength and the weakness of the Gallic tribes. On the one hand, they provided the flower of the Gallic armies ; on the other, surrounded by their retainers and sometimes even maintaining private armies, they intrigued so constantly for personal power that, in some of the tribes at least, they brought about a virtual anarchy. This lack of unity not only within, but also between, the tribes was a weakness which Caesar knew well how to exploit for his own advantage. So fierce a jealousy was felt in some cases between noble and noble, tribe and tribe, that they did not hesitate to call in a foreign invader, either German or Roman, to support their ambitions. It is true that there were a few signs of the development of national feeling and unity ; but the Gauls had not yet learned to combine in face of a common danger, nor had a leader arisen strong and capable enough to force union upon them. When he did arrive, in the person of Vercingetorix, he came too late.

There were other reasons, in addition to this lack of cohesion, why the Gauls failed to withstand the Romans. As soldiers they displayed ample courage and dash, but in comparison with the legionaries they were undisciplined, and were wanting in tenacity, losing heart at the first setback. They were deficient too in strategical planning and their organization of the vital matter of supply was rudimentary. In both these respects, Caesar's work was incomparably superior.

(iv) THE SEVENTH BOOK OF THE GALLIC WAR:
A SUMMARY

Preparations for Revolt

[B.C. 52]

Chs. 1-4. Whilst Caesar was in Northern Italy during the winter, he received reports of political disturbances in Rome, reports which on reaching Gaul encouraged the Gallic chieftains to make plans for a revolt against Roman rule. It was a good opportunity, they thought, before their plans were known, to prevent Caesar rejoining his army, now in winter quarters in Central Gaul. The Carnutes offered to take the initiative in the revolt, and, to lessen the risk of their being deserted by their fellow Gauls, asked for their action to be sanctioned by a most solemn oath. On the appointed day the Carnutes massacred all Roman traders at Cenabum (Orléans) and the report of this spread rapidly throughout all Gaul. Vercingetorix, an Arvernian, supported the rising by collecting his own dependents and clients and seizing power in his own tribe. He also obtained considerable help from many important tribes. On being appointed their commander, he vigorously organized his military forces and supplies, and established a very strict discipline among the troops under him.

[*February*]

Chs. 5-9. After taking these measures, Vercingetorix sent Lucterius with forces against the Rúteni to
protect his rear and distract Caesar's attention, while
he himself invaded the territory of the Bituriges,
who, though dependents of the Aedui, failed to
obtain assistance from them and so joined with the
Arverni. On his arrival in Transalpine Gaul, Caesar
was faced with the difficult problem of rejoining his
troops who were in their winter quarters in Central
Gaul. He decided, therefore, first that vigorous
counter-action should be taken against Lucterius who
was threatening to over-run the Roman province. He,
therefore, marched to Narbo, posted garrisons at
strategic points and ordered some of his troops with
the supplementary levy he had brought with him
from Northern Italy to assemble on the borders of
the Arverni. When these moves had succeeded in
their object, Caesar with his usual speed of action
crossed the Cevennes in spite of the snow to devas-
tate Arvernian territory, thus compelling Vercingetorix to return from his campaign among the
Bituriges to protect his own tribe. In this way
Caesar was able first to reach Vienna and by forced
marches to make his way through the country of the
Aedui to the Lingones to the winter quarters of two
of his legions. He ordered the rest of the legions to

concentrate in the neighbourhood of Agedincum. Vercingetorix replied by assaulting Gorgobina in the country of the Boii, a town friendly to Caesar.

Chs. 10-16. *Caesar's Dilemma.* If he remained inactive in face of this new threat, he would probably lose all Gaul, as it would seem that he could not protect his allies ; if on the other hand, he marched his legions out of their winter quarters, he might have serious difficulty with his corn supplies. Realizing that he must defend the Boii, he set off to relieve the town of Gorgobina, capturing Vellaunodunum and storming Cenabum on his way. Cenabum was plundered and sacked as a punishment for the murder of the Roman merchants. Noviodunum, a stronghold of the Bituriges, was also captured en route. Then Caesar prepared to besiege Avaricum, the most important town of the Bituriges, for success there would, he felt, be a great blow to Gallic morale.

After these setbacks, Vercingetorix suggested to his followers that they must apply guerilla tactics, especially with their cavalry, and destroy their hamlets and homesteads to prevent the Romans getting supplies. A scorched earth policy was inevitable, if they wished to avoid the loss of their liberty and the enslavement of their wives and children. His plan was approved and many towns were fired not only amongst the Bituriges but also amongst other tribes. Against the advice of Vercingetorix, however, the Gallic council decided to defend Avaricum because of its strong natural defences.

[March-April]

Chs. 17-21. *The siege of Avaricum.* Caesar completed his preparations to storm Avaricum on its one undefended side where there was a narrow gap. Although his troops suffered severe distress through lack of grain, no suggestion was made that they should relinquish the siege. On hearing that Vercingetorix had moved his camp nearer to Avaricum, Caesar marched off to meet him but found the Gauls in such a strong position surrounded by marshes that he refused his troops' demand that they should engage the enemy. On his return, Vercingetorix had to meet accusations of treachery from his impatient followers. In his reply, Vercingetorix emphasized that he had moved his base through lack of forage, that he had hoped to engage the Romans on ground unfavourable to them and that he had appointed no deputy through fear that he might engage with the enemy at an unfavourable time. He brought forward evidence that the Romans were suffering severe strain through shortage of supplies and that in three days they would withdraw. His words were received with tremendous enthusiasm and they all gave him their fullest confidence. It was decided that 10,000 men should be sent to reinforce Avaricum in order that the prestige of the victory they felt sure was theirs should not rest with the Bituriges alone.

Chs. 22-28. *The siege of Avaricum (continued).* The Gauls sought to impede the Roman siege works by many ingenious contrivances which included nooses, windlasses, mines, and the addition of scaffolding to their own towers. The walls of the town too were strongly made of wooden timbers banked up with earth and stones. (The structure is described in considerable detail in Chapter 23). None the less, in spite of enemy resistance and bad weather, Caesar's troops in just over three weeks completed the ramp 330 ft. broad and 80 ft. high. Just before its completion, the enemy made a last desperate sortie from two gates in an effort to set fire to the towers and the ramp. Effective counter measures were taken by Caesar's troops as there were always two legions on the alert. A desperate battle ensued, in which a remarkable feat of bravery on the part of the enemy was described by Caesar. Defeated again, the Gauls decided to try to escape from the doomed town but their plan was hindered by the hysteria of their womenfolk who besought them not to abandon them to the enemy. The next day during a heavy shower, Caesar launched storming parties on the town and succeeded in mounting the walls, but instead of descending into the town itself to join battle, his men occupied the whole wall and so demoralized the defenders that, in fear of being trapped, they rushed for the farthest parts of the town. Many were cut down at the gates and those who got out were destroyed by the cavalry. Nobody was spared, not even the aged, women or children and all but 800 of the 40,000 inhabitants were slaughtered. The refugees were intercepted by Vercingetorix and distributed amongst their friends in his camp.

Chs. 29-31. At a conference the next day Vercingetorix encouraged the desperate Gauls not to lose heart and pointed out that the loss of Avaricum was due mainly to their not following his advice. By promising to win over those Gallic tribes which had not yet joined them and to follow a single policy, he won the confidence of his compatriots and established discipline amongst them. He so convinced them that for the first time, as Caesar noticed, they began to fortify their camp in the Roman fashion. By vigorous action Vercingetorix maintained morale amongst the tribal contingents, tried to win over the remaining tribes, armed and re-equipped the refugees from Avaricum and requisitioned more troops from the tribes themselves, including large numbers of archers. He was joined by Teutomatus, King of the Nitiobriges, and large numbers of his cavalry.

Chs. 32-36. After a few days' stay at Avaricum to allow his army to recuperate, Caesar received a deputation from Aeduan chieftains who reported that two magistrates, Convictolitavis and Cotus, were claiming to be the Chief Magistrate and that their senate and tribe were divided on this issue and likely to settle it by civil war. Although Caesar did not wish to give up his plan either to bring the enemy to battle or to reduce them by blockade, he felt that he could not afford to run the risk of losing the support of the most powerful state in Gaul. He therefore invited the senate to meet him in their territory at Decetia where he declared in favour of Convictolitavis who had been elected Chief Magistrate constitutionally. He asked the Aedui to give him their support in the coming campaign and to send him all their cavalry and 10,000 infantry in order that he might protect his supply route. He then gave four legions to Labienus to march into the territory of the Senones and Parisii, while he took six along the river Allier in the direction of Gergovia, the most important stronghold of the Arverni. His army was followed on the opposite bank by the troops of Vercingetorix who destroyed all the bridges. Caesar crossed the river by a well judged stratagem to get to the same side as Vercingetorix and reached in five days the district of Gergovia at which Vercingetorix had concentrated his forces. Unable to storm the town, he made preparations for a blockade. The troops of Vercingetorix were established on the heights to the South West of the town whilst Caesar established his camp to the North East of Orcet. Caesar secured a position to the South of the town, La Roche Blanche, and joined it to his main base by a double ditch.

Chs. 37-43. Meanwhile, Convictolitavis, bribed by the Arverni, discussed revolt with Litaviccus on the plea that, should the tribes of the Aedui join Vercingetorix, the Romans could be dislodged from Gaul. They decided that Litaviccus should command the 10,000 soldiers that the Aedui had promised to Caesar. About thirty miles from Gergovia, Litaviccus persuaded his men in a passionate speech

which accused Caesar of having treacherously
butchered the Aeduan cavalry and their Commanders Eporedorix and Viridomarus, to avenge
their deaths by killing the Roman citizens in their
column and by rousing the rest of the Aedui to rise
in rebellion against the power of Rome. These plans
were reported by Eporedorix to Caesar who, realising
the seriousness of the situation, marched four legions
and all his cavalry, met the Aeduan troops in time to
quell the revolt, and after giving his men three
hours' rest, began the return march the same night
to Gergovia. On news from Fabius, whom he had
left in charge at Gergovia with two legions, that they
had been hard-pressed by attacks in full force by
the enemy, Caesar called for tremendous efforts
from his troops and reached camp before dawn.
The Aedui at home, unaware that their army had
surrendered to Caesar, rebelled and killed and
plundered Romans in their territory, aided and
abetted by Convictolitavis, who hoped to commit his
people too deeply for them to return to their loyalty
to Rome. Envoys were sent by the Aedui, however,
when they knew the truth, to offer apologies and
explanations, to disclaim responsibility for the riots
and to offer compensation. Secretly they continued
to plot rebellion. Caesar who was undeceived, and
had no choice but to receive them politely, found

himself in a cleft stick. How was he to retire from
Gergovia without loss of face and join up with
Labienus—a move that was essential—, while there
was so much restlessness among the Gauls and the
loyalty of the Aedui was so uncertain?

[*May to the end of June*]

Chs. 44-53. *The operations around Gergovia.* One
day Caesar noticed that Vercingetorix had withdrawn
his troops from the defences in front of the town.
Later on he learned that the Gallic chieftain, alarmed
lest the Romans seized the saddle which linked
Gergovia with the heights of Risolles, had decided
to avoid the danger of being cut off from his water
supplies by fortifying the western approach to
Risolles—the only place where an attack was possible. Thereupon Caesar devised the following
stratagem and attempted to capture the town by a
coup-de-main. Sending the cavalry and one legion
from the larger camp westwards as if he intended to
attack the Gallic entrenchments at Risolles, he also
diverted attention from his main attack from the east
by sending small parties of men from the larger
camps to the smaller. Then he launched his attack
from the east, in the hope that if the legions acted
decisively and speedily, he would be able to sweep

through the town and roll up the Gallic levies at Risolles.[1]

The Roman attack was so successful that they not only captured three Gallic camps and surprised the half-clad Teutomatus who was having a nap, but became so elated as not to hear, so they claimed, the order to retreat which Caesar gave as soon as he realized that his surprise attack must fail. For, hearing the din, the Gauls had returned from Risolles and began to press the legionaries hard. Caesar, now somewhat anxious, ordered T. Sextius with cohorts of the 13th legion to leave the smaller camp and cover the legionaries on their left flank while he moved his 10th nearer the walls in support. The gallant conduct of a centurion of the 8th legion won particular mention in Caesar's dispatches. Confusion was caused when the Romans saw troops moving up the hill on their right. Actually they were Aeduans with right shoulder bared, sent by Caesar to make a secondary attack on the right but suspected as enemy troops by the hard pressed legionaries.

The Gauls followed hard on the withdrawing Romans, but were halted on their right by Sextius and on their left by the veterans of the 10th legion

---

[1] See Appendix A for a different theory as to Caesar's plan and its execution.

which changed its position to suit the conditions of the fighting. Thus aided, the Roman troops were able to reform on level ground after losing 46 centurions and 700 men—a serious reverse.

Next day Caesar paraded his men and rebuked them for not obeying his orders, not however without paying tribute to their spirit and valour. After successful cavalry skirmishes and two challenges to Vercingetorix to join battle, Caesar felt he had done enough to restore morale and abandoned the blockade of Gergovia. Without being pursued by the enemy, he repaired the bridges over the Allier and got his army across.

Chs. 54-62. *Caesar's critical position and the operation of Labienus against Lutetia.* After the desertion of Litaviccus, Caesar met Viridomarus and Eporedorix and appealed to them to maintain the loyalty of their tribe. The Aeduan chieftains, however, were by now so disaffected that on their arrival at Noviodunum, an important base and supply depot of Caesar, they threw in their lot with the rebels, plundered his baggage, stores and treasure, and burned the town to the ground, massacring the garrison and Italian traders. Efforts were then made to prevent Caesar crossing the Loire and to drive him back into the Province by cutting him off from his supplies. Caesar's dilemma is discussed in Ch. 56. To join Labienus, he had to cross the river which he reached a few miles south of Nevers by an extraordinary feat of forced marches and, finding a ford and breaking the force of the current by a skilful use of his cavalry, he got his infantry to wade across.

Leaving his base of Agedincum, Labienus marched upon Lutetia to control the important tribes of the Senones and the Carnutes. Finding his way barred by the Gallic forces under their aged but able chieftain Camulogenus who was strongly encamped behind a wide marsh, Labienus retraced his steps, captured Metiosedum (Melun), crossed the Seine, and moved up stream towards Lutetia. His camp opposite the island on which Lutetia stood, was faced across the river by the enemy on the southern bank. Grim news about Caesar's plight after his withdrawal from Gergovia and the revolt of the Bellovaci made Labienus decide to return to his base at Agedincum. But how to recross the river?

By making a feint of crossing north of his position while his main forces marched to a point four miles down stream, Labienus extricated himself from his position, crossed the river, and engaged and defeated the enemy. He was thus able to return to his base and baggage and to join Caesar with his forces intact two days later.

[*End of July*]

Chs. 63-68. The Aedui who had by now joined the rebellion were resentful at finding Vercingetorix unanimously elected commander-in-chief at the Gallic council at Bibracte. In continuance of his policy of harassing the Romans and cutting them off from supplies, Vercingetorix first called upon his fellow countrymen to burn their crops and home-steads and then sent detachments to cut Caesar off from his communications with the Province and to win over the Allobroges. The latter, however, maintained the frontier lines with a string of outposts, and Lucius Caesar, cousin of Julius, had ready to oppose the enemy attack about 10,000 men (22 cohorts). Realizing the enemy's superiority in cavalry, Caesar got an efficient force of troopers from German tribes across the Rhine and gave them Gallic mounts to replace the inferior German ones. Meanwhile Vercingetorix, leaving Bibracte with 80,000 infantry and strong cavalry, continued to dog Caesar and took up a position on a stream, the Suzon (not far north of Dijon), Caesar being about ten miles away and unsuspecting that he was so near. Vercingetorix, abandoning his previous policy, now launched a cavalry attack on the Roman columns, hampered by its large baggage—an attack which in its failure enabled Caesar not only to inflict

a sharp reverse on the enemy but also to deal a
heavy blow to Gallic morale. Despondently Vercingetorix was compelled to fall back on the fortress
of Alesia, hotly pursued by Caesar.

[*Mid-August to the end of September*]

Chs. 69-90. *The Siege of Alesia.* The story of the
investment and siege of Alesia, one of the greatest
operations and most famous exploits in military
history, begins with a description of the town, situated on an oval plateau, 500 ft. high, a mile in
length and one half-mile wide, and connected with
the neighbouring hills with a saddle on the eastern
slope. Beneath the western slope there was an
open plain—now that of Les Laumes—three miles
in length. This natural fortress, now occupied by a
Gallic force 80,000 strong, Caesar decided to invest—
to storm it was out of the question—with a force of
about 45,000 men. Caesar placed his infantry camp
in the hills[1] north, south and east of the town and his
cavalry in the plain in the west, all protected by a
ring of twenty-three forts, placed at intervals of about
a third of a mile. As soon as Caesar began his lines,
Vercingetorix launched a cavalry attack on the plain
in the west and a fierce action developed in which
Caesar's German units, supported by the legions

[1] Mt. Réa, Flavigny, Bussy.

drawn up outside the camp, inflicted heavy losses on the enemy. An advance by the Roman legions caused panic amongst the Gauls encamped outside the town.

Vercingetorix, not willing to risk an open engagement with the legions, sent away his cavalry through the uncompleted Roman lines to raise a relief force. He then had 80,000 men in Alesia and provisions for about thirty days, if strictly rationed.

Caesar's lines of contravallation and circumvallation were as follows : first on the western side in the plain—his most vulnerable spot—a trench 20 ft. wide with perpendicular sides to serve as a screen behind which at a distance of 400 yds. the main works could be dug. These were : two parallel trenches 15 ft. wide, 8 ft. deep (the outer only across the plain) and the inner[1] one filled where possible with water from the Ozerain and the Rabutin—then a rampart with palisade 12 ft. high with fence of wattle work and projecting branches. Wooden towers were also erected at intervals of 80 ft. To prevent sudden sallies on the part of the enemy Caesar also constructed these subsidiary defences in front of his main lines : five rows of slit trenches 5 ft. deep in which strong boughs were sunk so that the branches protruded above ground and could be

[1] I.e. the one nearer the town.

interlaced; in front, small conical pits 3 ft. deep and 3 ft. apart arranged in quincunx with sharp pointed logs embedded in them and in front again, concealed beneath the turf, barbed spikes in pieces of wood.[1]

To repel the relieving forces, Caesar constructed a second line of exterior defence works on a similar plan to cover a circuit of twelve miles.

The tribes of central and northern Gaul organized a great army of relief and gave the command to Commius of the Atrebates, Viridomarus and Eporedorix of the Aedui and Vercassivellaunus of the Arverni. Meanwhile in Alesia, the besieged were reduced to such straits through lack of food that Critognatus suggested that the garrison should maintain their strength by feeding on the bodies of aged non-combatants, a suggestion which was rejected. It was resolved, however, to send away the women and children but they were refused passage by the Romans. At last after seven weeks the relieving forces arrived. The garrison of Alesia made ready to support them by moving down into the plain, to the first Roman trench, furnished with the necessary equipment to break through the Roman lines. A stubborn engagement for most of the day between Caesar's German cavalry and the Gallic troopers

[1] See Appendix B for a different siting of the defence lines.

ended in the victory of the former and the disconsolate retirement of the garrison. After one day's lull there followed a second attack launched at midnight by the relieving force and a sortie by the garrison. Fierce fighting continued until dawn but the Roman soldiers in spite of many casualties stood firm, doing much good work with their heavy artillery.

Somewhat discouraged by the failure of these two attacks, the Gauls now decided on a final all out effort. After a thorough reconnaissance of the Roman lines which surrounded Alesia, they decided that there was a chance of a break through on the north-west side of the town at Mont Réa, a hill which had not been included by the Romans in their lines of circumvallation. They therefore assembled 60,000 picked men, and after making a circuit of about ten or twelve miles around the northern hills to avoid being seen, they mustered in a hollow ravine at the north-eastern slope of Mont Réa preparatory to an attack at noon under the command of Vercassivellaunus. Their attack upon the Roman camp near by, held by two legions, was timed to coincide with an attack by their cavalry against the Roman defences in the plain and movements on the part of the remaining relief forces the purpose of which was to pin down the Roman defenders. At the same time the Gallic garrison descended the hill and advanced towards

the Roman defence works on the plain, equipped
with scaling ladders, grappling hooks and other
implements. A desperate battle followed with
Caesar directing the fighting and sending reserves to
every point where he saw his men hard pressed.
When the Gallic attack on the circumvallation in the
plain was held, Caesar realized that in the fierce
fighting at the north-west camp the Roman lines
might be pierced at the weak point below Mont Réa,
where the Roman troops had to face heavy missile
fire directed from higher ground by the enemy's
shock troops. A mounted messenger was sent to
Caesar for help. Immediately he ordered Labienus
with six cohorts to move from the Bussy Hill camp
in support and to counter attack against the enemy's
right flank. In his turn, Vercingetorix abandoning
his attempt to break through the Roman lines in the
plain, crossed the Ozerain and made a fresh attack
on the slighter defences of the Roman lines at the
foot of Flavigny hill in the hope of pinning down
Roman troops and preventing Caesar sending
reserves for the fight against Vercassivellaunus. In
reply Caesar sent young Decimus Brutus with six
cohorts to support these threatened defenders. Gaius
Fabius also followed with seven more cohorts. Only
the throwing in of more reserves enabled Caesar to
restore his lines here.

Meanwhile, the situation at Mont Réa became critical. Caesar called out four cohorts from the nearest fort, ordered his cavalry to follow him and sent a trooper with orders that some of the cavalry squadrons from the north camp at Grésigny should fall on the enemy's flank or rear. Labienus too collected every man he could from nearby forts, so that as much as two fifths of the Roman army must have been concentrated at this point. A desperate battle followed with the Romans heartened and cheered by Caesar's personal appearance. The sight of the Roman cavalry on the heights above and a vigorous charge by the legionaries and their reserves finally broke the Gallic assault. Panic seized the Gauls as they attempted to flee from the battle field and the relieving army soon melted away with the exhausted legionaries unable to follow up their victory and exterminate the enemy. Seeing the hopelessness of his position, Vercingetorix sent envoys to Caesar in submission and obeyed the Roman General's command for an unconditional surrender.

(v) NOTE ON ILLUSTRATION

Plate of Coins, p. xiii.

No. 1. Roman silver coin (denarius) issued by L. Aemilius Bucca in 44 B.C. In the British Museum. Julius Caesar, who is here described as CAESAR

DICT(ator) PERPETVO, is represented wearing a thick laurel wreath. This is one of the latest portraits executed during the Dictator's lifetime.

Compare this coin with the bust, p. x.

No. 2. Silver coins (denarii) of L. Hostilius, struck in 48 B.C.

It is possible that these two heads in some way represent conquered Gaul : the male head may even be meant for Vercingetorix himself, while the female head is the personification of Gallia. The two symbols are a Gaulish war-trumpet and an oval shield.

No. 3. Gaulish coin (gold) in the British Museum.
About second century B.C.

These gold coins were introduced into Gaul towards the end of the second century B.C. as a result of direct intercourse between the tribes of Central Gaul and Rome. They were modelled on the gold staters of Macedon which, as a result of the Roman victories in the East during the first half of the second century B.C., flooded Rome and became almost an international currency.

These Macedonian gold coins of Philip II (fourth century B.C.) consisted of : obverse (head), head of Apollo (with laurel wreath) ; reverse (tail), two-horsed chariot with the king's name underneath.

In this Gaulish copy, the details of the original have been debased, but they are still fairly clear.

C. IULI CAESARIS
COMMENTARIORUM
DE BELLO GALLICO
LIBER SEPTIMUS

1. Quieta Gallia, Caesar, ut constituerat, in Italiam
ad conventus agendos proficiscitur.   Ibi cognoscit de
Clodi caede, de senatusque consulto certior factus,
ut omnes iuniores Italiae coniurarent, dilectum tota
provincia habere instituit. Eae res in Galliam Trans- 5
alpinam celeriter perferuntur. Addunt ipsi et adfingunt rumoribus Galli, quod res poscere videbatur,
retineri urbano motu Caesarem neque in tantis dissensionibus ad exercitum venire posse. Hac impulsi
occasione qui iam ante se populi Romani imperio 1
subiectos dolerent liberius atque audacius de bello
consilia inire incipiunt. Indictis inter se principes
Galliae conciliis silvestribus ac remotis locis queruntur de Acconis morte ; posse hunc casum ad ipsos
recidere demonstrant ; miserantur communem Gal- 1
liae fortunam ; omnibus pollicitationibus ac praemiis
deposcunt qui belli initia faciant et sui capitis periculo
Galliam in libertatem vindicent. In primis rationem
esse habendam dicunt, prius quam eorum clandestina

20 consilia efferantur, ut Caesar ab exercitu intercludatur. Id esse facile, quod neque legiones audeant
absente imperatore ex hibernis egredi neque imperator sine praesidio ad legiones pervenire possit.
Postremo in acie praestare interfici quam non veterem
25 belli gloriam libertatemque quam a maioribus acceperint reciperare.

2. His rebus agitatis, profitentur Carnutes se
nullum periculum communis salutis causa recusare,
principesque ex omnibus bellum facturos pollicentur ; et, quoniam in praesentia obsidibus cavere inter
5 se non possint ne res efferatur, ut iure iurando ac
fide sanciatur petunt, collatis militaribus signis, quo
more eorum gravissima caerimonia continetur, ne
facto initio belli ab reliquis deserantur. Tum, col-
laudatis Carnutibus, dato iure iurando ab omnibus
10 qui aderant, tempore eius rei constituto ab concilio
disceditur.

3. Ubi ea dies venit, Carnutes, Cotuato et
Conconnetodumno ducibus, desperatis hominibus,
Cenabum signo dato concurrunt civesque Romanos
qui negotiandi causa ibi constiterant, in his C. Fufium
5 Citam, honestum equitem Romanum, qui rei
frumentariae iussu Caesaris praeerat, interficiunt
bonaque eorum diripiunt. Celeriter ad omnes Galliae civitates fama perfertur. Nam, ubique maior
atque inlustrior incidit res, clamore per agros region-

esque significant; hunc alii deinceps excipiunt et proximis tradunt, ut tum accidit. Nam quae Cenabi oriente sole gesta essent ante primam confectam vigiliam in finibus Arvernorum audita sunt, quod spatium est milium passuum circiter centum LX.

4. Simili ratione ibi Vercingetorix, Celtilli filius, Arvernus, summae potentiae adulescens, cuius pater principatum Galliae totius obtinuerat et ob eam causam, quod regnum appetebat, ab civitate erat interfectus, convocatis suis clientibus facile incendit. Cognito eius consilio ad arma concurritur. Prohibetur ab Gobannitione, patruo suo, reliquisque principibus, qui hanc temptandam fortunam non existimabant; expellitur ex oppido Gergovia; non destitit tamen, atque in agris habet dilectum egentium ac perditorum. Hac coacta manu, quoscumque adit ex civitate ad suam sententiam perducit; hortatur ut communis libertatis causa arma capiant, magnisque coactis copiis adversarios suos a quibus paulo ante erat eiectus expellit ex civitate. Rex ab suis appellatur. Dimittit quoque versus legationes; obtestatur ut in fide maneant. Celeriter sibi Senones, Parisios, Pictones, Cadurcos, Turonos, Aulercos, Lemovices, Andos reliquosque omnes qui Oceanum attingunt adiungit; omnium consensu ad eum defertur imperium. Qua oblata potestate omnibus his civitatibus obsides imperat, certum numer-

um militum ad se celeriter adduci iubet, armorum
quantum quaeque civitas domi quodque ante tem-
25 pus efficiat constituit ; in primis equitatui studet.
Summae diligentiae summam imperi severitatem
addit ; magnitudine supplici dubitantes cogit.
Nam maiore commisso delicto igne atque omnibus
tormentis necat, leviore de causa auribus desectis
30 aut singulis effossis oculis domum remittit, ut sint
reliquis documento et magnitudine poenae perter-
reant alios.

5. His suppliciis celeriter coacto exercitu, Luc-
terium Cadurcum, summae hominem audaciae, cum
parte copiarum in Rutenos mittit ; ipse in Bituriges
proficiscitur. Eius adventu Bituriges ad Aeduos,
5 quorum erant in fide, legatos mittunt subsidium
rogatum, quo facilius hostium copias sustinere possint. Aedui de consilio legatorum, quos Caesar ad
exercitum reliquerat, copias equitatus peditatusque
subsidio Biturigibus mittunt. Qui cum ad flumen
10 Ligerim venissent, quod Bituriges ab Aeduis dividit,
paucos dies ibi morati neque flumen transire ausi
domum revertuntur legatisque nostris renuntiant se
Biturigum perfidiam veritos revertisse, quibus id
consili fuisse cognoverint ut, si flumen transissent,
15 una ex parte ipsi, altera Arverni se circumsisterent.
Id eane de causa, quam legatis pronuntiarunt, an
perfidia adducti fecerint, quod nihil nobis constat,

non videtur pro certo esse proponendum. Bituriges eorum discessu statim cum Arvernis iunguntur. *motion*

6. His rebus in Italiam Caesari nuntiatis, cum iam ille urbanas res virtute Cn. Pompei commodiorem in statum pervenisse intellegeret, in Transalpinam Galliam profectus est. Eo cum venisset, magna difficultate adficiebatur, qua ratione ad exercitum pervenire posset. Nam, si legiones in provinciam arcesseret, se absente in itinere proelio dimicaturas intellegebat ; si ipse ad exercitum contenderet, ne eis quidem eo tempore qui quieti viderentur, suam salutem recte committi videbat.

7. Interim Lucterius Cadurcus in Rutenos missus eam civitatem Arvernis conciliat. Progressus in Nitiobriges et Gabalos ab utrisque obsides accipit et magna coacta manu in provinciam Narbonem versus eruptionem facere contendit. Qua re nuntiata Caesar omnibus consiliis antevertendum existimavit, ut Narbonem proficisceretur. Eo cum venisset, timentes confirmat, praesidia in Rutenis provincialibus, Volcis Arecomicis, Tolosatibus circumque Narbonem, quae loca hostibus erant finitima, constituit ; partem copiarum ex provincia supplementumque quod ex Italia adduxerat in Helvios, qui fines Arvernorum contingunt, convenire iubet.

8. His rebus comparatis, represso iam Lucterio et remoto, quod intrare intra praesidia periculosum

putabat, in Helvios proficiscitur. Etsi mons Cevenna,
qui Arvernos ab Helviis discludit, durissimo tempore
5 anni, altissima nive iter impediebat, tamen discussa
nive sex in altitudinem pedum atque ita viis patefactis summo militum sudore ad fines Arvernorum
pervenit. Quibus oppressis inopinantibus, quod se
Cevenna ut muro munitos existimabant, ac ne singu-
10 lari quidem umquam homini eo tempore anni semitae
patuerant, equitibus imperat ut quam latissime possint vagentur et quam maximum hostibus terrorem
inferant. Celeriter haec fama ac nuntii ad Vercingetorigem perferuntur ; quem perterriti omnes Arverni
15 circumsistunt atque obsecrant ut suis fortunis consulat neve ab hostibus diripiantur, praesertim cum
videat omne ad se bellum translatum. Quorum ille
precibus permotus castra ex Biturigibus movet in
Arvernos versus.

9. At Caesar biduum in his locis moratus, quod
haec de Vercingetorige usu ventura opinione praeceperat, per causam supplementi equitatusque cogendi ab exercitu discedit ; Brutum adulescentem
5 his copiis praeficit ; hunc monet ut in omnes partes
equites quam latissime pervagentur ; daturum se
operam ne longius triduo ab castris absit. His constitutis rebus, suis inopinantibus quam maximis
potest itineribus Viennam pervenit. Ibi nactus
10 recentem equitatum, quem multis ante diebus eo

praemiserat, neque diurno neque nocturno itinere
intermisso per fines Aeduorum in Lingones contendit,
ubi duae legiones hiemabant, ut, si quid etiam de sua
salute ab Aeduis iniretur consili, celeritate praecurreret. Eo cum pervenisset, ad reliquas legiones 15
mittit priusque omnes in unum locum cogit quam
de eius adventu Arvernis nuntiari posset. Hac re
cognita, Vercingetorix rursus in Bituriges exercitum
reducit atque inde profectus Gorgobinam, Boiorum
oppidum, quos ibi Helvetico proelio victos Caesar col- 20
locaverat Aeduisque attribuerat, oppugnare instituit.

10. Magnam haec res Caesari difficultatem ad consilium capiendum adferebat : si reliquam partem
hiemis uno loco legiones contineret, ne stipendiariis
Aeduorum expugnatis cuncta Gallia deficeret, quod
nullum amicis in eo praesidium videret positum esse ; 5
si maturius ex hibernis educeret, ne ab re frumentaria
duris subvectionibus laboraret. Praestare visum est
tamen omnes difficultates perpeti quam tanta contumelia accepta omnium suorum voluntates alien-
are. Itaque cohortatus Aeduos de supportando com- 10
meatu, praemittit ad Boios qui de suo adventu doceant hortenturque ut in fide maneant atque hostium
impetum magno animo sustineant. Duabus Agedinci legionibus atque impedimentis totius exercitus
relictis, ad Boios proficiscitur. 15

11. Altero die cum ad oppidum Senonum Vel-

launodunum venisset, ne quem post se hostem relin-
queret, quo expeditiore re frumentaria uteretur,
oppugnare instituit idque biduo circumvallavit ;
5 tertio die missis ex oppido legatis de deditione, arma
conferri, iumenta produci, sescentos obsides dari
iubet. Ea qui conficeret, C. Trebonium legatum relinquit. Ipse, ut quam primum iter faceret,
Cenabum Carnutum proficiscitur. Qui tum primum
10 allato nuntio de oppugnatione Vellaunoduni, cum
longius eam rem ductum iri existimarent, praesidium
Cenabi tuendi causa quod eo mitterent comparabant. Huc biduo pervenit. Castris ante oppidum
positis, diei tempore exclusus in posterum oppugna-
15 tionem differt, quaeque ad eam rem usui sint militibus imperat, et quod oppidum Cenabum pons fluminis
Ligeris contingebat, veritus ne noctu ex oppido pro-
fugerent, duas legiones in armis excubare iubet.
Cenabenses paulo ante mediam noctem silentio ex
20 oppido egressi flumen transire coeperunt. Qua re per
exploratores nuntiata, Caesar legiones quas expeditas
esse iusserat portis incensis intromittit atque oppido
potitur, perpaucis ex hostium numero desideratis
quin cuncti caperentur, quod pontis atque itinerum
25 angustiae multitudinis fugam intercluserant. Oppidum diripit atque incendit, praedam militibus
donat, exercitum Ligerim traducit atque in Biturigum fines pervenit.

12. Vercingetorix, ubi de Caesaris adventu cognovit, oppugnatione destitit atque obviam Caesari proficiscitur. Ille oppidum Biturigum positum in via Noviodunum oppugnare instituerat. Quo ex oppido cum legati ad eum venissent oratum ut sibi 5 ignosceret suaeque vitae consuleret, ut celeritate reliquas res conficeret, qua pleraque erat consecutus, arma conferri, equos produci, obsides dari iubet. Parte iam obsidum tradita, cum reliqua administrarentur, centurionibus et paucis militibus intro- 10 missis qui arma iumentaque conquirerent, equitatus hostium procul visus est, qui agmen Vercingetorigis antecesserat. Quem simul atque oppidani conspexerunt atque in spem auxili venerunt, clamore sublato arma capere, portas claudere, murum complere coe- 15 perunt. Centuriones in oppido, cum ex significatione Gallorum novi aliquid ab eis iniri consili intellexissent, gladiis destrictis portas occupaverunt suosque omnes incolumes receperunt.

13. Caesar ex castris equitatum educi iubet, proelium equestre committit; laborantibus iam suis Germanos equites circiter CCCC summittit, quos ab initio habere secum instituerat. Eorum impetum Galli sustinere non potuerunt atque in fugam coiecti 5 multis amissis se ad agmen receperunt. Quibus profligatis, rursus oppidani perterriti comprehensos eos quorum opera plebem concitatam existimabant ad

Caesarem perduxerunt seseque ei dediderunt. Quibus
10 rebus confectis Caesar ad oppidum Avaricum, quod
erat maximum munitissimumque in finibus Biturigum atque agri fertilissima regione, profectus est,
quod eo oppido recepto civitatem Biturigum se in
potestatem redacturum confidebat.

14. Vercingetorix, tot continuis incommodis Vellaunoduni, Cenabi, Novioduni acceptis, suos ad concilium convocat. Docet longe alia ratione esse bellum
gerendum atque antea gestum sit. Omnibus modis
5 huic rei studendum ut pabulatione et commeatu
Romani prohibeantur. Id esse facile, quod equitatu
ipsi abundent et quod anni tempore subleventur.
Pabulum secari non posse ; necessario dispersos
hostes ex aedificiis petere ; hos omnes cotidie ab
10 equitibus deligi posse. Praeterea salutis causa rei
familiaris commoda neglegenda : vicos atque aedifi-
cia incendi oportere hoc spatio ab via quoqueversus
quo pabulandi causa adire posse videantur. Harum
ipsis rerum copiam suppetere, quod quorum in finibus
15 bellum geratur, eorum opibus subleventur ; Romanos aut inopiam non laturos aut magno periculo
longius ab castris processuros ; neque interesse ipsosne interficiant impedimentisne exuant, quibus
amissis bellum geri non possit. Praeterea oppida
20 incendi oportere, quae non munitione et loci natura
ab omni sint periculo tuta, neu suis sint ad detrect-

andam militiam receptacula neu Romanis proposita
ad copiam commeatus praedamque tollendam. Haec
si gravia aut acerba videantur, multo illa gravius
aestimare, liberos, coniuges in servitutem abstrahi, 25
ipsos interfici ; quae sit necesse accidere victis.

15. Omnium consensu hac sententia probata, uno
die amplius XX urbes Biturigum incenduntur. Hoc
idem fit in reliquis civitatibus ; in omnibus partibus
incendia conspiciuntur ; quae etsi magno cum
dolore omnes ferebant, tamen hoc sibi solaci propone- 5
bant, quod se prope explorata victoria celeriter amissa
reciperaturos confidebant. Deliberatur de Avarico
in communi concilio, incendi placeret an defendi.
Procumbunt omnibus Gallis ad pedes Bituriges, ne
pulcherrimam prope totius Galliae urbem, quae prae- 10
sidio et ornamento sit civitati, suis manibus succen-
dere cogerentur ; facile se loci natura defensuros
dicunt, quod prope ex omnibus partibus flumine et
palude circumdata unum habeat et perangustum
aditum. Datur petentibus venia, dissuadente primo 15
Vercingetorige, post concedente et precibus ipsorum
et misericordia vulgi. Defensores oppido idonei
deliguntur.

16. Vercingetorix minoribus Caesarem itineribus
subsequitur et locum castris deligit paludibus silvisque munitum ab Avarico longe milia passuum
XVI. Ibi per certos exploratores in singula diei

5 tempora quae ad Avaricum agerentur cognoscebat
et quid fieri vellet imperabat. Omnes nostras pabu-
lationes frumentationesque observabat dispersosque,
cum longius necessario procederent, adoriebatur magnoque incommodo adficiebat, etsi quantum ratione
10 provideri poterat ab nostris occurrebatur, ut incertis
temporibus diversisque itineribus iretur.

17. Castris ad eam partem oppido positis Caesar,
quae intermissa a flumine et a paludibus aditum, ut
supra diximus, angustum habebat, aggerem apparare,
vineas agere, turres duas constituere coepit ; nam cir-
5 cumvallare loci natura prohibebat. De re frumentaria Boios atque Aeduos adhortari non destitit ;
quorum alteri, quod nullo studio agebant, non multum adiuvabant, alteri non magnis facultatibus,
quod civitas erat exigua et infirma, celeriter quod
10 habuerunt consumpserunt. Summa difficultate rei
frumentariae adfecto exercitu tenuitate Boiorum,
indiligentia Aeduorum, incendiis aedificiorum, usque
eo ut complures dies frumento milites caruerint et
pecore ex longinquioribus vicis adacto extremam
15 famem sustentarent, nulla tamen vox est ab eis audita populi Romani maiestate et superioribus victoriis
indigna. Quin etiam Caesar cum in opere singulas
legiones appellaret et, si acerbius inopiam ferrent, se
dimissurum oppugnationem diceret, universi ab eo ne
20 id faceret petebant : sic se complures annos illo

imperante meruisse ut nullam ignominiam acciperent,
nusquam incepta re discederent ; hoc se ignominiae
laturos loco, si inceptam oppugnationem reliquis-
sent ; praestare omnes perferre acerbitates quam
non civibus Romanis qui Cenabi perfidia Gallorum 25
interissent parentarent. Haec eadem centurionibus
tribunisque militum mandabant, ut per eos ad
Caesarem deferrentur.

18. Cum iam muro turres appropinquassent, ex
captivis Caesar cognovit Vercingetorigem consumpto
pabulo castra movisse propius Avaricum atque ipsum
cum equitatu expeditisque qui inter equites proe-
liari consuessent insidiarum causa eo profectum quo 5
nostros postero die pabulatum venturos arbitraretur.
Quibus rebus cognitis media nocte silentio profectus
ad hostium castra mane pervenit. Illi celeriter per
exploratores adventu Caesaris cognito carros impedi-
mentaque sua in artiores silvas abdiderunt, copias 10
omnes in loco edito atque aperto instruxerunt. Qua
re nuntiata Caesar celeriter sarcinas conferri, arma
expediri iussit.

19. Collis erat leniter ab infimo acclivis. Hunc ex
omnibus fere partibus palus difficilis atque impedita
cingebat, non latior pedibus quinquaginta. Hoc se
colle interruptis pontibus Galli fiducia loci continebant generatimque distributi in civitates omnia vada 5
ac saltus eius paludis obtinebant, sic animo parati

ut, si eam paludem Romani perrumpere conarentur,
haesitantes premerent ex loco superiore ; ut qui pro-
pinquitatem loci videret paratos prope aequo Marte
10 ad dimicandum existimaret, qui iniquitatem con-
dicionis perspiceret inani simulatione sese ostentare
cognosceret. Indignantes milites Caesar, quod conspectum suum hostes perferre possent tantulo spatio
interiecto, et signum proeli exposcentes edocet quanto
15 detrimento et quot virorum fortium morte necesse
sit constare victoriam ; quos cum sic animo paratos
videat ut nullum pro sua laude periculum recusent,
summae se iniquitatis condemnari debere, nisi eorum vitam sua salute habeat cariorem. Sic milites
20 consolatus eodem die reducit in castra reliquaque
quae ad oppugnationem pertinebant oppidi administrare instituit.

20. Vercingetorix, cum ad suos redisset, prodi-
onis insimulatus, quod castra propius Romanos
movisset, quod cum omni equitatu discessisset, quod
sine imperio tantas copias reliquisset, quod eius dis-
5 cessu Romani tanta opportunitate et celeritate venissent : non haec omnia fortuito aut sine consilio accidere potuisse ; regnum illum Galliae malle Caesaris
concessu quam ipsorum habere beneficio : tali modo
accusatus ad haec respondit : quod castra movisset,
10 factum inopia pabuli, etiam ipsis hortantibus ; quod
propius Romanos accessisset, persuasum loci oppor-

tunitate, qui se ipsum munitione defenderet ;
equitum vero operam neque in loco palustri desiderari
debuisse et illic fuisse utilem quo sint profecti. Summam imperi se consulto nulli discedentem tradidisse, 15
ne is multitudinis studio ad dimicandum impellere-
tur ; cui rei propter animi mollitiem studere omnes
videret, quod diutius laborem ferre non possent.
Romani si casu intervenerint, fortunae, si alicuius
indicio vocati, huic habendam gratiam, quod et pauci- 20
tatem eorum ex loco superiore cognoscere et virtutem despicere potuerint, qui dimicare non ausi turpiter se in castra receperint. Imperium se ab Caesare
per proditionem nullum desiderare, quod habere
victoria posset quae iam esset sibi atque omnibus 25
Gallis explorata ; quin etiam ipsis remittere, si sibi
magis honorem tribuere quam ab se salutem accipere
videantur. ' Haec ut intellegatis,' inquit, ' a me sincere pronuntiari, audite Romanos milites.' Producit
servos, quos in pabulatione paucis ante diebus ex- 30
ceperat et fame vinculisque excruciaverat. Hi iam
ante edocti quae interrogati pronuntiarent, milites
se esse legionarios dicunt ; fame atque inopia adductos clam ex castris exisse, si quid frumenti aut pecoris
in agris reperire possent ; simili omnem exercitum 35
inopia premi, nec iam vires sufficere cuiusquam nec
ferre operis laborem posse ; itaque statuisse imperatorem, si nihil in oppugnatione oppidi profecissent,

triduo exercitum deducere. ' Haec,' inquit, ' a me,'
40 Vercingetorix, ' beneficia habetis, quem proditionis
insimulatis ; cuius opera sine vestro sanguine tantum exercitum victorem fame consumptum videtis ;
quem turpiter se ex fuga recipientem ne qua civitas
suis finibus recipiat a me provisum est.'

21. Conclamat omnis multitudo et suo more
armis concrepat, quod facere in eo consuerunt cuius
orationem approbant : summum esse Vercingetorigem ducem, nec de eius fide dubitandum, nec maiore
5 ratione bellum administrari posse. Statuunt ut X
milia hominum delecta ex omnibus copiis in oppidum
mittantur, nec solis Biturigibus communem salutem
committendam censent, quod penes eos, si id oppidum retinuissent, summam victoriae constare in-
10 tellegebant.

22. Singulari militum nostrorum virtuti consilia
cuiusque modi Gallorum occurrebant, ut est summae
genus sollertiae atque ad omnia imitanda et effici-
enda quae ab quoque traduntur aptissimum. Nam
5 et laqueis falces avertebant, quas cum destinaverant
tormentis introrsus reducebant, et aggerem cuniculis
subtrahebant, eo scientius quod apud eos magnae
sunt ferrariae atque omne genus cuniculorum notum
atque usitatum est. Totum autem murum ex omni
10 parte turribus contabulaverant atque has coriis in-
texerant. Tum crebris diurnis nocturnisque erupti-

onibus aut aggeri ignem inferebant aut milites occu-
patos in opere adoriebantur et nostrarum turrium
altitudinem, quantum has cotidianus agger expres-
serat, commissis suarum turrium malis adaequabant, 15
et apertos cuniculos praeusta et praeacuta materia et
pice fervefacta et maximi ponderis saxis morabantur
moenibusque appropinquare prohibebant.

23. Muri autem omnes Gallici hac fere forma sunt.
Trabes directae perpetuae in longitudinem paribus
intervallis distantes inter se binos pedes in solo col-
locantur. Hae revinciuntur introrsus et multo aggere vestiuntur ; ea autem quae diximus intervalla 5
grandibus in fronte saxis effarciuntur. His collocatis
et coagmentatis alius insuper ordo additur, ut idem
illud intervallum servetur neque inter se contingant
trabes, sed paribus intermissae spatiis singulae singulis saxis interiectis arte contineantur. Sic deinceps 10
omne opus contexitur, dum iusta muri altitudo ex-
pleatur. Hoc cum in speciem varietatemque opus
deforme non est, alternis trabibus ac saxis quae rectis
lineis suos ordines servant, tum ad utilitatem et
defensionem urbium summam habet opportunitatem, 15
quod et ab incendio lapis et ab ariete materia defen-
dit, quae perpetuis trabibus pedes quadragenos plerumque introrsus revincta neque perrumpi neque
distrahi potest.

24. His tot rebus impedita oppugnatione milites,

cum toto tempore frigore et assiduis imbribus tar-
darentur, tamen continenti labore omnia haec super-
averunt et diebus XXV aggerem latum pedes
5 CCCXXX, altum pedes LXXX exstruxerunt. Cum
is murum hostium paene contingeret et Caesar ad
opus consuetudine excubaret militesque hortaretur
ne quod omnino tempus ab opere intermitteretur,
paulo ante tertiam vigiliam est animadversum fum-
10 are aggerem, quem cuniculo hostes succenderant ;
eodemque tempore toto muro clamore sublato, duabus
portis ab utroque latere turrium eruptio fiebat. Alii
faces atque aridam materiem de muro in aggerem
eminus iaciebant, picem reliquasque res quibus
15 ignis excitari potest fundebant, ut quo primum curreretur aut cui rei ferretur auxilium vix ratio iniri
posset. Tamen, quod instituto Caesaris semper duae
legiones pro castris excubabant pluresque partitis
temporibus erant in opere, celeriter factum est ut
20 alii eruptionibus resisterent, alii turres reducerent
aggeremque interscinderent, omnis vero ex castris
multitudo ad restinguendum concurreret.

25. Cum in omnibus locis, consumpta iam reliqua
parte noctis, pugnaretur semperque hostibus spes
victoriae redintegraretur, eo magis quod deustos
pluteos turrium videbant nec facile adire apertos ad
5 auxiliandum animadvertebant, semperque ipsi recentes defessis succederent omnemque Galliae salu-

tem in illo vestigio temporis positam arbitrarentur,
accidit inspectantibus nobis quod dignum memoria
visum praetereundum non existimavimus. Quidam
ante portam oppidi Gallus per manus sebi ac picis 10
traditas glaebas in ignem e regione turris proiciebat ;
scorpione ab latere dextro traiectus exanimatusque
concidit. Hunc ex proximis unus iacentem trans-
gressus eodem illo munere fungebatur ; eadem
ratione ictu scorpionis exanimato alteri successit ter- 15
tius et tertio quartus ; nec prius ille est a propugna-
toribus vacuus relictus locus quam restincto aggere
atque omni ex parte summotis hostibus finis est pug-
andi factus.

26. Omnia experti Galli, quod res nulla suc-
cesserat, postero die consilium ceperunt ex oppido
profugere, hortante et iubente Vercingetorige. Id
silentio noctis conati non magna iactura suorum sese
effecturos sperabant, propterea quod neque longe ab 5
oppido castra Vercingetorigis aberant et palus, quae
perpetua intercedebat, Romanos ad insequendum
tardabat. Iamque hoc facere noctu apparabant
cum matres familiae repente in publicum procurrer-
unt flentesque proiectae ad pedes suorum omnibus 10
precibus petierunt ne se et communes liberos hostibus
ad supplicium dederent quos ad capiendam fugam
naturae et virium infirmitas impediret. Ubi eos in
sententia perstare viderunt, quod plerumque in sum-

15 mo periculo timor misericordiam non recipit, conclamare et significare de fuga Romanis coeperunt. Quo
timore perterriti Galli ne ab equitatu Romanorum
viae praeoccuparentur consilio destiterunt.

27. Postero die Caesar, promota turri derectisque
operibus quae facere instituerat, magno coorto imbre,
non inutilem hanc ad capiendum consilium tempesta-
tem arbitratus est, quod paulo incautius custodias in
5 muro dispositas videbat, suosque languidius in
opere versari iussit et quid fieri vellet ostendit ;
legionibusque extra castra intra vineas in occulto
expeditis, cohortatus ut aliquando pro tantis labori-
bus fructum victoriae perciperent eis qui primi
10 murum ascendissent praemia proposuit militibusque
signum dedit. Illi subito ex omnibus partibus evol-
averunt murumque celeriter compleverunt.

28. Hostes re nova perterriti, muro turribusque
deiecti in foro ac locis patentioribus cuneatim constiterunt, hoc animo ut, si qua ex parte obviam
[contra] veniretur, acie instructa depugnarent. Ubi
5 neminem in aequum locum sese demittere sed toto
undique muro circumfundi viderunt, veriti ne omnino
spes fugae tolleretur, abiectis armis ultimas oppidi
partes continenti impetu petiverunt, parsque ibi,
cum angusto exitu portarum se ipsi premerent, a
10 militibus, pars iam egressa portis ab equitibus est
interfecta ; nec fuit quisquam qui praedae studeret.

Sic et Cenabi caede et labore operis incitati non aetate confectis, non mulieribus, non infantibus pepercerunt. Denique ex omni numero, qui fuit circiter milium XL, vix DCCC, qui primo clamore audito se 15 ex oppido eiecerunt, incolumes ad Vercingetorigem pervenerunt. Quos ille multa iam nocte silentio ex fuga excepit veritus ne qua in castris ex eorum concursu et misericordia vulgi seditio oreretur, ut procul in via dispositis familiaribus suis principi- 20 busque civitatum disparandos deducendosque ad suos curaret, quae cuique civitati pars castrorum ab initio obvenerat.

29. Postero die concilio convocato, consolatus cohortatusque est ne se admodum animo demitterent, ne perturbarentur incommodo. Non virtute neque in acie vicisse Romanos, sed artificio quodam et scientia oppugnationis, cuius rei fuerint ipsi im- 5 periti. Errare, si qui in bello omnes secundos rerum proventus exspectent. Sibi numquam placuisse Avaricum defendi, cuius rei testes ipsos haberet ; sed factum imprudentia Biturigum et nimia obsequentia reliquorum uti hoc incommodum 10 acciperetur. Id tamen se celeriter maioribus commodis sanaturum. Nam quae ab reliquis Gallis civitates dissentirent, has sua diligentia adiuncturum atque unum consilium totius Galliae effecturum, cuius consensui ne orbis quidem terrarum possit 15

obsistere ; idque se prope iam effectum habere. Interea aequum esse ab eis communis salutis causa impetrari ut castra munire instituerent, quo facilius re-
pentinos hostium impetus sustinerent.

30. Fuit haec oratio non ingrata Gallis, et maxime,
quod ipse animo non defecerat tanto accepto incommodo neque se in occultum abdiderat et conspectum
multitudinis fugerat ; plusque animo providere et
5 praesentire existimabatur, quod re integra primo incendendum Avaricum, post deserendum censuerat.
Itaque ut reliquorum imperatorum res adversae au-
ctoritatem minuunt, sic huius ex contrario dignitas
incommodo accepto in dies augebatur. Simul in spem
10 veniebant eius adfirmatione de reliquis adiungendis
civitatibus ; primumque eo tempore Galli castra
munire instituerunt ; et sic sunt animo consternati
homines insueti laboris ut omnia quae imperarentur
sibi patienda existimarent.

31. Nec minus quam est pollicitus Vercingetorix
animo laborabat ut reliquas civitates adiungeret,
atque eas donis pollicitationibusque alliciebat. Huic
rei idoneos homines deligebat quorum quisque aut
5 oratione subdola aut amicitia facillime capere posset.
Qui Avarico expugnato refugerant, armandos ves-
tiendosque curat ; simul, ut deminutae copiae re-
dintegrarentur, imperat certum numerum militum
civitatibus, quem et quam ante diem in castra adduci

velit, sagittariosque omnes, quorum erat permagnus 10
numerus in Gallia, conquiri et ad se mitti iubet. His
rebus celeriter id quod Avarici deperierat expletur.
Interim Teutomatus, Olloviconis filius, rex Nitiobrigum, cuius pater ab senatu nostro amicus erat appellatus, cum magno equitum suorum numero et quos 15
ex Aquitania conduxerat ad eum pervenit.

32. Caesar Avarici complures dies commoratus
summamque ibi copiam frumenti et reliqui commeatus nactus exercitum ex labore atque inopia reficit.
Iam prope hieme confecta, cum ipso anni tempore ad
gerendum bellum vocaretur et ad hostem proficisci 5
constituisset, sive eum ex paludibus silvisque elicere
sive obsidione premere posset, legati ad eum principes Aeduorum veniunt oratum ut maxime necessario tempore civitati subveniat : summo esse in periculo rem, quod, cum singuli magistratus antiquitus 10
creari atque regiam potestatem annum obtinere consuessent, duo magistratum gerant et se uterque
eorum legibus creatum esse dicat. Horum esse alterum
Convictolitavem, florentem et inlustrem adulescentem ; alterum Cotum, antiquissima familia natum 15
atque ipsum hominem summae potentiae et magnae
cognationis, cuius frater Valetiacus proximo anno
eundem magistratum gesserit. Civitatem esse omnem in armis ; divisum senatum, divisum populum,
suas cuiusque eorum clientelas. Quod si diutius 20

alatur controversia, fore uti pars cum parte civitatis
configat.   Id ne accidat, positum in eius diligentia
atque auctoritate.

33. Caesar, etsi a bello atque hoste discedere detri-
mentosum esse existimabat, tamen non ignorans
quanta ex dissensionibus incommoda oriri consuessent, ne tanta et tam coniuncta populo Romano civi-
5 tas, quam ipse semper aluisset omnibusque rebus
ornasset, ad vim atque arma descenderet atque ea
pars quae minus sibi confideret auxilia a Vercingetorige arcesseret, huic rei praevertendum existimavit,
et, quod legibus Aeduorum eis qui summum magis-
0 tratum obtinerent excedere ex finibus non liceret, ne
quid de iure aut de legibus eorum deminuisse videretur, ipse .in Aeduos proficisci statuit senatumque
omnem et quos inter controversia esset ad se Decetiam evocavit. Cum prope omnis civitas eo con-
5 venisset, docereturque paucis clam convocatis alio
loco, alio tempore atque oportuerit fratrem a fratre
renuntiatum, cum leges duo ex una familia vivo
utroque non solum magistratus creari vetarent sed
etiam in senatu esse prohiberent, Cotum imperium
0 deponere coegit ; Convictolitavem, qui per sacer-
dotes more civitatis intermissis magistratibus esset
creatus, potestatem obtinere iussit.

34. Hoc decreto interposito, cohortatus Aeduos
ut controversiarum ac dissensionis obliviscerentur

atque omnibus omissis his rebus huic bello servirent,
eaque quae meruissent praemia ab se devicta Gallia
exspectarent, equitatumque omnem et peditum milia 5
X sibi celeriter mitterent quae in praesidiis rei frumentariae causa disponeret, exercitum in duas partes
divisit : quattuor legiones in Senones Parisiosque
Labieno ducendas dedit, sex ipse in Arvernos ad
oppidum Gergoviam secundum flumen Elaver duxit ; 10
equitatus partem illi attribuit, partem sibi reliquit.
Qua re cognita Vercingetorix omnibus interruptis
eius fluminis pontibus ab altera fluminis parte iter
facere coepit.

35. Cum uterque utrimque exisset exercitus, in
conspectu fereque e regione castris castra ponebant,
dispositis exploratoribus necubi effecto ponte Romani
copias traducerent. Erat in magnis Caesari difficultatibus res, ne maiorem aestatis partem flumine 5
impediretur, quod non fere ante autumnum Elaver
vado transiri solet. Itaque, ne id accideret, silvestri
loco castris positis e regione unius eorum pontium
quos Vercingetorix rescindendos curaverat, postero
die cum duabus legionibus in occulto restitit ; re- 10
liquas copias cum omnibus impedimentis, ut consue-
verat, misit, apertis quibusdam cohortibus, uti
numerus legionum constare videretur. His quam
longissime possent egredi iussis, cum iam ex diei
tempore coniecturam ceperat in castra perventum, 15

isdem sublicis, quarum pars inferior integra remane-
bat, pontem reficere coepit. Celeriter effecto opere
legionibusque traductis et loco castris idoneo delecto,
reliquas copias revocavit. Vercingetorix re cognita,
20 ne contra suam voluntatem dimicare cogeretur, magnis itineribus antecessit.

36. Caesar ex eo loco quintis castris Gergoviam
pervenit equestrique eo die proelio levi facto, perspecto urbis situ, quae posita in altissimo monte
omnes aditus difficiles habebat, de expugnatione
5 desperavit; de obsessione non prius agendum constituit quam rem frumentariam expedisset. At Vercingetorix, castris prope oppidum positis, mediocribus
circum se intervallis separatim singularum civitatum copias collocaverat atque omnibus eius
10 iugi collibus occupatis, qua dispici poterat, hor-
ribilem speciem praebebat; principesque earum civitatum quos sibi ad consilium capiendum delegerat
prima luce cotidie ad se convenire iubebat, seu quid
communicandum seu quid administrandum videre-
15 tur; neque ullum fere diem intermittebat quin
equestri proelio interiectis sagittariis quid in quoque
esset animi ac virtutis suorum periclitaretur. Erat
e regione oppidi collis sub ipsis radicibus montis
egregie munitus atque ex omni parte circumcisus;
20 quem si tenerent nostri, et aquae magna parte et
pabulatione libera prohibituri hostes videbantur.

Sed is locus praesidio ab his, non nimis firmo tamen, tenebatur. Silentio noctis Caesar ex castris egressus, prius quam subsidio ex oppido veniri posset, deiecto praesidio, potitus loco duas ibi legiones col- 25 locavit fossamque duplicem duodenum pedum a maioribus castris ad minora perduxit, ut tuto ab repentino hostium incursu etiam singuli commeare possent.

37. Dum haec ad Gergoviam geruntur, Convictolitavis Aeduus, cui magistratum adiudicatum a Caesare demonstravimus, sollicitatus ab Arvernis pecunia cum quibusdam adulescentibus colloquitur; quorum erat princeps Litaviccus atque eius fratres, 5 amplissima familia nati adulescentes. Cum his praemium communicat hortaturque eos ut se liberos et imperio natos meminerint. Unam esse Aeduorum civitatem quae certissimam Galliae victoriam distineat; eius auctoritate reliquas contineri; qua 10 traducta, locum consistendi Romanis in Gallia non fore. Esse non nullo se Caesaris beneficio adfectum, sic tamen ut iustissimam apud eum causam obtinuerit; sed plus communi libertati tribuere. Cur enim potius Aedui de suo iure et de legibus ad Caesarem 15 disceptatorem quam Romani ad Aeduos veniant? Celeriter adulescentibus et oratione magistratus et praemio deductis, cum se vel principes eius consili fore profiterentur, ratio perficiendi quaerebatur,

20 quod civitatem temere ad suscipiendum bellum adduci posse non confidebant. Placuit ut Litaviccus decem illis milibus quae Caesari ad bellum mitterentur praeficeretur atque ea ducenda curaret, fratresque eius ad Caesarem praecurrerent. Reliqua qua ratione 25 agi placeat constituunt.

38. Litaviccus accepto exercitu, cum milia passuum circiter XXX ab Gergovia abesset, convocatis subito militibus lacrimans : ' quo proficiscimur ', inquit, ' milites? Omnis noster equitatus, omnis 5 nobilitas interiit ; principes civitatis, Eporedorix et Viridomarus, insimulati proditionis ab Romanis indicta causa interfecti sunt. Haec ab ipsis cognoscite qui ex ipsa caede fugerunt ; nam ego fratribus atque omnibus meis propinquis interfectis dolore prohibeor 10 quae gesta sunt pronuntiare.' Producuntur ei quos ille edocuerat quae dici vellet, atque eadem quae Litaviccus pronuntiaverat multitudini exponunt : multos equites Aeduorum interfectos, quod collocuti cum Arvernis dicerentur ; ipsos se inter multitu-15 dinem militum occultasse atque ex media caede fugisse. Conclamant Aedui et Litaviccum obsecrant ut sibi consulat. ' Quasi vero', inquit ille, ' consili sit res, ac non necesse sit nobis Gergoviam contendere et cum Arvernis nosmet coniungere. An 20 dubitamus quin nefario facinore admisso Romani iam ad nos interficiendos concurrant ? Proinde, si quid in nobis animi est, persequamur eorum mortem qui indignissime interierunt, atque hos latrones interficiamus.' Ostendit cives Romanos, qui eius praesidi fiducia una erant; magnum numerum 25 frumenti commeatusque diripit; ipsos crudeliter excruciatos interficit. Nuntios tota civitate Aeduorum dimittit, eodem mendacio de caede equitum et principum permovet; hortatur ut simili ratione atque ipse fecerit suas iniurias persequantur. 30

39. Eporedorix Aeduus, summo loco natus adulescens et summae domi potentiae, et una Viridomarus, pari aetate et gratia sed genere dispari, quem Caesar ab Diviciaco sibi traditum ex humili loco ad summam dignitatem perduxerat, in equitum numero 5 convenerant nominatim ab eo evocati. His erat inter se de principatu contentio, et in illa magistratuum controversia alter pro Convictolitavi, alter pro Coto summis opibus pugnaverant. Ex his Eporedorix cognito Litavicci consilio media fere 10 nocte rem ad Caesarem defert; orat ne patiatur civitatem pravis adulescentium consiliis ab amicitia populi Romani deficere; quod futurum provideat, si se tot hominum milia cum hostibus coniunxerint, quorum salutem neque propinqui neglegere neque 15 civitas levi momento aestimare posset.

40. Magna adfectus sollicitudine hoc nuntio Caesar, quod semper Aeduorum civitati praecipue indulserat,

nulla interposita dubitatione legiones expeditas
quattuor equitatumque omnem ex castris educit;
5 nec fuit spatium tali tempore ad contrahenda castra,
quod res posita in celeritate videbatur; C. Fabium
legatum cum legionibus duabus castris praesidio
relinquit. Fratres Litavicci, cum comprehendi
iussisset, paulo ante reperit ad hostes fugisse.
10 Adhortatus milites ne necessario tempore itineris
labore permoveantur, cupidissimis omnibus progressus milia passuum XXV, agmen Aeduorum conspicatus, immisso equitatu iter eorum moratur atque
impedit; interdicitque omnibus ne quemquam
15 interficiant. Eporedorigem et Viridomarum, quos
illi interfectos existimabant, inter equites versari
suosque appellare iubet. His cognitis et Litavicci
fraude perspecta Aedui manus tendere et deditionem significare et proiectis armis mortem deprecari
20 incipiunt. Litaviccus cum suis clientibus, quibus
more Gallorum nefas est etiam in extrema fortuna
deserere patronos, Gergoviam profugit.

41. Caesar, nuntiis ad civitatem Aeduorum missis
qui suo beneficio conservatos docerent quos iure belli
interficere potuisset, tribusque horis noctis exercitui
ad quietem datis, castra ad Gergoviam movit. Medio
5 fere itinere equites a Fabio missi quanto res in periculo fuerit exponunt. Summis copiis castra oppugnata demonstrant, cum crebro integri defessis suc-

cederent nostrosque assiduo labore defatigarent,
quibus propter magnitudinem castrorum perpetuo
esset isdem in vallo permanendum. Multitudine 10
sagittarum atque omnis generis telorum multos vul-
neratos ; ad haec sustinenda magno usui fuisse tormenta. Fabium discessu eorum duabus relictis
portis obstruere ceteras pluteosque vallo addere et
se in posterum diem similemque casum apparare. 15
His rebus cognitis, Caesar summo studio militum
ante ortum solis in castra pervenit.

42. Dum haec ad Gergoviam geruntur, Aedui
primis nuntiis ab Litavicco acceptis nullum sibi ad
cognoscendum spatium relinquunt. Impellit alios
avaritia, alios iracundia et temeritas quae maxime
illi hominum generi est innata, ut levem auditionem 5
habeant pro re comperta. Bona civium Romanorum
diripiunt, caedes faciunt, in servitutem abstrahunt.
Adiuvat rem proclinatam Convictolitavis plebemque
ad furorem impellit, ut facinore admisso ad sanitatem
reverti pudeat. M. Aristium, tribunum militum, iter 10
ad legionem facientem fide data ex oppido Cabillono
educunt ; idem facere cogunt eos qui negotiandi
causa ibi constiterant. Hos continuo in itinere
adorti omnibus impedimentis exuunt ; repugnantes
diem noctemque obsident ; multis utrimque inter- 15
fectis maiorem multitudinem ad arma concitant.

43. Interim nuntio allato omnes eorum milites in

potestate Caesaris teneri, concurrunt ad Aristium ;
nihil publico factum consilio demonstrant ; quaes-
tionem de bonis direptis decernunt, Litavicci fratrum-
5 que bona publicant, legatos ad Caesarem sui purgandi gratia mittunt. Haec faciunt reciperandorum
suorum causa ; sed contaminati facinore et capti
compendio ex direptis bonis, quod ea res ad multos
pertinebat, timore poenae exterriti consilia clam de
10 bello inire incipiunt civitatesque reliquas legationi-
bus sollicitant. Quae tametsi Caesar intellegebat,
tamen quam mitissime potest legatos appellat :
nihil se propter inscientiam levitatemque vulgi gravius de civitate iudicare neque de sua in Aeduos bene-
15 volentia deminuere. Ipse maiorem Galliae motum
exspectans,. ne ab omnibus civitatibus circumsister-
etur, consilia inibat quem ad modum ab Gergovia
discederet ac rursus omnem exercitum contraheret,
ne profectio nata ab timore defectionis similis fugae
20 videretur.

44. Haec cogitanti accidere visa est facultas bene
rei gerendae. Nam cum in minora castra operis
perspiciendi causa venisset, animadvertit collem,
qui ab hostibus tenebatur, nudatum hominibus, qui
5 superioribus diebus vix prae multitudine cerni poterat. Admiratus quaerit ex perfugis causam, quorum
magnus ad eum cotidie numerus confluebat. Constabat inter omnes, quod iam ipse Caesar per ex-

ploratores cognoverat, dorsum esse eius iugi prope
aequum, sed hunc silvestrem et angustum, qua esset 10
aditus ad alteram partem oppidi ; vehementer huic
illos loco timere nec iam aliter sentire, uno colle ab
Romanis occupato, si alterum amisissent, quin paene
circumvallati atque omni exitu et pabulatione inter-
clusi viderentur : ad hunc muniendum omnes a 15
Vercingetorige evocatos.

45. Hac re cognita, Caesar mittit complures equitum turmas eo de media nocte. Imperat his ut paulo
tumultuosius omnibus locis pervagentur. Prima
luce magnum numerum impedimentorum ex castris
mulorumque produci deque his stramenta detrahi 5
mulionesque cum cassidibus equitum specie ac simulatione collibus circumvehi iubet. His paucos addit
equites qui latius ostentationis causa vagarentur.
Longo circuitu easdem omnes iubet petere regiones.
Haec procul ex oppido videbantur, ut erat a Ger- 10
govia despectus in castra, neque tanto spatio certi
quid esset explorari poterat. Legionem unam eodem
iugo mittit et paulum progressam inferiore constituit loco silvisque occultat. Augetur Gallis suspicio
atque omnes illo ad munitionem copiae traducuntur. 15
Vacua castra hostium Caesar conspicatus, tectis
insignibus suorum occultatisque signis militaribus
raros milites, qui ex oppido animadverterentur, ex
maioribus castris in minora traducit ; legatisque,

quos singulis legionibus praefecerat, quid fieri velit 20
ostendit ; in primis monet ut contineant milites, ne
studio pugnandi aut spe praedae longius progredian-
tur ; quid iniquitas loci habeat incommodi proponit ;
hoc una celeritate posse mutari ; occasionis esse rem,
non proeli. His rebus expositis signum dat et ab 25
dextra parte alio ascensu eodem tempore Aeduos
mittit.

46. Oppidi murus ab planitie atque initio ascensus
recta regione, si nullus anfractus intercederet, mille
CC passus aberat ; quidquid huc circuitus ad mollien-
dum clivum accesserat, id spatium itineris augebat.
A medio fere colle in longitudinem, ut natura montis 5
ferebat, ex grandibus saxis sex pedum murum, qui
nostrum impetum tardaret praeduxerant Galli
atque inferiore omni spatio vacuo relicto superiorem
partem collis usque ad murum oppidi densissimis
castris compleverant. Milites dato signo celeriter ad 10
munitionem perveniunt eamque transgressi trinis
castris potiuntur ; ac tanta fuit in castris capiendis
celeritas ut Teutomatus, rex Nitiobrigum, subito in
tabernaculo oppressus, ut meridie conquieverat,
superiore corporis parte nudata, vulnerato equo vix 15
se ex manibus praedantium militum eriperet.

47. Consecutus id quod animo proposuerat Caesar
receptui cani iussit legionisque decimae, quacum erat,
continuo signa constituit ; ac reliquarum legionum

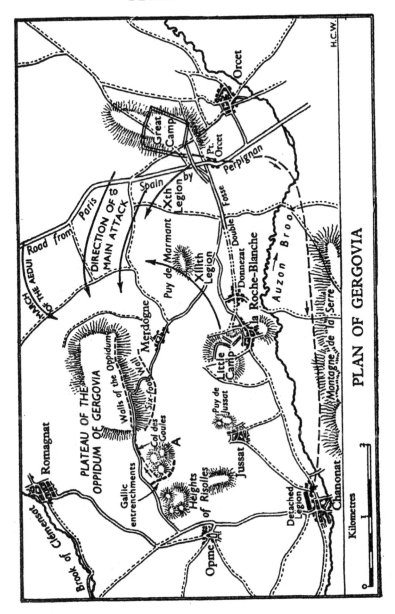

PLAN OF GERGOVIA

milites, non exaudito sono tubae, quod satis magna
valles intercedebat, tamen ab tribunis militum legat- 5
isque, ut erat a Caesare praeceptum, retinebantur.
Sed elati spe celeris victoriae et hostium fuga et superiorum temporum secundis proeliis, nihil adeo arduum
sibi esse existimaverunt quod non virtute consequi
possent, neque finem prius sequendi fecerunt quam 10
muro oppido portisque appropinquarunt. Tum
vero ex omnibus urbis partibus orto clamore, qui
longius aberant repentino tumultu perterriti, cum
hostem intra portas esse existimarent, sese ex oppido
eiecerunt. Matres familiae de muro vestem argen- 15
tumque iactabant, et pectore nudo prominentes
passis manibus obtestabantur Romanos ut sibi
parcerent neu, sicut Avarici fecissent, ne a mulieribus quidem atque infantibus abstinerent; non nullae
de muro per manus demissae sese militibus trade- 20
bant. L. Fabius, centurio legionis VIII., quem inter
suos eo die dixisse constabat excitari se Avaricensi-
bus praemiis neque commissurum ut prius quisquam
murum ascenderet, tres suos nactus manipulares
atque ab eis sublevatus murum ascendit; hos ipse 25
rursus singulos exceptans in murum extulit.

48. Interim ei qui ad alteram partem oppidi, ut
supra demonstravimus, munitionis causa convenerant, primo exaudito clamore, inde etiam crebris nuntiis incitati oppidum a Romanis teneri, praemissis

5 equitibus magno concursu eo contenderunt. Eorum
ut quisque primus venerat, sub muro consistebat
suorumque pugnantium numerum augebat. Quorum
cum magna multitudo convenisset, matres familiae,
quae paulo ante Romanis de muro manus tende-
10 bant, suos obtestari et more Gallico passum capillum
ostentare liberosque in conspectum proferre coeperunt. Erat Romanis nec loco nec numero aequa contentio ; simul et cursu et spatio pugnae defatigati
non facile recentes atque integros sustinebant.

49. Caesar, cum iniquo loco pugnari hostiumque
augeri copias videret, praemetuens suis ad T. Sextium legatum, quem minoribus castris praesidio
reliquerat, misit, ut cohortes ex castris celeriter
5 educeret et sub infimo colle ab dextro latere hostium
constitueret, ut, si nostros loco depulsos vidisset,
quo minus libere hostes insequerentur terreret.
Ipse paulum ex eo loco cum legione progressus, ubi
constiterat, eventum pugnae exspectabat.

50. Cum acerrime comminus pugnaretur, hostes
loco et numero, nostri virtute confiderent, subito
sunt Aedui visi ab latere.nostris aperto, quos Caesar
ab dextra parte alio ascensu manus distinendae
5 causa miserat. Hi similitudine armorum vehementer
nostros perterruerunt, ac, tametsi dextris umeris
exsertis animadvertebantur, quod insigne pacatum
esse consuerat, tamen id ipsum sui fallendi causa

milites ab hostibus factum existimabant. Eodem
tempore L. Fabius centurio quique una murum 10
ascenderant circumventi atque interfecti muro
praecipitabantur. M. Petronius, eiusdem legionis
centurio, cum portas excidere conatus esset, a multitudine oppressus ac sibi desperans, multis iam vulneribus acceptis, manipularibus suis, qui illum secuti 15
erant, ' Quoniam ', inquit, ' me una vobiscum servare
non possum, vestrae quidem certe vitae prospiciam,
quos cupiditate gloriae adductus in periculum de-
duxi. Vos data facultate vobis consulite.' Simul in
medios hostes irrupit duobusque interfectis reliquos 20
a porta paulum summovit. Conantibus auxiliari
suis, ' Frustra ', inquit, ' meae vitae subvenire con-
amini, quem iam sanguis viresque deficiunt. Proinde
abite, dum est facultas, vosque ad legionem recipite.'
Ita pugnans post paulum concidit ac suis saluti fuit. 25

51. Nostri, cum undique premerentur, XLVI
centurionibus amissis deiecti sunt loco. Sed intolerantius Gallos insequentes legio decima tardavit,
quae pro subsidio paulo aequiore loco constiterat.
Hanc rursus XIII. legionis cohortes exceper- 5
unt, quae ex castris minoribus eductae cum T.
Sextio legato ceperant locum superiorem. Legiones,
ubi primum planitiem attigerunt, infestis contra
hostes signis constiterunt. Vercingetorix ab radicibus collis suos intra munitiones reduxit. Eo die 10

milites sunt paulo minus septingenti desiderati.

52. Postero die Caesar contione advocata temeri-
tatem cupiditatemque militum reprehendit, quod
sibi ipsi iudicavissent quo procedendum aut quid
agendum videretur neque signo recipiendi dato con-
5 stitissent neque ab tribunis militum legatisque
retineri potuissent. Exposuit quid iniquitas loci
posset, quid ipse ad Avaricum sensisset, cum sine
duce et sine equitatu deprehensis hostibus explora-
tam victoriam dimisisset ne parvum modo detrimen-
10 tum in contentione propter iniquitatem loci accideret;
quanto opere eorum animi magnitudinem admiraretur, quos non castrorum munitiones, non altitudo
montis, non murus oppidi tardare potuisset, tanto
opere licentiam arrogantiamque reprehendere, quod
15 plus se quam imperatorem de victoria atque exitu
rerum sentire existimarent ; nec minus se ab milite
modestiam et continentiam quam virtutem atque
animi magnitudinem desiderare.

53. Hac habita contione et ad extremam orationem
confirmatis militibus, ne ob hanc causam animo per-
moverentur neu quod iniquitas loci attulisset id virtuti hostium tribuerent, eadem de profectione cogi-
5 tans quae ante senserat legiones ex castris eduxit
aciemque idoneo loco constituit. Cum Vercingetorix nihilo minus in aequum locum descenderet,
levi facto equestri proelio atque secundo in castra

exercitum reduxit. Cum hoc idem postero die fecis-
set, satis ad Gallicam ostentationem minuendam 10
militumque animos confirmandos factum existimans
in Aeduos movit castra. Ne tum quidem insecutis
hostibus, tertio die ad flumen Elaver pontes reficit
eoque exercitum traducit.

54. Ibi a Viridomaro atque Eporedorige Aeduis
appellatus discit cum omni equitatu Litaviccum ad
sollicitandos Aeduos profectum ; opus esse ipsos
antecedere ad confirmandam civitatem. Etsi multis
iam rebus perfidiam Aeduorum perspectam habebat 5
atque horum discessu admaturari defectionem civitatis existimabat, tamen eos retinendos non constituit, ne aut inferre iniuriam videretur aut daret
timoris aliquam suspicionem. Discedentibus his
breviter sua in Aeduos merita exposuit : quos et 10
quam humiles accepisset, compulsos in oppida, multatos agris, omnibus ereptis copiis, imposito stipen-
dio, obsidibus summa cum contumelia extortis, et
quam in fortunam quamque in amplitudinem deduxisset, ut non solum in pristinum statum redissent 15
sed omnium temporum dignitatem et gratiam antecessisse viderentur. His datis mandatis eos ab se
dimisit.

55. Noviodunum erat oppidum Aeduorum ad ripas
Ligeris opportuno loco positum. Huc Caesar omnes
obsides Galliae, frumentum, pecuniam publicam,

suorum atque exercitus impedimentorum magnam
5 partem contulerat ; huc magnum numerum equorum
huius belli causa in Italia atque Hispania coemptum
miserat. Eo cum Eporedorix Viridomarusque venissent et de statu civitatis cognovissent, Litaviccum
Bibracte ab Aeduis receptum, quod est oppidum apud
10 eos maximae auctoritatis, Convictolitavem magistratum magnamque partem senatus ad eum conven-
isse, legatos ad Vercingetorigem de pace et amicitia
concilianda publice missos, non praetermittendum
tantum commodum existimaverunt. Itaque inter-
15 fectis Novioduni custodibus quique eo negotiandi
causa convenerant, pecuniam atque equos inter se
partiti sunt ; obsides civitatum Bibracte ad magistratum deducendos curaverunt ; oppidum, quod a se
teneri non posse iudicabant, ne cui esset usui Rom-
20 anis, incenderunt ; frumenti quod subito potuerunt
navibus avexerunt, reliquum flumine atque incendio
corruperunt. Ipsi ex finitimis regionibus copias cogere,
praesidia custodiasque ad ripas Ligeris disponere
equitatumque omnibus locis iniciendi timoris causa
25 ostentare coeperunt, si ab re frumentaria Romanos
excludere aut adductos inopia ex provincia expellere
possent. Quam ad spem multum eos adiuvabat
quod Liger ex nivibus creverat, ut omnino vado non
posse transiri videretur.

56. Quibus rebus cognitis Caesar maturandum sibi

censuit, si esset in perficiendis pontibus periclitandum, ut prius quam essent maiores eo coactae copiae dimicaret. Nam, ut commutato consilio iter in provinciam converteret, ut ne metu quidem necessario 5 faciendum existimabat, cum infamia atque indignitas rei et oppositus mons Cevenna viarumque difficultas impediebat, tum maxime quod abiuncto Labieno atque eis legionibus quas una miserat vehementer timebat. Itaque admodum magnis diurnis noctur- 10 nisque itineribus confectis contra omnium opinionem ad Ligerem venit, vadoque per equites invento pro rei necessitate opportuno, ut bracchia modo atque umeri ad sustinenda arma liberi ab aqua esse possent, disposito equitatu qui vim fluminis refringeret 15 atque hostibus primo aspectu perturbatis incolumem exercitum traduxit; frumentumque in agris et pecoris copiam nactus, repleto his rebus exercitu iter in Senones facere instituit.

57. Dum haec apud Caesarem geruntur, Labienus eo supplemento, quod nuper ex Italia venerat, relicto Agedinci, ut esset impedimentis praesidio, cum IIII legionibus Lutetiam proficiscitur. Id est oppidum Parisiorum, quod positum est in insula fluminis 5 Sequanae. Cuius adventu ab hostibus cognito, magnae ex finitimis civitatibus copiae convenerunt. Summa imperi traditur Camulogeno Aulerco, qui prope confectus aetate tamen propter singularem

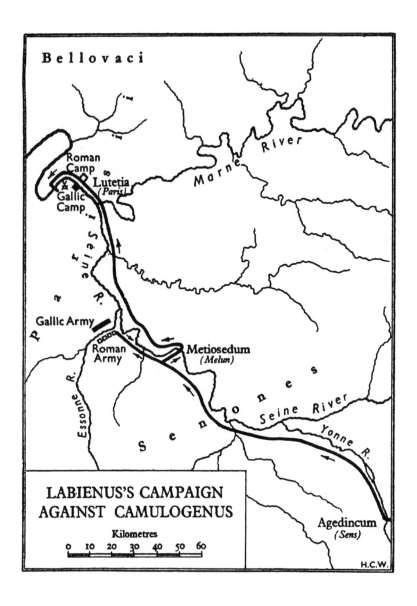

Bellovaci

Marne River

Roman
Camp

Lutetia
(Paris)

Gallic
Camp.

Seine R.

P a r i s i i

Gallic Army

Roman
Army

Metiosedum
(Melun)

Essonne R.

S e n o n e s

Seine River

Yonne R.

LABIENUS'S CAMPAIGN
AGAINST CAMULOGENUS

Kilometres

0   10   20   30   40   50   60

Agedincum
(Sens)

H.C.W.

scientiam rei militaris ad eum est honorem evocatus. 10
Is cum animadvertisset perpetuam esse paludem
quae influeret in Sequanam atque illum omnem locum magnopere impediret, hic consedit nostrosque
transitu prohibere instituit.

58. Labienus primo vineas agere, cratibus atque
aggere paludem explere atque iter munire conabatur.
Postquam id difficilius fieri animadvertit, silentio e
castris tertia vigilia egressus eodem quo venerat
itinere Metiosedum pervenit. Id est oppidum Sen- 5
onum, in insula Sequanae positum, ut paulo ante de
Lutetia diximus. Deprensis navibus circiter quinquaginta celeriterque coniunctis atque eo militibus
iniectis et rei novitate perterritis oppidanis, quorum
magna pars erat ad bellum evocata, sine contentione 10
oppido potitur. Refecto ponte, quem superioribus
diebus hostes resciderant, exercitum traducit et
secundo flumine ad Lutetiam iter facere coepit.
Hostes, re cognita ab eis qui Metiosedo fugerant,
Lutetiam incendi pontesque eius oppidi rescindi 15
iubent ; ipsi profecti a palude ad ripas Sequanae e
regione Lutetiae contra Labieni castra considunt.

59. Iam Caesar a Gergovia discessisse audiebatur,
iam de Aeduorum defectione et secundo Galliae motu
rumores adferebantur, Gallique in colloquiis interclusum itinere et Ligere Caesarem inopia frumenti
coactum in provinciam contendisse confirmabant. 5

Bellovaci autem, defectione Aeduorum cognita, qui
iam ante erant per se infideles, manus cogere atque
aperte bellum parare coeperunt. Tum Labienus
tanta rerum commutatione longe aliud sibi capien-
10 dum consilium atque antea senserat intellegebat,
neque iam ut aliquid adquireret proelioque hostes
lacesseret sed ut incolumem exercitum Agedincum
reduceret cogitabat. Namque altera ex parte Bellovaci, quae civitas in Gallia maximam habet opinion-
15 em virtutis, instabant, alteram Camulogenus parato
atque instructo exercitu tenebat ; tum legiones a
praesidio atque impedimentis interclusas maximum
flumen distinebat. Tantis subito difficultatibus
obiectis ab animi virtute auxilium petendum
20 videbat.

60. Sub vesperum consilio convocato, cohortatus
ut ea quae imperasset diligenter industrieque ad-
ministrarent, naves quas Metiosedo deduxerat
singulas equitibus Romanis attribuit et prima con-
5 fecta vigilia IIII milia passuum secundo flumine
silentio progredi ibique se exspectari iubet. Quinque
cohortes, quas minime firmas ad dimicandum esse
existimabat, castris praesidio relinquit ; quinque
eiusdem legionis reliquas de media nocte cum omni-
10 bus impedimentis adverso flumine magno tumultu
proficisci imperat. Conquirit etiam lintres ; has
magno sonitu remorum incitatas in eandem partem

mittit. Ipse post paulo silentio egressus cum tribus legionibus eum locum petit quo naves appelli ius- serat. 15

61. Eo cum esset ventum, exploratores hostium, ut omni fluminis parte erant dispositi, inopinantes, quod magna subito erat coorta tempestas, ab nostris op- primuntur ; exercitus equitatusque equitibus Rom- anis administrantibus quos ei negotio praefecerat 5 celeriter transmittitur. Uno fere tempore sub lucem hostibus nuntiatur in castris Romanorum praeter consuetudinem tumultuari et magnum ire agmen ad- verso flumine sonitumque remorum in eadem parte exaudiri et paulo infra milites navibus transportari. 10 Quibus rebus auditis, quod existimabant tribus locis transire legiones atque omnes perturbatos defectione Aeduorum fugam parare, suas quoque copias in tres partes distribuerunt. Nam praesidio e regione cas- trorum relicto et parva manu Metiosedum versus 15 missa, quae tantum progrediatur quantum naves processissent, reliquas copias contra Labienum duxerunt.

62. Prima luce et nostri omnes erant transportati et hostium acies cernebatur. Labienus milites cohortatus ut suae pristinae virtutis et secundissimo- rum proeliorum retinerent memoriam atque ipsum Caesarem, cuius ductu saepe numero hostes superas- 5 sent, praesentem adesse existimarent, dat signum

proeli. Primo concursu ab dextro cornu, ubi septima
legio constiterat, hostes pelluntur atque in fugam
coiciuntur ; ab sinistro, quem locum duodecima
10 legio tenebat, cum primi ordines hostium transfixi
telis concidissent, tamen acerrime reliqui resistebant
nec dabat suspicionem fugae quisquam. Ipse dux
hostium Camulogenus suis aderat atque eos cohorta-
batur. At incerto etiam nunc exitu victoriae, cum
15 septimae legionis tribunis esset nuntiatum quae in
sinistro cornu gererentur, post tergum hostium
legionem ostenderunt signaque intulerunt. Ne eo
quidem tempore quisquam loco cessit, sed circumventi omnes interfectique sunt. Eandem fortunam
20 tulit Camulogenus. At ei qui praesidio contra castra
Labieni erant relicti, cum proelium commissum audis-
sent, subsidio suis ierunt collemque ceperunt, neque
nostrorum militum victorum impetum sustinere
potuerunt. Sic cum suis fugientibus permixti, quos
25 non silvae montesque texerunt, ab equitatu sunt
interfecti. Hoc negotio confecto Labienus revertitur
Agedincum, ubi impedimenta totius exercitus relicta
erant ; inde tertio die cum omnibus copiis ad Caesarem pervenit.

63. Defectione Aeduorum cognita bellum augetur.
Legationes in omnes partes circummittuntur ; quantum gratia, auctoritate, pecunia valent ad sollici-
tandas civitates nituntur ; nacti obsides quos Caesar

apus eos deposuerat, horum supplicio dubitantes 5
territant. Petunt a Vercingetorige Aedui ut ad se
veniat rationesque belli gerendi communicet. Re
impetrata contendunt ut ipsis summa imperi trada-
tur et re in controversiam deducta totius Galliae concilium Bibracte indicitur. Eodem conveniunt un- 10
dique frequentes. Multitudinis suffragiis res permit-
titur; ad unum omnes Vercingetorigem probant
imperatorem. Ab hoc concilio Remi, Lingones,
Treveri afuerunt ; illi, quod amicitiam Romanorum
sequebantur ; Treveri, quod aberant longius et ab 15
Germanis premebantur, quae fuit causa quare toto
abessent bello et neutris auxilia mitterent. Magno
dolore Aedui ferunt se deiectos principatu, queruntur
fortunae commutationem et Caesaris indulgentiam
in se requirunt; neque tamen suscepto bello suum 20
consilium ab reliquis separare audent. Inviti summae
spei adulescentes Eporedorix et Viridomarus Ver-
cingetorigi parent.

64. Ipse imperat reliquis civitatibus obsides
diemque ei rei constituit ; omnes equites, XV milia
numero celeriter convenire iubet ; peditatu, quem
antea habuerit, se fore contentum dicit, neque fortunam temptaturum aut in acie dimicaturum sed, 5
quoniam abundet equitatu, perfacile esse factu
frumentationibus pabulationibusque Romanos prohibere ; aequo modo animo sua ipsi frumenta cor-

rumpant aedificiaque incendant, qua rei familiaris
10 iactura perpetuum imperium libertatemque se consequi videant. His constitutis rebus, Aeduis Segus-
iavisque, qui sunt finitimi provinciae, decem milia
peditum imperat ; huc addit equites octingentos.
His praeficit fratrem Eporedorigis, bellumque inferri
15 Allobrogibus iubet. Altera ex parte Gabalos prox-
imosque pagos Arvernorum in Helvios, item Rutenos
Cadurcosque ad fines Volcarum Arecomicorum
depopulandos mittit. Nihilo minus clandestinis
nuntiis legationibusque Allobrogas sollicitat, quorum
20 mentes nondum ab superiore bello resedisse sperabat. Horum principibus pecunias, civitati autem
imperium totius provinciae pollicetur.

65. Ad hos omnes casus provisa erant praesidia
cohortium duarum et XX, quae ex ipsa coacta provincia ab L. Caesare legato ad omnes partes opponebantur. Helvii sua sponte cum finitimis proelio
5 congressi pelluntur et C. Valerio Donnotauro, Caburi
filio, principe civitatis compluribusque aliis interfectis intra oppida ac muros compelluntur. Allobroges crebris ad Rhodanum dispositis praesidiis
magna cum cura et diligentia suos fines tuentur.
10 Caesar, quod hostes equitatu superiores esse intellegebat et interclusis omnibus itineribus nulla re ex
provincia atque Italia sublevari poterat, trans
Rhenum in Germaniam mittit ad eas civitates quas

superioribus annis pacaverat equitesque ab his ar-
cessit et levis armaturae pedites, qui inter eos proe- 15
liari consuerant. Eorum adventu, quod minus
idoneis equis utebantur, a tribunis militum reliquisque equitibus Romanis atque evocatis equos
sumit Germanisque distribuit.

66. Interea, dum haec geruntur, hostium copiae
ex Arvernis equitesque qui toti Galliae erant imperati conveniunt. Magno horum coacto numero,
cum Caesar in Sequanos per extremos Lingonum fines
iter faceret quo facilius subsidium provinciae ferri 5
posset, circiter milia passuum X ab Romanis trinis
castris Vercingetorix consedit; convocatisque ad
concilium praefectis equitum venisse tempus victoriae demonstrat: fugere in provinciam Romanos
Galliaque excedere; id sibi ad praesentem obtinen- 10
dam libertatem satis esse, ad reliqui temporis pacem
atque otium parum profici: maioribus enim coactis
copiis reversuros neque finem bellandi facturos.
Proinde agmine impeditos adoriantur; si pedites
suis auxilium ferant atque in eo morentur, iter 15
facere non posse; si, id quod magis futurum confidat, relictis impedimentis suae saluti consulant, et
usu rerum necessariarum et dignitate spoliatum iri.
Nam de equitibus hostium quin nemo eorum progredi modo extra agmen audeat, ipsos quidem non 20
debere dubitare; id quo maiore faciant animo, copi-

as se omnes pro castris habiturum et terrori hostibus
futurum. / Conclamant equites, sanctissimo iure
iurando confirmari oportere, ne tecto recipiatur, ne
25 ad liberos, ne ad parentes, ne ad uxorem aditum
habeat qui non bis per agmen hostium perequitasset.

67. Probata re atque omnibus iure iurando adactis,
postero die in tres partes distributo equitatu duae
se acies ab duobus lateribus ostendunt, una a primo
agmine iter impedire coepit. Qua re nuntiata Caesar
5 suum quoque equitatum tripertito divisum contra
hostem ire iubet. Pugnatur una omnibus in partibus. Consistit agmen ; impedimenta intra legiones
recipiuntur. Si qua in parte nostri laborare aut
gravius premi videbantur, eo signa inferri Caesar
10 aciemque constitui iubebat , quae res et hostes ad
insequendum tardabat et nostros spe auxili con-
firmabat. Tandem Germani ab dextro latere summum iugum nacti hostes loco depellunt ; fugientes
usque ad flumen, ubi Vercingetorix cum pedestribus
15 copiis consederat, persequuntur compluresque
interficiunt. Qua re animadversa reliqui ne circumirentur veriti se fugae mandant. Omnibus locis
fit caedes. Tres nobilissimi Aedui capti ad Caesarem
perducuntur : Cotus, praefectus equitum, qui con-
20 troversiam cum Convictolitavi proximis comitiis
habuerat, et Cavarillus, qui post defectionem Litavicci pedestribus copiis praefuerat, et Eporedorix,

quo duce ante adventum Caesaris Aedui cum Sequanis bello contenderant.

68. Fugato omni equitatu, Vercingetorix copias, ut pro castris collocaverat, reduxit protinusque Alesiam, quod est oppidum Mandubiorum, iter facere coepit celeriterque impedimenta ex castris educi et se subsequi iussit. Caesar impedimentis in 5 proximum collem deductis, duabus legionibus praesidio relictis secutus quantum diei tempus est passum, circiter tribus milibus hostium ex novissimo agmine interfectis altero die ad Alesiam castra fecit. Perspecto urbis situ perterritisque hostibus, quod equi- 10 tatu, qua maxime parte exercitus confidebant, erant pulsi, adhortatus ad laborem milites circumvallare instituit.

69. Ipsum erat oppidum Alesia in colle summo, admodum edito loco, ut nisi obsidione expugnari non posse videretur; cuius collis radices duo duabus ex partibus flumina subluebant. Ante id oppidum planities circiter milia passuum III in longitudinem 5 patebat ; reliquis ex omnibus partibus colles mediocri interiecto spatio pari altitudinis fastigio oppidum cingebant. Sub muro, quae pars collis ad orientem solem spectabat, hunc omnem locum copiae Gallorum compleverant fossamque et maceriam sex in alti- 10 tudinem pedum praeduxerant. Eius munitionis quae ab Romanis instituebatur circuitus XI milia

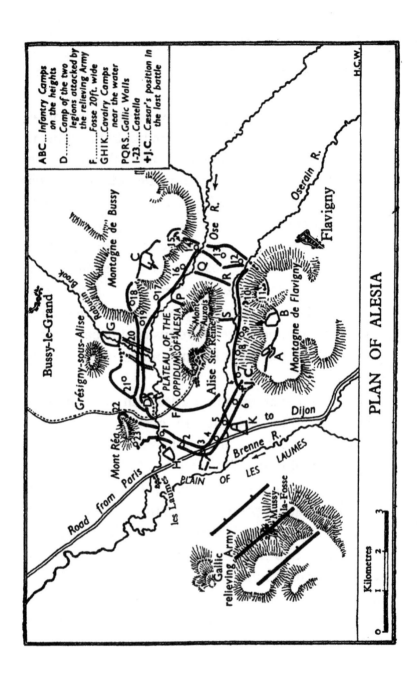

PLAN OF ALESIA

ABC..Infantry Camps
       on the heights
D........Camp of the two
       legions attacked by
       the relieving Army
F........Fosse 20ft. wide
GHIK..Cavalry Camps
       near the water
PQRS..Gallic Walls
1-23....Castella
+J.C...Cæsar's position in
       the last battle

Kilometres
0   1   2   3

passuum tenebat. Castra opportunis locis erant
posita, ibique castella XXIII facta, quibus in castellis interdiu stationes ponebantur, ne qua subito 15
eruptio fieret; haec eadem noctu excubitoribus ac
firmis praesidiis tenebantur.

70. Opere instituto, fit equestre proelium in ea
planitie quam intermissam collibus tria milia passuum in longitudinem patere supra demonstravimus.
Summa vi ab utrisque contenditur. Laborantibus
nostris Caesar Germanos summittit legionesque pro 5
castris constituit, ne qua subito irruptio ab hostium
peditatu fiat. Praesidio legionum addito nostris
animus augetur : hostes in fugam coiecti se ipsi
multitudine impediunt atque angustioribus portis
relictis coacervantur. Germani acrius usque ad 10
munitiones sequuntur. Fit magna caedes ; non nulli
relictis equis fossam transire et maceriam trans-
cendere conantur. Paulum legiones Caesar quas pro
vallo constituerat promoveri iubet. Non minus qui
intra munitiones erant perturbantur Galli : veniri 15
ad se confestim existimantes ad arma conclamant ;
non nulli perterriti in oppidum irrumpunt. Vercingetorix iubet portas claudi, ne castra nudentur.
Multis interfectis, compluribus equis captis Germani sese recipiunt. 20

71. Vercingetorix, prius quam munitiones ab
Romanis perficiantur, consilium capit omnem ab se

equitatum noctu dimittere. Discedentibus mandat
ut suam quisque eorum civitatem adeat omnesque
5 qui per aetatem arma ferre possint ad bellum cogant.
Sua in illos merita proponit obtestaturque ut suae
salutis rationem habeant, neu se optime de communi
libertate meritum hostibus in cruciatum dedant.
Quod si indiligentiores fuerint, milia hominum
10 delecta LXXX una secum interitura domonstrat.
Ratione inita exigue dierum se habere XXX frumentum, sed paulo etiam longius tolerare posse
parcendo. His datis mandatis, qua nostrum opus
erat intermissum, secunda vigilia silentio equitatum
15 dimittit. Frumentum omne ad se referri iubet;
capitis poenam eis qui non paruerint constituit;
pecus, cuius magna erat copia ab Mandubiis com-
pulsa, viritim distribuit; frumentum parce et
paulatim metiri instituit; copias omnes quas pro
20 oppido collocaverat in oppidum recipit. His rationibus auxilia Galliae exspectare et bellum parat administrare.

72. Quibus rebus cognitis ex perfugis et captivis,
Caesar haec genera munitionis instituit. Fossam
pedum XX derectis lateribus duxit, ut eius fossae
solum tantundem pateret quantum summae fossae
5 labra distarent. Reliquas omnes munitiones ab ea
fossa passus quadringentos reduxit, id hoc consilio,
quoniam tantum esset necessario spatium complexus

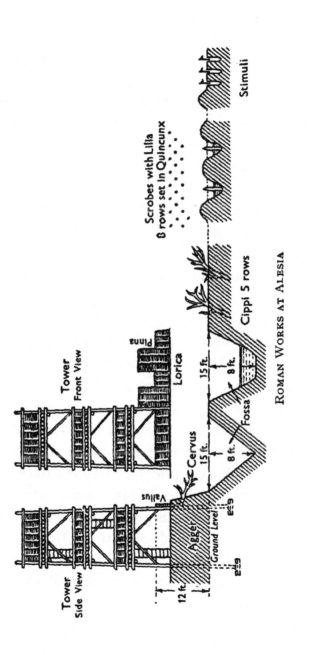

ROMAN WORKS AT ALESIA

Tower Side View

Tower Front View

Pinna

Lorica

Cervus

Vallus

Agger

Ground Level

12 ft.

15 ft.

8 ft.

Fossa

8 ft.

15 ft.

Cippi 5 rows

Scrobes with Lilia
8 rows set in Quincunx

Stimuli

nec facile totum opus corona militum cingeretur, ne
de improviso aut noctu ad munitiones hostium multi-
10 tudo advolaret aut interdiu tela in nostros operi
destinatos coicere possent. Hoc intermisso spatio
duas fossas quindecim pedes latas eadem altitudine
perduxit, quarum interiorem campestribus ac de-
missis locis aqua ex flumine derivata complevit.
15 Post eas aggerem ac vallum XII pedum exstruxit.
Huic loricam pinnasque adiecit, grandibus cervis
eminentibus ad commissuras pluteorum atque ag-
geris qui ascensum hostium tardarent, et turres toto
opere circumdedit quae pedes LXXX inter se dis-
20 tarent.

73. Erat eodem tempore et materiari et frumentari
et tantas munitiones fieri necesse deminutis nostris
copiis, quae longius ab castris progrediebantur; ac
non numquam opera nostra Galli temptare atque
5 eruptionem ex oppido pluribus portis summa vi
facere conabantur. Quare ad haec rursus opera ad-
dendum Caesar putavit, quo minore numero militum
munitiones defendi possent. Itaque truncis arborum
aut admodum firmis ramis abscisis atque horum
10 delibratis ac praeacutis cacuminibus perpetuae fossae
quinos pedes altae ducebantur. Huc illi stipites
demissi et ab infimo revincti, ne revelli possent, ab
ramis eminebant. Quini erant ordines coniuncti
inter se atque implicati; quo qui intraverant, se

CAESAR'S WORK AT ALESIA—RECONSTRUCTION

15 ipsi acutissimis vallis induebant ; hos cippos appellabant. Ante hos obliquis ordinibus in quincuncem
dispositis scrobes tres in altitudinem pedes fodie-
bantur paulatim angustiore ad infimum fastigio.
Huc teretes stipites feminis crassitudine ab summo
20 praeacuti et praeusti demittebantur ita ut non amplius digitis quattuor ex terra eminerent ; simul con-
firmandi et stabiliendi causa singuli ab infimo solo
pedes terra exculcabantur ; reliqua pars scrobis ad
occultandas insidias viminibus ac virgultis intege-
25 batur. Huius generis octoni ordines ducti ternos
inter se pedes distabant. Id ex similitudine floris
lilium appellabant. Ante haec taleae pedem longae
ferreis hamis infixis totae in terram infodiebantur
mediocribusque intermissis spatiis omnibus locis
30 disserebantur ; quos stimulos nominabant.

74. His rebus perfectis, regiones secutus quam
potuit aequissimas pro loci natura, XIIII milia
passuum complexus pares eiusdem generis munitiones, diversas ab his, contra exteriorem hostem per-
5 fecit, ut ne magna quidem multitudine, si ita accidat,
eius discessu munitionum praesidia circumfundi
possent ; ne autem cum periculo ex castris egredi
cogatur, dierum XXX pabulum frumentumque
habere omnes convectum iubet.

75. Dum haec apud Alesiam geruntur, Galli, concilio principum indicto, non omnes eos qui arma ferre

possent, ut censuit Vercingetorix, convocandos statuunt sed certum numerum cuique ex civitate imperandum, ne tanta multitudine confusa nec 5 moderari nec discernere suos nec frumentationem habere possent. Imperant Aeduis atque eorum clientibus, Segusiavis, Ambluaretis, Aulercis Branno-vicibus, Blannoviis milia XXXV; parem numerum Arvernis adiunctis Eleutetis, Cadurcis, Gabalis, Vel- 10 laviis, qui sub imperio Arvernorum esse consuerunt; Sequanis, Senonibus, Biturigibus, Santonis, Rutenis, Carnutibus duodena milia; Bellovacis decem; totidem Lemovicibus; octona Pictonibus et Turonis et Parisiis et Helvetiis; Senonibus, Ambianis, 15 Mediomatricis, Petrocoriis, Nerviis, Morinis, Nitio-brigibus quina milia; Aulercis Cenomanis totidem; Atrebatibus IV; Veliocassis Lexoviis et Aulercis Eburovicibus terna; Rauricis et Boiis bina; XXX milia universis civitatibus quae Oceanum attingunt 20 quaeque eorum consuetudine Aremoricae appellan-tur, quo sunt in numero Curiosolites, Redones, Ambibarii, Caletes, Osismi, Veneti, Lemovices, Venelli. Ex his Bellovaci suum numerum non com-pleverunt, quod se suo nomine atque arbitrio cum 25 Romanis bellum gesturos dicebant, neque cuiusquam imperio obtemperaturos; rogati tamen ab Commio pro eius hospitio duo milia una miserunt.

76. Huius opera Commi, ut antea demonstravimus, fideli atque utili superioribus annis erat usus in Britannia Caesar ; quibus ille pro meritis civitatem eius immunem esse iusserat, iura legesque reddiderat 5 atque ipsi Morinos attribuerat. Tamen tanta universae Galliae consensio fuit libertatis vindicandae et pristinae belli laudis reciperandae, ut neque beneficiis neque amicitiae memoria moverentur, omnesque et animo et opibus in id bellum incumberent. 10 Coactis equitum VIII milibus et peditum circiter CCXL, haec in Aeduorum finibus recensebantur, numerusque inibatur, praefecti constituebantur. Commio Atrebati, Viridomaro et Eporedorigi Aeduis, Vercassivellauno Arverno, consobrino Vercingetori-15 gis, summa imperi traditur. His delecti ex civitatibus attribuuntur quorum consilio bellum administraretur. Omnes alacres et fiduciae pleni ad Alesiam proficiscuntur, neque erat omnium quisquam qui aspectum modo tantae multitudinis sustineri posse 20 arbitraretur, praesertim ancipiti proelio, cum ex oppido eruptione pugnaretur, foris tantae copiae equitatus peditatusque cernerentur.

77. At ei qui Alesiae obsidebantur, praeterita die qua auxilia suorum exspectaverant, consumpto omni frumento, inscii quid in Aeduis gereretur, concilio coacto de exitu suarum fortunarum consultabant. 5 Ac variis dictis sententiis, quarum pars deditionem, pars, dum vires suppeterent, eruptionem censebat,

non praetereunda oratio Critognati videtur propter
eius singularem et nefariam crudelitatem. Hic,
summo in Arvernis ortus loco et magnae habitus
auctoritatis, 'nihil', inquit, 'de eorum sententia 10
dicturus sum, qui turpissimam servitutem deditionis
nomine appellant, neque hos habendos civium loco
neque ad concilium adhibendos censeo. Cum his
mihi res sit qui eruptionem probant; quorum in
consilio omnium vestrum consensu pristinae residere 15
virtutis memoria videtur. Animi est ista mollitia,
non virtus, paulisper inopiam ferre non posse. Qui
se ultro morti offerant facilius reperiuntur quam qui
dolorem patienter ferant. Atque ego hanc sententiam probarem (tantum apud me dignitas potest), 20
si nullam praeterquam vitae nostrae iacturam fieri
viderem; sed in consilio capiendo omnem Galliam
respiciamus, quam ad nostrum auxilium concitavi-
mus. Quid hominum milibus LXXX uno loco interfectis propinquis consanguineisque nostris animi 25
fore existimatis, si paene in ipsis cadaveribus proelio
decertare cogentur? Nolite hos vestro auxilio ex-
spoliare, qui vestrae salutis causa suum periculum
neglexerunt, nec stultitia ac temeritate vestra aut
animi imbecillitate omnem Galliam prosternere et 30
perpetuae servituti subicere. An, quod ad diem non
venerunt, de eorum fide constantiaque dubitatis?
Quid ergo? Romanos in illis ulterioribus munitioni-

bus animine causa cotidie exerceri putatis ? Si
35 illorum nuntiis confirmari non potestis omni aditu
praesepto, his utimini testibus appropinquare eorum
adventum ; cuius rei timore exterriti diem noctemque
in opere versantur. Quid ergo mei consili est ?
Facere, quod nostri maiores nequaquam pari bello
40 Cimbrorum Teutonumque fecerunt ; qui in oppida
compulsi ac simili inopia subacti eorum corporibus
qui aetate ad bellum inutiles videbantur vitam toler-
averunt neque se hostibus tradiderunt. Cuius rei
si exemplum non haberemus, tamen libertatis causa
45 institui et posteris prodi pulcherrimum iudicarem.
Nam quid illi simile bello fuit ? Depopulata Gallia
Cimbri magnaque inlata calamitate finibus quidem
nostris aliquando excesserunt atque alias terras
petierunt ; iura, leges, agros, libertatem nobis reli-
50 querunt.   Romani vero quid petunt aliud aut quid
volunt, nisi invidia adducti, quos fama nobiles potentesque bello cognoverunt, horum in agris civitatibusque considere atque his aeternam iniungere servitutem ? Neque enim ulla alia condicione bella
55 gesserunt. Quod si ea quae in longinquis nationibus
geruntur ignoratis, respicite finitimam Galliam, quae
in provinciam redacta, iure et legibus commutatis,
securibus subiecta perpetua premitur servitute.'

78. Sententiis dictis constituunt, ut ei qui valetudine aut aetate inutiles sunt bello oppido excedant

atque omnia prius experiantur quam ad Critognati
sententiam descendant ; illo tamen tempore potius
utendum consilio, si res cogat atque auxilia moren- 5
tur, quam aut deditionis aut pacis subeundam condicionem. Mandubii, qui eos oppido receperant,
cum liberis atque uxoribus exire coguntur. Hi cum
ad munitiones Romanorum accessissent, flentes
omnibus precibus orabant ut se in servitutem receptos 10
cibo iuvarent. At Caesar dispositis in vallo custo-
diis recipi prohibebat.

79. Interea Commius reliquique duces quibus
summa imperi permissa erat cum omnibus copiis ad
Alesiam perveniunt, et colle exteriore occupato non
longius mille passibus ab nostris munitionibus considunt. Postero die equitatu ex castris educto, 5
omnem eam planitiem quam in longitudinem tria
milia passuum patere demonstravimus complent,
pedestresque copias paulum ab eo loco abditas in
locis superioribus constituunt. Erat ex oppido
Alesia despectus in campum. Concurrunt his auxiliis 10
visis ; fit gratulatio inter eos atque omnium animi
ad laetitiam excitantur. Itaque productis copiis
ante oppidum considunt et proximam fossam cratibus integunt atque aggere explent seque ad eruptionem atque omnes casus comparant. 15

80. Caesar, omni exercitu ad utramque partem
munitionum disposito, ut, si usus veniat, suum

quisque locum teneat et noverit, equitatum ex castris
educi et proelium committi iubet. Erat ex omnibus
5 castris, quae summum undique iugum tenebant,
despectus, atque omnes milites intenti pugnae pro-
ventum exspectabant. Galli inter equites raros
sagittarios expeditosque levis armaturae interiecer-
ant, qui suis cedentibus auxilio succurrerent et nos-
10 trorum equitum impetus sustinerent. Ab his complures de improviso vulnerati proelio excedebant.
Cum suos pugna superiores esse Galli confiderent et
nostros multitudine premi viderent, ex omnibus partibus et ei qui munitionibus continebantur et hi qui ad
15 auxilium convenerant clamore et ululatu suorum
animos confirmabant. Quod in conspectu omnium
res gerebatur neque recte ac turpiter factum celari
poterat, utrosque et laudis cupiditas et timor ignominiae ad virtutem excitabat. Cum a meridie
20 prope ad solis occasum dubia victoria pugnaretur,
Germani una in parte confertis turmis in hostes impetum fecerunt eosque propulerunt ; quibus in fugam
coiectis, sagittarii circumventi interfectique sunt.
Item ex reliquis partibus nostri cedentes usque in
25 castra insecuti sui colligendi facultatem non deder-
unt. At ei qui ab Alesia processerant maesti prope
victoria desperata se in oppidum receperunt.

81. Uno die intermisso Galli atque hoc spatio magno cratium, scalarum, harpagonum numero effecto,

media nocte silentio ex castris egressi ad campestres
munitiones accedunt. Subito clamore sublato, qua
significatione qui in oppido obsidebantur de suo ad- 5
ventu cognoscere possent, crates proicere, fundis,
sagittis, lapidibus nostros de vallo proturbare reliquaque quae ad oppugnationem pertinent parant
administrare. Eodem tempore clamore exaudito
dat tuba signum suis Vercingetorix atque ex oppido 10
educit. Nostri, ut superioribus diebus, ut cuique
erat locus attributus, ad munitiones accedunt ; fundis librilibus sudibusque, quas in opere disposuerant,
ac glandibus Gallos proterrent. Prospectu tenebris
adempto multa utrimque vulnera accipiuntur. 15
Complura tormentis tela coiciuntur. At M. Antonius
et C. Trebonius legati, quibus hae partes ad
defendendum obvenerant, qua ex parte nostros
premi intellexerant, eis auxilio ex ulterioribus castellis deductos summittebant. 20

82. Dum longius ab munitione aberant Galli,
plus multitudine telorum proficiebant ; postea
quam propius successerunt, aut se stimulis inopinantes induebant aut in scrobes delati transfodie-
bantur aut ex vallo ac turribus traiecti pilis murali- 5
bus interibant. Multis undique vulneribus acceptis,
nulla munitione perrupta, cum lux appeteret, veriti
ne ab latere aperto ex superioribus castris eruptione
circumvenirentur se ad suos receperunt. At in-

10 teriores, dum ea quae a Vercingetorige ad eruptionem
praeparata erant proferunt, priores fossas explent,
diutius in his rebus administrandis morati prius suos
discessisse cognoverunt quam munitionibus appropinquarent. Ita re infecta in oppidum reverterunt.

83. Bis magno cum detrimento repulsi Galli quid
agant consulunt ; locorum peritos adhibent ; ex his
superiorum castrorum situs munitionesque cognos-
cunt. Erat a septentrionibus collis, quem propter
5 magnitudinem circuitus opere circumplecti non
potuerant nostri ; necessario paene iniquo loco et
leniter declivi castra fecerant. Haec C. Antistius
Reginus et C. Caninius Rebilus legati cum duabus
legionibus obtinebant. Cognitis per exploratores
10 regionibus, duces hostium LX milia ex omni numero
deligunt earum civitatum quae maximam virtutis
opinionem habebant , quid quoque pacto agi placeat
occulte inter se constituunt , adeundi tempus de-
finiunt, cum meridies esse videatur. His copiis
15 Vercassivellaunum Arvernum, unum ex quattuor
ducibus, propinquum Vercingetorigis, praeficiunt.
Ille ex castris prima vigilia egressus prope confecto
sub lucem itinere post montem se occultavit militesque ex nocturno labore sese reficere iussit. Cum
20 iam meridies appropinquare videretur, ad ea castra
quae supra demonstravimus contendit ; eodemque
tempore equitatus ad campestres munitiones accedere

et reliquae copiae pro castris sese ostendere coeperunt.

84. Vercingetorix ex arce Alesiae suos conspicatus ex oppido egreditur, crates, longurios, musculos, falces reliquaque quae eruptionis causa paraverat profert. Pugnatur uno tempore omnibus locis atque omnia temptantur : quae minime visa pars firma 5 est, huc concurritur. Romanorum manus tantis munitionibus distinetur nec facile pluribus locis occurrit. Multum ad terrendos nostros valet clamor, qui post tergum pugnantibus exstitit, quod suum periculum in aliena vident salute constare ; omnia 10 enim plerumque quae absunt vehementius hominum mentes perturbant.

85. Caesar idoneum locum nactus quid quaque ex parte geratur cognoscit ; laborantibus summittit. Utrisque ad animum occurrit unum esse illud tempus quo maxime contendi conveniat : Galli, nisi perfregerint munitiones, de omni salute desperant ; 5 Romani, si rem obtinuerint, finem laborum omnium exspectant. Maxime ad superiores munitiones laboratur, quo Vercassivellaunum missum demonstravimus. Iniquum loci ad declivitatem fastigium magnum habet momentum. Alii tela coiciunt, alii 10 testudine facta subeunt ; defatigatis in vicem integri succedunt. Agger ab universis in munitionem coiectus et ascensum dat Gallis et ea quae in terra

occultaverant Romani contegit ; nec iam arma
15 nostris nec vires suppetunt.

86. His rebus cognitis Caesar Labienum cum
cohortibus sex subsidio laborantibus mittit ; imperat, si sustinere non possit, deductis cohortibus,
eruptione pugnet ; id, nisi necessario, ne faciat.
5 Ipse adit reliquos, cohortatur ne labori succumbant ;
omnium superiorum dimicationum fructum in eo die
atque hora docet consistere. Interiores, desperatis
campestribus locis propter magnitudinem munitionum, loca praerupta ex ascensu temptant ; huc ea
10 quae paraverant conferunt. Multitudine telorum
ex turribus propugnantes deturbant, aggere et cratibus fossas explent, falcibus vallum ac loricam rescin-
dunt.

87. Mittit primo Brutum adulescentem cum
cohortibus Caesar, post cum aliis C. Fabium legatum ; postremo ipse, cum vehementius pugnaretur,
integros subsidio adducit. Restituto proelio ac re-
5 pulsis hostibus eo quo Labienum miserat contendit ;
cohortes IIII ex proximo castello deducit, equitum
partem se sequi, partem circumire exteriores munitiones et ab tergo hostes adoriri iubet. Labienus,
postquam neque aggeres neque fossae vim hostium
10 sustinere poterant, coactis una XI cohortibus, quas
ex proximis praesidiis deductas fors obtulit, Caesarem per nuntios facit certiorem quid faciendum

existimet. Accelerat Caesar, ut proelio intersit.

88. Eius adventu ex colore vestitus cognito, quo insigni in proeliis uti consuerat, turmisque equitum et cohortibus visis quas se sequi iusserat, ut de locis superioribus haec declivia et devexa cernebantur, hostes proelium committunt. Utrimque clamore 5 sublato excipit rusus ex vallo atque omnibus munitionibus clamor. Nostri omissis pilis gladiis rem gerunt. Repente post tergum equitatus cernitur; cohortes aliae appropinquant. Hostes terga verterunt; fugientibus equites occurrunt. Fit magna 10 caedes. Sedulius, dux et princeps Lemovicum, occiditur; Vercassivellaunus Arvernus vivus in fuga comprehenditur; signa militaria LXXIIII ad Caesarem referuntur; pauci ex tanto numero se incolumes in castra recipiunt. Conspicati ex oppido caedem 15 et fugam suorum desperata salute copias a munitionibus reducunt. Fit protinus hac re audita ex castris Gallorum fuga. Quod nisi crebris subsidiis ac totius diei labore milites essent defessi, omnes hostium copiae deleri potuissent. De media nocte missus 20 equitatus novissimum agmen consequitur; magnus numerus capitur atque interficitur, reliqui ex fuga in civitates discedunt.

89. Postero die Vercingetorix consilio convocato id bellum se suscepisse non suarum necessitatum sed communis libertatis causa demonstrat et, quoniam

sit fortunae cedendum, ad utramque rem se illis
offere, seu morte sua Romanis satisfacere seu vivum 5
tradere velint. Mittuntur de his rebus ad Caesarem
legati. Iubet arma tradi, principes produci. Ipse in
munitione pro castris consedit ; eo duces producuntur. Vercingetorix deditur, arma proiciuntur. Re-
servatis Aeduis atque Arvernis, si per eos civitates 10
reciperare posset, ex reliquis captivis toto exercitui
capita singula praedae nomine distribuit.

90. His rebus confectis, in Aeduos proficiscitur ;
civitatem recipit. Eo legati ab Arvernis missi quae
imperaret se facturos pollicentur. Imperat magnum
numerum obsidum. Legiones in hiberna mittit.
Captivorum circiter XX milia Aeduis Arvernisque 5
reddit. T. Labienum duabus cum legionibus et
equitatu in Sequanos proficisci iubet ; huic M. Sem-
pronium Rutilum attribuit. C. Fabium legatum et
L. Minucium Basilum cum legionibus duabus in
Remis collocat, ne quam a finitimis Bellovacis cala- 10
mitatem accipiant. C. Antistium Reginum in
Ambibaretos, T. Sextium in Bituriges, C. Caninium
Rebilum in Rutenos cum singulis legionibus mittit.
Q. Tullium Ciceronem et P. Sulpicium Cabilloni et
Matiscone in Aeduis ad Ararim rei frumentariae 15
causa collocat. Ipse Bibracte hiemare constituit.
His litteris cognitis Romae dierum viginti suppli-
catio redditur.

NOTES

NOTES

CHAPTER 1

Line 1. **quieta Gallia,** abl. of attendant circumstances, (abl. absol.), having the force of a temporal clause, ' when Gaul was quiet '. Note that the verb **sum** has no present participle and that when an abl. absol. which would naturally include it, as in the present case, is used, only the subject and complement appear. Cf. **absente imperatore,** l. 22.

l. 1. **ut** with the indicative means ' as ' or ' when '.

l. 1. **in Italiam.** By ' Italy ' Caesar means Cisalpine Gaul (Gaul on this—the Roman side of the Alps), i.e. the Po valley which had been for nearly four centuries occupied by settled tribes of Gauls. Caesar's sphere of government included Cisalpine Gaul, Illyricum (north-east shores of the Adriatic), and Transalpine Gaul (south-east France). During the winter Caesar visited Cisalpine Gaul to hold assizes (**ad conventus agendos**) and to attend to the various civil duties which fell to the lot of a provincial governor.

l. 2. **ad conventus agendos,** *lit.,* ' for assizes to-be-held ', i.e. ' for holding, i.e. to hold, the assizes'.

l. 2. **proficiscitur.** Even when recording past events, Latin writers often use the present tense—the Historic Present. It may control primary or historic sequence. Translate by a past tense.

ll. 2–3. **de Clodi caede.** The anarchy then prevalent in Rome is well illustrated by the turbulent activities of Clodius, a ringleader in the riots that frequently occurred in the city. One of Caesar's agents, he was killed 52 B.C. in a scuffle with Milo, one of the supporters of Pompey.

l. 4. **ut ... coniurarent** is explanatory of the senate's decree

' that all the younger-men-of-military-age (**iuniores**) in Italy should be sworn in en masse (*con*)' ; ' men of military age ', i.e. 17 to 45.

ll. 4–5. **tota provincia,** ' throughout his whole province ', i.e. Cisalpine Gaul. See the note above.

Observe that with **totus, omnis,** and **medius,** the abl. of *the place where* is generally used without the prep. **in.**

ll. 6–7. **addunt . . . Galli,** *lit.,* ' the Gauls themselves add and invent with rumours ', i.e. ' of their own invention the Gauls created additional rumours '.

l. 7. **quod,** ' as '.

l. 7. **res,** ' the situation '.

ll. 8–9. **retineri . . . posse,** acc. and infin. dependent upon **addunt et adfingunt,** ' that Caesar was detained by the disturbance in-the-city (i.e. Rome) and could not . . .'.

Here we have another reference to the political discord in Rome. Caesar's army is stationed in winter quarters at strategic points in Gaul.

l. 9. **impulsi,** nom. pl. masc., perf. part. pass. of **impello.**

ll. 10–11. **qui . . . dolerent,** ' inasmuch as they resented even before that they were . . .'. Note **qui** introducing an adverbial clause of reason—hence the subjunctive mood.

l. 12. **incipiunt,** historic present again.

ll. 12–13. **indictis inter se conciliis,** ' having convened meetings amongst themselves '. The abl. absol. may be turned into English in a variety of ways of which the commonest are : (i) a temporal clause, ' when they had convened . . .'. (ii) a participial phrase, as in the translation above. (iii) a finite verb, ' they convened meetings (and) . . .'.

l. 13. **silvestribus . . . locis,** ' in remote spots in-the-forests ', abl. of place where *without* a preposition.

l. 14. **de Acconis morte.** Acco was a chieftain of the Senones who had been the ringleader in a rebellion of his tribe in 53 B.C. Caesar tells us in Book VI, Ch. 44 that he had pronounced unusually severe sentence upon him and executed punishment in the traditional Roman fashion, i.e. had had him flogged to death.

l. 16. **omnibus . . . ,** ' by all-kinds-of . . . '.

l. 17. **qui . . . faciant,** ' (men) to make beginnings of the campaign', i.e. ' men to begin the campaign '. Note again **qui** introducing an adverbial clause, this time of result.

ll. 17–18. **et sui . . . vindicent,** ' and at the peril of their own head (i.e. lives) to claim Gaul for freedom, (i.e. to champion the freedom of Gaul) '.

ll. 18–19. **rationem . . . dicunt,** *lit.,* ' they said that a plan (was) to-be-had ', i.e. ' that they must form a plan '.

Note : (i) the necessity to supply **esse.** (ii) the use of the gerundive in the nom. and acc. in Oratio Obliqua as here to express ' ought ', ' must ', ' should '.

l. 19. **eorum.** The use of **eorum** where we might expect **sua** suggests that the **priusquam** clause is an addition of Caesar and not part of what the Gauls said. In this case the subj. is due to the idea of anticipation contained in it, ' before their . . . could be noised abroad ', and not to the dependence of the clause in indirect speech.

ll. 20–1. **ut . . . intercludatur.** This **ut** clause is explanatory of the plan : ' namely that . . . '.

l. 21. **id esse facile,** ' it was easy, (they said) '.

l. 21. **neque audeant** =' would not dare '. The present and imperfect subj. are often used in this way.

l. 22. **absente imperatore,** ' in the absence of their commander ', *lit.,* ' the commander (being) absent '. See also the note on l. 1.

l. 23. **possit,** ' would be able '.

l. 24. **postremo praestare,** still acc. and infin. ; ' finally, (they said) it was better '.

l. 24. **in acie** goes with **interfici,** pres. infin. passive.

l. 24. **non** goes with **reciperare.**

ll. 25–6. **quam acceperint,** ' which they had received '. It may have been noticed that in passages of indirect speech

(Oratio Obliqua), Caesar retains the primary subjunctives, present and perfect in subordinate clauses, where strict usage would demand the imperfect and pluperfect tenses of that mood.

CHAPTER 2

l. 1. **his ... agitatis.** For this abl. absol., use method (i) with the verb in the passive. See Ch. 1, ll. 12–13.

l. 2. **communis salutis causa.** Note this use of the abl. sing. of **causa** as a preposition and that it *follows* its case (gen.) : ' for the sake of ... '.

ll. 1–4. **profitentur, pollicentur,** etc. In this and the next chapter, Caesar uses the historic present with primary sequence.

l. 3. **principes ... facturos,** *lit.,* ' that they would first of all make ... ', i.e. ' that they would be the first of all to make ... '.

ll. 4–5. **quoniam non possint,** ' since they could not '. The subj. mood shows that the causal clause is *virtually* in indirect speech and represents the reason as being in the minds of the conspirators.

l. 4. **obsidibus,** ' by means of hostages ', abl. of the instrument.

l. 5. **ne res efferatur,** a negative purpose clause, ' that the matter should not ... ', i.e. ' to prevent the matter from ... '.

ll. 5–6. **ut sanciatur** depends upon **petunt,** ' that an assurance be given with a solemn oath '.

l. 6. **collatis ... signis,** ' the military standards massed together', i.e., ' in the presence of the massed military standards '.

ll. 6–7. **quo ... continetur.** This clause is, as the indicative shows, an addition by Caesar in parenthesis ; ' by which (= ' and by this') practice their most solemn ceremony is made binding '.

l. 8. **facto initio belli,** *lit.*, ' a beginning made of the campaign ', i.e. ' once the campaign had begun '.

ll. 8–11. **tum ... disceditur.** Translate the abl. absol. by main verbs with **omnibus qui aderant,** ' all those present ' as the subject.

Finally note **disceditur,** an excellent example of the impersonal passive of an intransitive verb—a very common use in Latin, which having no parallel in English must usually be rendered by a personal verb in the active, ' they departed ', for *lit.*, ' it was departed '.

CHAPTER 3

l. 1. **ea dies. dies** in the meaning ' a fixed day ' is nearly always feminine.

ll. 1–2. **Cotuato et ... ducibus,** ' under the leadership of ... '.

l. 3. **Cenabum** is the modern Orléans.

l. 4. **negotiandi causa,** *lit.*, ' for the sake of trading ', i.e. ' as traders ': probably as bankers or money-lenders. They were always unpopular.

l. 4. **in his,** ' among them '.

l. 5. **honestum ... Romanum,** ' a respectable Roman knight '. The latter term was given to those who ranked in the state socially below the senators. They were the business men in Rome and large Italian towns. In the early days of Rome, the ' knights ' were those who could afford to equip themselves as cavalry in the Roman army.

ll. 8–9. **maior ... res,** ' an incident more important and remarkable (than usual) happens '. **incidit** is perfect, for Latin idiom is more precise than English in tense-usage.

ll. 9–10. **clamore significant,** ' they (i.e. the Gauls) proclaim (it) by shouting ', i.e. ' they shout it abroad '.

l. 11. **tum,** ' on that occasion '.

ll. 11–12. **quae ... essent.** Note: (i) **Cenabi,** loc. case, ' at Cenabum '. (ii) **quae** + the subj., the relative clause being adverbial (concessive) for **quae = cum ea,** 'although such things'.

ll. 12-13. **ante . . . vigiliam,** *lit.,* 'before the first watch finished', i.e. 'before the end of the . . .'.

The Romans divided the night into four 'watches' which naturally varied in length according to the time of the year. As it was roughly, mid-winter, the first watch would end sometime after 8 p.m.

CHAPTER 4

l. 1. **ibi,** i.e. among the Arveni.

l. 2. **summae . . . adulescens,** 'a youth of outstanding influence'. For Vercingetorix, the 'hero' of Book VII, see the Introduction pp. xx, xxiii, xxiv-xliii.

l. 3. **obtinuerat,** 'had held'. Note the meaning of **obtineo.**

ll. 3-4. **ob eam causam** is explained by **quod . . . appetebat.**

l. 5. **convocatis . . . .** Use method (iii), 'called his own dependents together (and) . . .'. For the position of these dependents or retainers in the Gallic tribes, see the Introduction p. xxii.

l. 6. **incendit,** 'inflamed (them)'.

l. 6. **concurritur,** impersonal passive ; in English, *personal and active,* 'they rushed'.

l. 7. **prohibetur,** 'he was hindered'.

ll. 8-9. **qui . . . existimabant,** *lit.,* 'who did not think that this fortune (was) to-be-tried', i.e. 'that they should run this risk'.

Note : (i) the gerundive in the nom. and acc. (in acc. and infin.) expresses 'ought', 'must', 'should'. (ii) it is *passive* in Latin : English prefers the active. (iii) **esse** has to be supplied.

l. 9. **ex oppido Gergovia,** 'from the town (of) Gergovia'. Latin uses apposition where we have dependent genitive.

Gergovia is placed by commentators at a mountain about 4 miles south of Clermont-Ferrand.

l. 11. **hac ... manu.** Use method (ii). See Ch. 1, ll. 12–13.

ll. 11–12. **quoscumque ... perducit** : order for translation, **perducit ad suam sententiam quoscumque ex civitate** (=all of his tribe) **adit.**

l. 14. **magnis ... copiis.** Use the participle again, ' having collected . . . '.

l. 14. **adversarios suos,** i.e. his uncle and the other chieftains who were probably Caesar's supporters.

l. 15. **paulo ante,** ' a little before '. Latin says ' by a little before ', the abl. being that of the measure of difference and commonly used with comparatives or words like **ante** which have a comparative idea.

l. 17. **ut in fide maneant,** ' to remain in good faith (i.e. loyal) '.

ll. 17–19. **Senones ... Andos.** The Cadurci lie to the south-west of the Arverni, the rest are north-west and north.

ll. 19–20. **omnes qui . . . attingunt.** By ' all those who border on the Ocean ', Caesar means the sea-board tribes between the mouth of the Seine and the Loire, i.e. the Lexovii, Esuvii, Venelli, Osismi, Veneti and Namnetes.

l. 21. **qua . . . potestate.** Use a ' when ' clause with the verb in the passive. **oblata** from **offero.**

qua, *lit.,* ' which '. English, however, has not the fondness of Latin for beginning new sentences with a relative word referring to something in the sentence before, and it will be more in our idiom to substitute ' this ', for ' which '. This use of the relative will be referred to in this book as ' relative connection ', and in every case demonstrative or personal pronouns should be used in the English translation.

l. 22. **imperat.** Note that this verb can mean *de*mand as well as *com*mand and that the dative associated with it will then be translated ' from '.

ll. 23–5. **armorum . . . constituit,** ' he decided how much

(=what amount) of arms each tribe was-to-furnish, and before (=at) what time '. Note **quodque = et quod. efficiat**, indirect deliberative subjunctive.

l. 27. **dubitantes**, acc. pl. masc., ' the waverers '.

l. 28. **maiore . . . delicto**, *lit.*, ' a greater offence having been committed '. We may, however, translate, ' those who committed a greater offence ' as the object of **necat**.

ll. 29–30. **leviore . . . remittit**, *lit.*, ' for a lighter reason he sent (them) home, the ears cut off or one eye each put out '.

ll. 30–1. **ut sint . . . documento**, ' in order that they might be (for) a warning to the rest '. Note **documento**, a good instance of the predicative dative.

CHAPTER 5

l. 1. **his suppliciis**, ' by such kind of punishments '.

l. 1. **coacto exercitu**. For this abl. absol., use the participle in the active.

It is probable that Caesar is being less than just to Vercingetorix. It was the latter's personal qualities rather than his fierce discipline that held his forces together.

l. 2. **Cadurcum**, ' a Cadurcan '. The Cadurci were very near neighbours of the Arverni.

l. 3. **in Rutenos = in fines Rutenorum**, ' into (the country) of the Ruteni '. This is a brachylogy (condensed form of expression) often met with. The Ruteni lie south of the Arverni.

l. 3. **in**, ' against '. As Vercingetorix moved north-west to attack the Bituriges, he wished to protect his rear against any action by Caesar from the south-east, and to keep his attention as occupied as possible.

l. 5. **quorum in fide**, ' under whose protection they were '. The Aedui, most powerful tribe in central Gaul, occupied territory between the Loire (**Liger**) and the Saône (**Araris**), and relied chiefly on their friendship and loyalty to Rome to maintain their supremacy.

l. 6. **rogatum.** The supine (in the acc.) often expresses purpose after a verb of motion like **mitto.**

l. 6. **quo** . . . . Purpose clauses which contain a comparative (**facilius,** here, ' the more easily '), are regularly introduced by **quo.**

l. 7. **de,** ' acting on '.

l. 9. **subsidio,** predicative dative, or dative of purpose, ' for a help', i.e. ' to help the Bituriges '. Notice that it is followed by a second dative **Biturigibus.**

l. 9. **qui cum.** Note : (i) the relative connection ; see Ch. 4, l. 21. (ii) the distaste the Romans seem to have had for putting **cum** first in a sentence. ' When they . . . '.

l. 10. **Ligerim.** The Loire.

l. 10. **quod.** Caesar makes the relative pronoun agree in gender with the neuter noun **flumen.** Sometimes in such cases he makes it agree in gender with the name of the river (masc. or fem.).

l. 11. **neque . . . ausi,** ' nor having ventured to cross the river ', i.e. ' without venturing . . . '.

l. 13. **Biturigum . . . veritos,** ' having feared the treachery of the Bituriges ', i.e. ' through fear of . . . '.

Biturigum perfidiam, ' treachery on-the-part-of-the Bituriges '. Note that in Latin a noun that is made to depend upon another noun must be put in the genitive case. The particular use of the case here is called the subjective genitive, because it stands in the same relation to **perfidiam** as would **Bituriges** to a verb of similar meaning, i.e. ' The Bituriges were treacherous '.

ll. 13–14. **quibus . . . cognoverint,** *lit.,* ' to whom they had learned this of purpose to be ', i.e. ' whose purpose was they had learned '.

Note : (i) **id consili.** The gen. **consili** is called *partitive,* seen in its simplest form in **pars civium,** ' part of the citizens '. It is also called by a longer and clumsier, but more expressive name, ' the genitive of the divided whole '. (ii) **cognoverint,** subj. in subordinate clause in indirect speech. Caesar retains the perfect tense (primary) after the historic present **renuntiant.**

ll. 14–15. **ut . . . circumsisterent.** This **ut** clause explains their purpose : ' namely that if they (the Aedui) . . . , they themselves (i.e. the Bituriges) on the one side, the Arverni on the other . . . '. **se,** acc. pl., object of **circumsisterent,** refers to the subject of the verb **renuntiant.**

ll. 16–17. **id eane . . . constat.** Order for translation : **quod** (because) **nihil constat nobis -ne** (whether) **fecerint id de ea causa quam . . . pronuntiarunt an** (or) **adducti perfidia.** The indicative **pronuntia(ve)runt** is used, though in a subordinate clause in indirect speech, because it refers to a fact, not to any thought in the mind of the Aedui.

l. 18. **non videtur . . . proponendum,** ' it does not seem to-be-stated as certain ', i.e. ' it does not seem that it should be stated as certain '.

CHAPTER 6

l. 1. **in Italiam,** i.e. in Cisalpine Gaul.

ll. 2–3. **urbanas . . . pervenisse,** *lit.,* ' that the things in-the-city had reached a more satisfactory state by the decision of Gnaeus Pompeius ', i.e. ' that the situation in Rome had been brought into . . . '. In February 52 B.C., Pompey had been made sole consul and in the following weeks restored some order to the political confusion which reigned in Rome at this time.

l. 4. **eo,** *lit.,* ' thither ', but we say, ' there '.

ll. 4–5. **magna difficultate adficiebatur,** *lit.,* ' he was affected by great difficulty ', i.e. ' he experienced great difficulty '. **adficio,** a favourite word, particularly with Cicero, is often used with an abstract noun where a simple verb would be quite adequate. ' To torture ', for example, may be **cruciatu adficere** instead of **cruciare.** Here Caesar might have written **magnopere laborabat.**

ll. 5–6. **qua ratione . . . posset,** ' in what way he could reach . . . ', i.e. ' as to the method in which he . . . '.

ll. 6–8. **nam . . . intellegebat.** Begin with **nam intellegebat si arcesseret legiones . . . .** Note : **se absente,** abl. absol.,
' himself (being) absent ', i.e. ' in his absence '. See the note
on Ch. 1, l. 1. (ii) **dimicaturas.** Supply **eas**='that they' (i.e.
the legions) as subject and **esse** to give future infin. act.
' would fight '='would have to fight '.

l. 6. **in provinciam.** Gallia Narbonensis was at this time
the only part of Gaul beyond the Alps which was a Roman
province. Hence it was often referred to as ' the Province '.
Cf. the modern name ' Provence '.

l. 8. **si . . . ,** ' if (on the other hand) . . . '. Latin obtains
contrast· by mere apposition of words, phrases, or clauses.
English has to supply the necessary conjunction or phrase.
This absence of conjunction is known as asyndeton.

ll. 8–10. **ne eis . . . videbat,** *lit.,* ' he saw that his personal
safety was rightly being entrusted not even to those at that
time who seemed (to be) at peace '. As the emphasis falls on
recte and **qui** may be adverbial here ='although they ', we
may render : ' he saw that it was not right that his personal
safety be entrusted to them at that time although they . . . '.

Caesar had stationed his army in three winter camps, six
legions at Agedincum (amongst the Senones), two among the
Lingones (immediately to the south-east) and two near the
western frontier of the Treveri (to the north-east).

CHAPTER 7

ll. 2–3. **in Nitiobriges . . . ,** ' into (the territory of) the
Nitiobriges . . . '. See note on Ch. 5, l. 3.

l. 4. **Narbonem versus,** ' in the direction of Narbo '. **versus** often follows its case. **Narbo** is the modern Narbonne.

l. 5. **qua** ='this ', relative connection again. Ch. 4, l. 21.

l. 6. **Caesar . . . existimavit,** *lit.,* ' Caesar thought that (it
was) to-be-adopted-before all plans ', i.e. ' that he should put
this plan in operation before all others '. See Ch. 4, ll. 8–9.

l. 7. **ut . . . proficisceretur** is the plan, ' (namely) that . . . '.

l. 7. **eo,** ' there '.

l. 8. **timentes,** ' the faint-hearted ', *lit.,* ' the fearers '.

ll. 8–9. **in Rutenis provincialibus,** ' amongst the Ruteni in the province '. Some of the Ruteni lived in the Roman province.

l. 10. **quae loca . . . ,** ' and these localities were . . . '.

l. 10. **constituit,** ' he stationed '.

l. 13. **convenire,** ' to muster '.

CHAPTER 8

ll. 1–2. **his rebus . . . remoto.** The second abl. absol. gives us the result of the first, **his rebus comparatis.** Translate literally first and then examine this rendering in which **his rebus comparatis** ' these measures' is made the subject of two active verbs : ' these measures now checked Lucterius and compelled him to retire (because he thought . . . , **quod putabat . . .)** ' .

l. 3. **in Helvios proficiscitur.** Insert ' and so ' before **in** and state **Caesar** as the subject. **in Helvios = in fines Helviorum.**

l. 3. **mons Cevenna,** the Cevennes. This range actually separates the Vellavii from the Helvii and Caesar seems, therefore, to include that tribe as part of their neighbours, the Arverni, to whom, in any case, they were subject.

ll. 4–5. **durissimo . . . anni.** This abl. absol., ' the season of the year (being) most severe ', is equivalent to a causal clause, ' since it was . . . '.

ll. 5–7. **discussa nive, viis patefactis.** These abl. absols. will sound best in English, if made into participles in the active, ' clearing the snow . . . , opening up the roads . . . '.

l. 6. **sex . . . pedum,** ' six feet in depth ', gen. of description qualifying **nive.**

l. 7. **ad fines.** Insert ' thus ' before **ad.**

l. 8. **quibus . . . inopinantibus,** ' catching them off their guard '.

l. 9. **Cevenna ut muro,** ' by the Cevennes as by a wall '.

ll. 9–11. **ac ne . . . patuerant,** *lit.,* ' and not even to a solitary man ever at that season of the year had the paths been open '.

ll. 11–12. **quam latissime possint.** The verb **possint** adds nothing to the meaning, the other two words being all that is necessary to say ' as widely as possible '. Nevertheless, as here, the appropriate part of **possum** is occasionally inserted : contrast, however, **quam maximum terrorem** in the next line.

l. 13. **haec fama ac nuntii,** ' rumour and news of this '.

l. 14. **quem,** relative connection again, = ' him '.

l. 16. **neve diripiantur,** ' and they should not be plundered '.

l. 17. **quorum,** relative connection, = ' their ', with **precibus.**

ll. 18–19. **ex Biturigibus, in Arvernos,** ' from (the territory of) the Bituriges,' ' into (the territory of) the Arverni '.

CHAPTER 9

l. 1. **biduum,** accusative of duration of time, ' for . . . '.

l. 1. **moratus.** Make this perf. partic. a main verb, and insert ' and so ' or ' then ' before **per causam.**

ll. 1–3. **quod . . . praeceperat. usu venit** commonly means, ' it happens *or* befalls '. **opinione praecipere** = ' to suspect '. Hence we get : ' because he had suspected that this would happen concerning Vercingetorix '. **ventura :** supply **esse.**

ll. 3–4. **per causam . . . cogendi,** *lit.,* ' on the pretext of the fresh draft and cavalry to-be-assembled ', i.e. ' of assembling . . . . '. Note the gerundive construction.

l. 4. **Brutum adulescentem.** See the note on Ch.87, l. 1.

l. 5. **in omnes partes,** ' in all directions '.

ll. 6–7. **daturum . . . absit,** *lit.,* ' he would take trouble that he should not be away from the camp . . . ' ; i.e. ' he would do his best not to be . . . . '. **daturum operam . . .** is acc. and infin. **daturum** : supply **esse. longius triduo,** ' longer than three days ' ; **triduo,** abl. of comparison.

l. 8. **suis inopinantibus,** abl. absol., *lit.,* ' his own (soldiers) not expecting ' = ' to the surprise of his own men ', to be taken after **Viennam pervenit.**

ll. 8–9. **quam . . . itineribus. magnum iter** is ' a forced march '. So **quam . . . itineribus** literally means ' by the greatest—forced marches possible '. Translate, however, ' as fast as he could possibly travel '.

The average daily march of a Roman legionary was between 15 to 20 miles, but by forced marching it was probably increased to 30 miles— a considerable achievement when we remember that a legionary carried in addition to his armour a heavy pack of about 45 lb.

In this passage we cannot be sure how Caesar travelled although it is probable that he used relays of horses to push on as fast as possible.

l. 10. **equitatum.** At this time, the cavalry attached to each Roman legion (300 in number) was enrolled entirely from Gauls and Spaniards. The Romans themselves had never been successful cavalrymen, but had relied for this branch of their fighting forces, first on their Italian allies, and later on as in Caesar's day on the provinces, particularly Gaul, Spain and N. Africa.

The cavalry mentioned here probably came from the Roman province, south-east Gaul (Gallia Transalpina).

ll. 11–12. **neque diurno . . . intermisso,** *lit.,* ' the march interrupted neither by day nor by night ', = ' without stopping either by day or by night '.

ll. 13–15. **ut . . . praecurreret,** *lit.,* ' so that if anything of plan were entered upon about his safety even by the Aedui, he might anticipate it by the speed (of his movements) '. We should prefer the first verb in the active, ' if the Aedui formed any plan . . . '. **quid consili,** ' any plan '. See the note in Ch. 5, ll. 13–14. **de salute,** i.e. ' against his safety '.

l. 16. **mittit,** ' he sent (orders) '.

l. 16. **prius** goes with **quam** at the end of the line.

l. 16. **in unum locum.** Most commentators place this either at or near Agedincum where six of the ten legions were in winter quarters.

l. 17. **posset.** The subjunctive is not normal in *purely* temporal clauses introduced by **priusquam.** In the type of **priusquam** clause which involves the notion of action prevented or anticipated, the subjunctive is regular.

ll. 20–1. **quos . . . collocaverat.** Note : (i) **Helvetico proelio,** ' in the campaign against the Helvetii '. See the Introduction p. xviii. The Latin prep. **in** is sometimes inserted with such phrases, sometimes not, no doubt according as **proelium** was felt to be a place, or an occasion. The general principle, not rigidly observed, is that ' place ' phrases require, and ' time ' phrases must not include the prep. **in.** (ii) **quos victos collocaverat,** *lit.,* ' whom having been conquered he had stationed ', = ' whom he had defeated and stationed,' or ' whom he had stationed after their defeat'. The Latin perfect participle passive is the most used of the three participles the Latin verb possesses. Unfortunately, English does not favour it to the same extent and our translation must be more in accordance with English idiom.

CHAPTER 10

ll. 1–2. **ad consilium capiendum,** ' for a plan to-be-formed ', i.e. ' for forming . . . '.

l. 2. **adferebat,** ' caused '.

l. 2. **si . . . .** Begin a fresh sentence here and insert, ' he was afraid ' before **ne** in l. 3. Similarly with **si** and **ne** in l. 6.

l. 2. **reliquam partem,** acc. of duration of time, ' for . . . '.

ll. 3–4. **stipendariis . . . expugnatis,** abl. absol.; best rendered here by a conditional clause, ' if the tributaries . . . '.

l. 5. **in eo,** ' in him ', i.e. in Caesar. **videret.** The subject is **Gallia,** i.e. the Gauls.

ll. 6–7. **ne . . . laboraret,** ' that he would be hard pressed in-respect-of (**ab**) his corn supply owing to the difficulties of transport '.

l. 7. **praestare** is the infinitive of **praestat,** ' it is better '.

ll. 8–9. **tanta . . . accepta,** abl. absol.; render as ' by enduring so grievous a disgrace ', viz. of being unable to protect his allies.

l. 9. **suorum,** ' of his (supporters) '.

ll. 10–11. **de supportando commeatu,** ' about supplies to-be-brought-up ', i.e. ' about bringing up . . . '. Note the gerundive which is necessary in this construction in the acc., dat. and abl. dependent upon a preposition.

ll. 11–12. **qui . . . doceant hortenturque.** **qui** is final here and expresses purpose.

l. 13. **magno animo,** ' with great courage ' = ' courageously '.

ll. 13–14. **Agedinci** is locative, ' at Agedincum '. It is the modern Sens.

CHAPTER 11

l. 1. **altero die,** ' on the next day '.

l. 1. **ad oppidum.** **oppidum** here means ' stronghold ' rather than a town on the Roman pattern.

l. 2. **quem,** ' any ' in agreement with **hostem.** It comes from the indefinite adj., **qui, quae, quod** = ' any ', after **si, nisi, num, ne.**

l. 3. **quo . . . uteretur,** *lit.,* ' that he might use a readier corn supply ' = 'that he might find it easier to maintain his corn supply '.

l. 4. **id** is the object of **oppugnare** as well as of **circumvallavit.**

l. 5. **de deditione,** ' to discuss terms of surrender '.

l. 7. **ea . . . conficeret ;** **qui** introduces a purpose clause : ' to attend to those matters '.

l. 8. **iter,** i.e. to Gorgobina.

l. 9. **Cenabum Carnutum,** 'to Cenabum, (a town) of the Carnutes '.

l. 9. **qui,** relative connection, 'they ', i.e. the Carnutes.

l. 10. **allato nuntio,** 'news having been brought ', will be best rendered here by a relative clause, 'who had received news '.

l. 10. **cum** is causal, 'since '.

l. 11. **longius . . . iri,** 'that that thing(=the investment) would be led longer (=would be somewhat prolonged) '.

ll. 11-13. **praesidium . . . comparabant :** order for translation : **comparabant praesidium quod mitterent eo causa tuendi Cenabi.** Note : (i) **comparabant** is imperfect, a tense which may express action commenced : 'were beginning-to-prepare '. (ii) **quod** introduces a purpose clause. (iii) in the genitive the gerundive is an alternative to the gerund : here Caesar might have written **Cenabum tuendi causa.**

l. 14. **diei tempore exclusus,** 'prevented by the time of day ', i.e. 'by the lateness of the hour '.

l. 14. **in posterum,** supply **diem.**

ll. 15-16. **quae . . . imperat,** 'he demanded from the soldiers such things as were useful for that thing (=for the operation) '. **sint** is a generic subjunctive.

ll. 16-17. **et quod . . . contingebat,** 'and because a bridge over the Loire extended to the town of Cenabum '.

l. 17. **veritus,** 'having feared '='he feared '. Insert 'and ' before **duas legiones.**

l. 21. **expeditas,** 'ready for action '.

l. 22. **portis incensis.** This abl. absol. will be best rendered by a main verb in the active before **legiones . . . intromittit ;** 'he set fire to the gates (and) . . . '.

ll. 23-4. **perpaucis . . . caperentur,** *lit.,* 'very few from the number of the enemy being wanting but that all were captured ', i.e. 'very few of the enemy's number escaping capture '.

l. 24. **itinerum,** i.e. the narrow streets in Cenabum.

l. 25. **multitudini . . . intercluserat,** ' had cut off the flight of most ', i.e. ' had prevented the population from fleeing '.

CHAPTER 12

l. 2. **oppugnatione,** i.e. on Gorgobina. The abl. after **destitit** is one of separation. Note **destitit,** perfect, immediately followed by **proficiscitur,** historic present.

l. 3. **ille,** i.e. Caesar.

ll. 4-5. **quo ex oppido,** ' from this stronghold '.

l. 5. **oratum,** acc. of the supine to express purpose.

ll. 5-6. **sibi, suae vitae.** The reflexive pronoun and adjective refer to the **legati,** the 3rd person introductory subject. Note **suae vitae,** dat. and sing. where we use the plural.

ll. 6-7. **ut . . . consecutus.** This purpose clause, ' in order that he might complete the rest of the business with the speed with which he had accomplished most of it ', should be translated *after* **arma . . . iubet.**

ll. 9-11. **parte . . . conquirerent.** Note the structure of the subordination in Latin : (1) abl. absol.; (2) **cum** clause ; (3) abl. absol. with dependent purpose clause introduced by **qui.** English prefers a less rigid construction : make (1) a main verb, ' part . . . ', insert ' and ' before **cum** which can be dropped, (3) may be turned by a ' while ' clause ; then the connection between the subordinate clauses and the main sentence **equitatus . . . antecesserat** may be brought out by the insertion of ' when suddenly ' or ' and then '.

This is not the only way of dealing with this type of Latin sentence ; the main principle is clear, however : the substitution of finite verbs for the participles and co-ordination to replace subordination.

l. 13. **quem,** ' him ', relative connection.

l. 13. **simul atque,** ' as soon as '.

l. 14. **sublato** from **tollo.**

l. 17. **novi . . . consili,** ' (that) something of new plan was

being entered upon by them ', = ' that they were forming
some new plan '. For **aliquid novi consili,** see Ch. 5, ll. 13–14.

ll. 18–19. **suos omnes incolumes,** ' all their men safe(ly) ',
i.e. the **pauci milites** of l. 10.

CHAPTER 13

ll. 3–4. **ab initio,** ' from the beginning ', probably means
from the first time that he employed German cavalry and
realised how good they were.

l. 6. **ad agmen,** ' to the main body '.

ll. 7–9. **comprehensos eos ad Caesarem perduxerunt,** ' led
to Caesar those . . . having been seized '—another case for
English to substitute a finite verb for the Latin participle—
' seized and led to Caesar those . . . '.

l. 8. **opera** is the abl. sing. of the 1st declension noun,
' service ', ' agency '.

l. 10. **Avaricum** is the modern Bourges.

l. 12. **atque . . . regione,** ' and in the most fertile part of
their country '. The abl. is governed by the **in** before **finibus.**

l. 13. **eo oppido recepto,** *lit.,* ' that town having been
recovered ', = ' by the recovery of that town '. Note how the
Latin participle is translated here, not by a finite verb as in
earlier passages, but by a noun. Cf. **urbs condita,** ' the city
having been founded ' = ' the foundation of the city '.

CHAPTER 14

ll. 1–2. **Vellaunoduni, Cenabi, Novioduni** are locatives.

l. 3. **docet . . . .** We now have a long passage of indirect
speech introduced by **docet,** historic present. Note ; (i) all
subordinate clauses have their verbs in the subj. (ii) Caesar
uses primary sequence (present or perfect subjunctive)
throughout. (iii) the frequent use of the gerundive to express
' ought ', ' must ', ' should '. In this construction, observe
that the Latin gerundive is *passive,* and is used *personally*

with transitive verbs, *impersonally*, i.e. in the neuter, with intransitive ones. English prefers, however, the active voice.

ll. 3–4. **longe . . . sit,** ' that in a far different way the campaign (was) to-be-waged from (the way) it had been waged previously ', i.e. ' that they should conduct the campaign . . . '.

Note : (i) **alius atque** ' different from '. (ii) **esse** is frequently omitted in Latin.

l. 5. **huic rei studendum (esse),** ' attention (was) to-be-paid to this ' = ' they should pay . . . '. The **ut** clause explains **huic rei.**

l. 5. **pabulatione et commeatu,** abl. of separation, ' from . . . '.

l. 6. **id esse facile,** ' it was easy, (he said) '.

l. 6. **equitatu,** abl. of respect, ' in . . . '.

l. 8. **pabulum . . . non posse.** As far as possible, an invading army tried to live on the country, i.e. to derive all its supplies from the neighbouring countryside. Thus in the normal campaigning season, the summer months, every legionary carried a sickle with which he used to provide himself with grain and the pack-animals with fodder. The season of the year, March, prevented foraging and so, as Vercingetorix pointed out, Caesar's men had to seek grain from the homesteads (**aedificiis**) in-scattered-groups (**dispersos**).

l. 10. **deligi** probably means ' picked off '.

l. 10. **salutis causa,** ' for the (common) good '.

ll. 10–11. **rei . . . neglegenda (esse),** ' the interests of private property (were) to-be-neglected ', i.e. ' they would have to neglect . . . '.

l. 12. **hoc spatio . . . quoqueversus,** ' over that distance from the road in every direction '.

l. 13. **quo . . . videantur,** ' to which they seemed capable of penetrating . . . ', *lit.,* ' seemed to be able . . . '.

ll. 14–15. **quorum . . . subleventur** : order for translation : **subleventur opibus eorum in quorum finibus . . . .**

l. 17. **neque interesse**, ' nor did it make (any) difference '.

ll. 17–18. **ipsosne ... impedimentisne**, i.e. **utrum ipsos ... an impedimentis**, ' whether ... or ... '.

ll. 18–19. **quibus ... possit**, *lit.*, ' which having been lost, the campaign could not be continued ', i.e. ' the loss of which made it impossible (for the Romans) to continue the campaign '. For this translation of the participle **amissis**, see the note on Ch. 13, l. 13.

ll. 20–1. **quae ... tuta**, ' which were not safe from every danger by their defences and their natural position '.

ll. 21–3. **neu ... tollendam**, ' that they might not be refuges for their own (followers) to shirk military service (*lit.*, for military service to-be-shirked) nor be accessible for the Romans for removing store of supplies or plunder (*lit.*, for store ... to-be-removed) '.

neu ... neu is rare for the more usual **ne ... neu**.

l. 25. **multo ... aestimare** : supply **se** as the subject : ' they should consider the following much more serious '.

ll. 25–6. **liberos ... interfici**, ' viz. that their children ... be dragged off ... , and themselves be slain ' : this acc. and infin. is in apposition with **illa**.

CHAPTER 15

l. 2. **amplius**. This comparative adverb is often used in this way, i.e. without grammatical influence on the following words.

l. 2. **urbes = oppida**.

l. 5. **hoc solaci**, gen. of the divided whole, or partitive gen. See Ch. 5, ll. 13–14.

l. 6. **prope explorata victoria**, abl. absol., ' victory practically assured ', = ' as victory was ... ' : or we could turn by English abstract noun ' the assurance of victory ' and continue ' made them confident that ... '.

l. 6. **amissa**, acc. pl. neut., ' their losses ', object of **reciperaturos**.

l. 8. **incendi** . . . . Supply **utrum** before **incendi**, ' whether it pleased (them) that it be burned or defended ', = ' whether it should be . . . '.

l. 9. **Bituriges**, i.e. their representatives.

ll. 10–11. **praesidio et ornamento**, ' (for) a protection and an ornament ', predicative datives. We omit the ' for '.

ll 13–14. **ex omnibus** . . . **circumdata**, *lit.*, ' surrounded by a river and a marsh on all sides '. **circumdata** is nom. sing. fem. in agreement with **urbs**, the understood subject of **habeat**.

l. 15. **petentibus**, ' to (them) requesting ', i.e. ' to their request '.

l. 15. **dissuadente** . . . . Make these abl. absols. concessive clauses, ' although at first V. . . . '.

ll. 16–17. **et precibus** . . . **vulgi**, ' in consequence of their entreaties and out of compassion for the multitude ' ; abl. of cause.

vulgi, objective gen. The relation between **misericordia** and its gen. is similar to that between a verb and its *object*.

CHAPTER 16

l. 1. **minoribus itineribus**, ' by easier stages '.

l. 2. **locum**. Vercingetorix encamped north or north-east of Avaricum.

ll. 3–4. **longe** . . . **XVI**, ' 16 miles distant from Avaricum '. **milia** is an acc. of extent of space.

l. 4. **certos**, ' fixed ' or ' organised '.

ll. 4–5. **in singula** . . . **tempora**, ' for each times of the day ', i.e. ' for each hour of the day '.

l. 8. **cum** . . . **procederent**, ' when of necessity they advanced further (than usual) ', = ' when they were compelled to advance . . . '. We might have expected Caesar to use **cum** + pluperfect indicative for repeated action, ' whenever '. **Cum** may, however, be regarded here as causal.

ll. 8–9. **magnoque . . . adficiebat,** ' he harassed them greatly '. See the note on Ch. 6, ll. 4–5.

ll. 9–11. **etsi . . . iretur,** *lit.,* ' although (as far) as by strategy it could be provided against, it was met by our men so that movement was made at irregular times and by uncertain routes '.

Note : (i) the *impersonal* passives **provideri, occurrebatur, iretur**—English idiom demands either active voice used *personally* or abstract noun. (ii) **tantum,** ' as far ', has to be supplied as the antecedent of **quantum.** Translate : ' although our men took such counter-action as strategy could provide them with, so that all movement took place along . . . '.

CHAPTER 17

l. 2. **intermissa . . . paludibus,** ' left open (i.e. unenclosed) by the river and the marshes '. The **a** may be due to an unconscious personification of the river and the marshes, or it may have the meaning of ' in regard to '.

l. 2. **ut,** ' as '

l. 3. **aggerem,** ' terrace '. What this was and how it was constructed is apparently a question of great difficulty and there are many different opinions. T. Rice Holmes[1] describes it as ' a terrace, composed of a core of earth and timber, supported by walls of logs piled cross-wise and built up at right-angles to the enemies' wall '.

l. 4. **vineas.** ' Mantlets ' were movable huts made of wood and wickerwork, and protected against fire by raw hides. Placed end to end both on the terrace and along it, they were intended to protect the soldiers who were engaged in making the **agger.**

l. 4. **turres.** The ' tower ' was erected on the ' terrace ', and from its stories, archers, slingers and artillery discharged their missiles at the defenders of the besieged town. It could be moved along the **agger** on rollers.

[1] *Caesar's Conquest of Gaul,* p. 58.

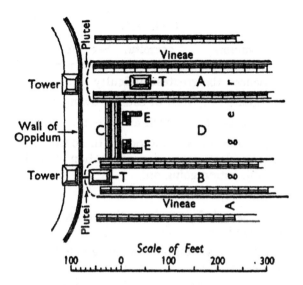

THE ROMAN AGGER AT AVARICUM

C = Terrace, level or nearly level with the top of the enemy's wall.

EE are steps from which the Roman troops can move to the level C.

TT = Towers.

A, B are ramps built up in inclined planes.

D is the area not built up but left at a natural level.

ll. 4–5. **circumvallare,** *lit.*, ' to invest ', is the direct obj. of **prohibebat** and may be translated by ' investment '.

l. 5. **natura,** nom.

l. 7. **alteri,** ' the one ', i.e. the Aedui.

l. 7. **nullo studio,** abl. of manner, ' with no enthusiasm ', i.e. ' without any enthusiasm '.

l. 8. **alteri,** ' the other ', *or* ' the former '.

l. 8. **non magnis facultatibus,** abl. absol., ' their resources not (being) great ', i.e. ' since they had no ... '. Some editors explain it as an abl. of quality, ' being people of slender resources '.

l. 9–10. **quod habuerunt** is the object of **consumpserunt.**

ll. 10–11. **summa . . . exercitu.** See the note on Ch. 6,
ll. 4–5, and make the abl. absol. a main verb : ' Thus the
army experienced the greatest difficulty . . . '.

l. 11. **tenuitate . . .,** abls. of cause, ' owing to . . . '.

ll. 12–13. **usque eo,** ' to such an extent '.

ll. 13–15. **caruerint, sustentarent.** In consecutive (result)
clauses, the perfect subj. denotes action completed, the
imperfect subj. action going on.

l. 15. **nulla vox,** ' no word '.

l. 17. **indigna. indignus** like **dignus** has the abl. case
dependent upon it.

l. 17. **quin.** This conjunction when followed by the
indicative means ' moreover ', ' nay more '.

l. 18. **si . . . ferrent** ' if they endured the scarcity too
bitterly ', = ' if they found the scarcity too bitter to endure '.

ll. 20–1. **illo imperante,** ' him commanding ', = ' under his
command '.

l. 22. **nusquam . . . discederent,** ' (that) in no instance did
they give up, once a task had been begun '.

ll. 22–3. **hoc . . . loco,** ' they would take it as a disgrace '.
ignominiae loco, ' in the place of a disgrace ' = ' as a disgrace '.

l. 24. **praestare,** ' it was better, (they said)'.

l. 25. **perfidia Gallorum,** abl. of cause, ' owing to the
treachery of the Gauls '.

l. 26. **pareatarent. Parento** (1), literally, ' I make a
solemn sacrifice in honour of deceased parents ', then came to
mean, ' I revenge the death of a parent *or* relative '.

l. 27. **tribunis militum.** There were six military tribunes
to a legion : their rank was lower than that of the **legati,** and
on occasion they commanded anything from a cohort to a
legion.

CHAPTER 18

l. 1. **appropinquassent,** = **appropinquavissent.** So also **consuessent** l. 5 = **consuevissent.** Verb forms containing the letter 'v' often drop that consonant and the following vowel.

ll. 2–3. **consumpto pabulo.** Translate as a finite verb in the active, 'had used up his forage (and)'.

l. 4. **expeditis.** For the help given by these light-armed troops to the Gallic cavalry, see Ch. 80, ll. 7–10.

l. 5. **insidiarum causa,** 'for the sake of an ambush', = 'to prepare an ambush'.

l. 5. **profectum.** Supply **esse** to give the perfect infinitive of this deponent verb.

l. 5. **eo . . . quo,** 'thither . . . whither', = 'to that place . . . where'.

l. 6. **pabulatum,** the acc. of the supine expressing purpose.

l. 8. **illi,** as often = 'the enemy'.

. 12. **sarcinas,** the soldiers' 'personal gear' or 'packs', of which they were relieved when fighting was in prospect.

l, 13, **expediri,** 'to be prepared for action'.

CHAPTER 19

l. 1. **collis . . . .** The hill is the **locus editus atque apertus** of Ch. 18.

l. 3–5. **hoc se colle continebant,** 'kept themselves (= were stationed) on this hill'. **fiducia loci,** 'with confidence of (= in) their position (hoc colle)'.

l. 4. **interruptis pontibus,** 'after breaking up the causeways'.

l. 5. **in civitates** seems merely to repeat **generatim** and may therefore be omitted in translation. It is possible that it may have been put in the margin by a copyist as an explanation of **generatim** and later been transferred mistakenly by later copyists into the text itself.

ll. 6–8. **sic ... animo parati ut premerent.** *lit.*, ' so prepared in their resolve that they overwhelmed,' = 'fully resolved to overwhelm '.

l. 8. **haesitantes** is in agreement with the unexpressed object of **premerent,** ' them ', i.e. the Romans : *lit.*, '(them) sticking fast ' = ' them as they stuck fast '.

ll. 8–10. **ut qui ... existimaret,** ' so that (a man) who saw (=anyone who saw) the proximity of their position would think (them) ready to fight on almost equal terms '.
Note : (i) **videret, existimaret.** The subjunctives are conditional. (ii) **aequo Marte.** The Romans often used especially in poetry the name of a deity for the activity or thing especially associated with him or her. Here, **Mars,** ' the god of war ', = ' war ', ' fighting '. So **Bacchus,** = ' wine '.

ll. 10–12. **qui ... cognosceret.** This sentence is exactly parallel to the preceding one and should be translated accordingly. Insert ' but ' or ' while ' to get the contrast which Latin obtains merely by apposition of words, phrases, or clauses. For the asyndeton, cf. also Ch. 6, l. 8.

ll. 11–12. **inani ... cognosceret,** ' would realise that they were parading themselves in empty show '.
In thus sneering at the Gauls, Caesar seems to be deliberately trying to mislead us here ; for it is obvious that Vercingetorix was hoping to entice Caesar to attack him as his speech in the next chapter shows. The whole manoeuvre was a trap and it is not therefore very convincing for Caesar to say that the Gauls offered battle only because they knew that the offer would not be accepted and thus could be regarded as ' mere empty show '.

ll. 12–14. **indignantes ... edocet ....** The skeleton of this sentence is **Caesar edocet milites.** The object **milites** has **indignantes** and **exposcentes** in agreement; dependent upon the former of the present participles is **quod ... interiecto.** It might be better then to say : ' as the soldiers were resentful that . . . and demanded the signal for battle, Caesar showed . . . '.

ll. 13–14. **tantulo spatio interiecto.** 'so little space lying between ', i.e. ' at so short a distance '.

ll. 14–16. **quanto . . . victoriam,** 'how great a loss and the death of how many brave men it was necessary that victory cost ', i.e. ' what a terrible loss, the death of so many brave men victory must cost '. **constare,** ' to cost ' is often found with an abl. of price.

ll. 16–19. **quos . . . cariorem :** the construction is still dependent upon **edocet. quos = eos. cum =** ' when '.

l. 18. **summae iniquitatis,** genitive of the matter charged, ' for the greatest injustice '.

ll. 18–19. **nisi . . . cariorem,** ' unless he regarded their lives dearer than his own well-being '.

CHAPTER 20

ll. 1–2. **proditionis,** gen. of the charge.

ll. 2–3. **quod movisset, quod discessisset,** etc. Each **quod** clause introduces a separate complaint. Note that the subjunctive is use in causal clauses when they are virtually in Indirect Speech, i.e. when the reason given is not the writer's, but is quoted from the words or thoughts of another.

l. 2. **propius Romanos,** ' too near the Romans '.

l. 4. **sine imperio,** 'without a command ', would be better in English as ' without a commander '.

ll. 4–5. **eius discessu,** ' on his departure ', abl. of time when. **tanta . . . celeritate,** ' so opportunely and at such speed'.

ll. 6–8. **non haec . . . beneficio.** The construction is acc. and infin. : ' they said ', being understood.

ll. 7–8. **regnum . . . beneficio ;** order for translation : **illum** (i.e. Vercingetorix) **malle habere regnum Galliae concessu Caesaris quam ipsorum.**
After **quam** supply ' by that '.

l. 8. **tali modo . . . .** The opening sentence of this chapter is excessively long by English standards : hence make

insimulatus a main verb, ' was accused ' and put a full stop at **beneficio.** We can then begin a fresh sentence with **tali modo.**

ll. 9–28. **quod** .... Vercingetorix answers each charge in turn. **quod,** ' as to the fact that '. **movisset,** subjunctive for the same reason as **movisset** in l. 3.

l. 10. **factum.** Supply **esse,** ' it had been done '.

l. 10. **inopia,** abl.

l. 10. **etiam . . . hortantibus,** ' even themselves encouraging (him)', abl. absol., =' even with their encouragement '.

l. 11. **persuasum.** Supply **esse sibi,** *lit.,* ' it was persuaded to him ', = ' he was persuaded '. Note that **persuadeo,** a verb which takes the dative, is used in the passive only *im*-personally.

ll. 11–12. **loci opportunitate,** ' by the favourable nature of the ground '.

l. 12. **qui . . . defenderet,** ' which could protect itself by its own defences '.

ll. 13–14. **equitum . . . debuisse,** ' the services of the cavalry ought not to have been missed . . . '.

l. 14. **illic quo,** ' in the place to which '.

l. 14. **sint profecti.** For the use of the primary tense, see the note on Ch. 1, ll. 25–6.

So also **intervenerint, potuerint, receperint** later.

ll. 14–15. **summam . . . tradidisse. nulli** is dative, ' to no-one '.

l. 15. **discedentem** agrees with **se.**

l. 16. **is,** ' he ' i.e. his deputy.

l. 17. **cui rei** is relative connection. The dative depends upon **studere,** ' they were all anxious for this '. **propter animi mollitiem,** ' through lack of energy '.

l. 18. **laborem,** ' the rigours (of the campaign) '.

ll. 19–20. **Romani . . . gratiam,** ' if the Romans had appeared by chance, gratitude should be paid (i.e. they should be grateful) to fortune, (but) if they had been summoned by the information of someone (i.e. by some informer), they should be grateful to that man '.

l. 22. **qui,** either ' (of those) who ', or if the relative introduces a causal clause, ' inasmuch as they '.

ll. 23–4. **se . . . desiderare,** ' he looked for '.

l. 25. **victoria** is abl.

ll. 25–6. **quae iam esset explorata,** ' which was already assured '.

l. 26. **quin,** ' nay more '.

l. 26. **remittere.** Supply **se,** ' he gave (it) back '.

l. 28. **videantur,** ' they seemed (to themselves) ', i.e. ' they thought '. **sibi** which has to be supplied with **videantur** is omitted because of the previous **sibi** referring as it does to Vercingetorix.

l. 32. **edocti quae interrogati pronuntiarent,** ' instructed (as to) what (when) questioned they were to say '. **pronuntiarent,** subj. in indirect question, was also subj. in the direct form, (deliberative subj.).

ll. 34–5. **si . . . possent,** ' (to see) if they could '.

l. 34. **quid frumenti aut pecoris,** ' any corn or cattle '. Note the genitive (partitive) for which see the note on Ch. 5, ll. 13–14.

l. 36. **cuiusquam** from **quisquam,** the regular word for 'anyone ' after a negative, depends upon **vires.**

ll. 36–7. **nec . . . posse.** Supply ' anyone ' from the preceding **cuiusquam** as the subject of **posse.**

l. 38. **si nihil profecissent,** ' if they made no progress '.

l. 41. **cuius opera,** ' by whose efforts '.

l. 41. **sine vestro sanguine,** ' without (loss of) your blood '.

ll. 43–4. **quem . . . provisum est :** order for translation : **provisum est a me ne qua civitas recipiat suis finibus quem turpiter se recipientem ex fuga.**

Note : (i) **provisum est a me,** ' it has been provided against

by me '; English would prefer the active : ' I have made pro-
vision '. (ii) **ne qua civitas,** ' that-not any tribe ' = ' that no
tribe '. (iii) **quem,** relative connection = ' this army '. (iv)
turpiter . . . fuga. We say : ' when it takes refuge in igno-
minious flight '.

CHAPTER 21

l. 1. **suo more,** ' in their native fashion '. The Germans
are said by another Roman historian (Tacitus[1]) to have had
the same custom.

l. 2. **quod,** ' as '.

l. 2. **in eo,** ' in (the case of) one '.

l. 3. **summum . . . :** acc. and infin., ' they said ' can easily
be supplied from the verb **approbant.**

ll. 4–5. **nec . . . posse,** ' nor (was) it to-be-doubted about
his loyalty nor could the campaign be conducted with greater
skill '. For the first part we may render : ' no one could
doubt his loyalty '.

ll. 7–8. **nec . . . censent,** ' and decide that the common
safety of all should not be entrusted . . . '.

ll. 8–10. **quod . . . intellegebant,** ' because they realised that
if they kept possession of that town, the whole of the victory
(i.e. all the glory of the victory) rested with them '.

CHAPTER 22

l. 2. **cuiusque modi,** ' of every kind ' depends upon **consilia.**

ll. 2–4. **ut . . . aptissimum,** ' for they are a race . . . and
most apt for . . . '.

l. 4. **ab quoque,** ' by anyone '.

l. 4. **tradere** means here ' to suggest ' or ' impart '.

ll. 5–7. **avertebant, reducebant, subtrahebant.** These im-

---

[1] End of 1st century A.D.

perfects mean, ' they tried to drag aside . . . '. This use of the tense is known as conative, (Latin **conor**, ' I try ').

l. 5. **falces**. The **falx** was a wooden beam with a piece of iron in the end, and shaped like a hook. It was used for loosening and dragging out stones and timber in an enemies' wall or palisade.

l. 5. **cum destinaverant**, ' whenever they secured (them) '. Note the pluperfect indicative, regular after **cum** : ' whenever '.

l. 6. **tormentis**, ' with windlasses '.

l. 7. **eo scientius**, ' *the* more skilfully '. **eo**, abl. of the measure of difference ; found with comparatives.

l. 10. **turribus contabulaverant**, ' they had furnished with storied towers '.

l. 10. **coriis**. The hides were soaked in water as a protection against fire.

l. 12. **ignem inferebant**. The imperfect is conative : ' they tried to set fire '. Caesar's terrace was mostly of timber.

ll. 13–15. **et nostrarum . . . adaequabant**, ' and the height of our towers (as far) as the daily terrace had raised them, they equalled, the scaffolding of their own towers joined together ' (abl. absol.) : i.e. ' they equalled the daily increase in the height of our towers which the raising of the terrace caused, by joining together the scaffolding of their own towers '. The **mali** are the four uprights to which the tiers of the towers are attached.

The passage will become clear, if it is remembered that the towers were moved along the terrace on their own rollers and that as the terrace rose daily, so the height of the towers would rise in respect of the enemies' wall. The Gauls countered this by adding new stories to their own towers. It has also been suggested that the terrace rose in height as it approached the enemies' wall.

l. 16. **apertos cuniculos**. The meaning of **cuniculos** here is strongly debated among editors. There are three possible meanings : (1) 'open trenches'. (2) 'gangways (where they were) exposed' (i.e. the gangways which were made by the mantlets that protected the soldiers who were making the **agger,** but which were exposed at the end that faced the enemy). (3) 'subterranean galleries'. In the case of (3), **apertos** is a participle and they must have been 'opened' by the Gauls who were digging subterranean galleries into the Roman ones. So the translation will run : 'they opened up our galleries and tried to check (their progress) by means of timbers . . .'.

ll. 17–18. **morabantur, prohibebant,** conative again : 'they tried to check and to prevent'.

CHAPTER 23

l. 1. **hac forma,** abl. of description, 'of this pattern'.

ll. 2–6. **trabes** . . . . As technical descriptions are always very difficult to follow, even in our own language, you will find this chapter hard to understand. The following is as close a translation as can be given. In several passages the meaning is very much disputed and the translation given represents one only of several views.

'Balks-of-timber are placed on the ground at right angles (**directae** i.e. to the line of the wall) in-a-continuous-line (**perpetuae**) along its length at equal intervals of 2 ft. (*lit.*, with equal intervals being distant among themselves as-to 2 ft. each). These balks are bound together on the inner side and covered with a great deal of rubble ; the intervals which we have mentioned are filled up on the front side with huge stones'.

The description so far is clear but there is one point to notice : the balks were bound together by 40 ft. long beams, placed upon them transversely so that they were in line with the wall : they were either clamped with iron clamps or mortised into the balks. Rubble was used to fill up the gaps between the balks 'except on the outer side where huge blocks of stones were employed.

ll. 6–12. **his collocatis** . . . . The first layer of the wall has

been described : now, we are told, a second layer exactly like
the first was placed upon it, but in such a way that the balks
of the second layer rest upon the rubble of the first.

' When these (i.e. balks and rubble of the first layer) have
been placed and fastened together, another row is added on
the top, so that that same interval is kept and the balks do
not touch each other but set apart at equal intervals each
balk is kept tightly in-its-place (**arte contineantur**), single
stones being set between them. In this way layer by layer
(**deinceps**) the whole work is knit together until the proper
height of the wall is reached '.

neque inter se contingant,   The simplest way of taking this
disputed sentence is that the balks of the second row were
placed on the rubble and stones of the first.

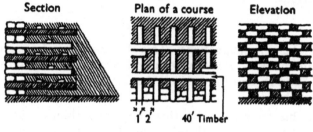

Section   Plan of a course   Elevation

GALLIC WALL

ll. 12–13. **hoc .... cum** followed by **tum** in l. 14 means ' not
only . . . but also '. Order for translation : **cum est hoc opus
non deforme in speciem varietatemque.** The last four words
mean : ' in regard to its variegated appearance '—a hendiadys.[1]

l. 13. **alternis . . . saxis,** ' with alternate balks and stones ',
almost an abl. of cause.

l. 14. **suos ordines,** ' their proper rows '.

ll. 14–15. **tum . . . opportunitatem,** ' but also it has the

[1] A figure of speech in which Latin expresses by two nouns in
the same case what English prefers to do by one noun and a
second dependent on it in the genitive or by a noun and an
adjective (as here).

greatest suitability (=it is extremely suitable) for usefulness and the defence of cities '. **ad ... urbium** may be taken as a hendiadys, ' for the useful (i.e. successful) defence of cities '.

l. 16. **ariete.** The battering-ram was a long beam, reinforced with a head of iron. It was suspended from the roof of a **testudo** (a sapper's hut), which thus gave protection both to the weapon and the soldiers whose task it was to give the ram momentum by pulling it backward and then letting it go.

ll. 17–19. **quae ... potest ;** ' which, bound fast on the inside by beams generally 40 ft. long placed-end-to-end (**continuis**), can neither be broken through nor pulled to pieces '.

l. 17. **pedes quadragenos** is an acc. of extent of space grammatically going with **revincta ;** in sense, however, it belongs to **trabibus.**

CHAPTER 24

l. 1. **his ... oppugnatione.** This abl. absol. may be rendered by a main verb. Begin a fresh sentence at **milites cum** with ' But ' and reverse the order of the Latin words : **cum** means ' although '.

l. 1. **his tot rebus,** ' by these so many things ', i.e. ' by many causes such as these '. **toto tempore,** ' constantly '; *lit.,* ' all the time '.

l. 3. **omnia haec,** ' all these difficulties '.

ll. 4–5. **aggerem ....** Some commentators refuse to accept these figures as accurate on the score that the construction of a ramp of such a size would have involved an enormous amount of labour. Perhaps the best explanation is as follows : the ramp consisted mainly of two parallel terraces at right angles to the enemies' wall and wide enough to support the two towers. The space in between was occupied by another terrace not so long as the two flanking ones but of sufficient size to enable the assaulting troops to pour over the enemies' wall into the town. The great height (80 ft.) may have been due to the depression one would naturally expect in front of the wall of Avaricum.

ll. 6–7. **ad opus,** ' close to the work ', i.e. the **agger.**

l. 7. **consuetudine,** ' according to his usual practice '.

l. 8. **ne quod . . . intermitteretur,** ' that-not any time at all be left off from the work ', = ' that no time at all be lost in their work '.

l. 9. **vigiliam.** See the note on Ch. 3, ll. 12–13.

l. 10. **quem . . . succenderant.** The indicative mood shows that this sentence is an addition by Caesar for explanatory purposes : ' for the enemy had set fire to it from a mine '.

l. 11. **sublato.** Look up **tollo. toto muro,** ' all along the wall '.

l. 12. **ab utroque . . . turrium,** ' on either side of the (Roman) towers '.

l. 14–15. **reliquas . . . potest,** ' and the remaining things by which a fire can be kindled ', i.e. ' and everything else that was inflammable '.

ll. 15–17. **ut quo . . . posset.** Order for translation : **ut ratio posset vix iniri quo primum . . . .**

Note : (i) **ut . . . iniri,** *lit.,* ' that a calculation could scarcely be formed ', i.e. ' that it could hardly be calculated '. (ii) **quo . . . curreretur**—impersonal passive. See the note on Ch. 2, ll. 8–11, and translate ' where the troops should run first '. (iii) **cui rei . . . auxilium,** ' to which thing help should be brought ', would sound better in the active in English : ' to which point they should bring . . . '.

l. 17. **instituto Caesaris,** ' in accordance with Caesar's arrangement '.

ll. 18–19. **partitis temporibus,** *lit.,* ' the times having been divided ', the perfect participle of the deponent **partior** being used in a passive meaning : translate : ' by turns '.

l. 21. **aggerem interscinderent,** i.e. to prevent the fire from spreading.

l. 22. **ad restinguendum,** ' to put out (the fire) '

CHAPTER 25

ll. 1–9. **cum . . . existimavimus.** This long sentence consists of a string of **cum,** 'when', clauses and a short main clause **accidit nobis inspectantibus.** It may be helpful to make the **cum** clauses main verbs and begin a new sentence at **accidit.**

ll. 1–2. **consumpta . . . noctis.** This abl. absol. is equivalent to a concessive clause, 'although . . .'.

l. 2. **pugnaretur,** 'the fighting continued'. **in omnibus locis** goes with it.

l. 4. **pluteos.** According to Rice Holmes, these **plutei** were most probably mantlets which protected the men who moved the towers.

ll. 4–5. **nec . . . animadvertebant,** 'and noticed that they did not easily advance without-cover (**apertos**) to render-assistance'.

ll. 6–7. **omnemque . . . arbitrarentur,** 'and they believed that all the deliverance of Gaul depended upon that instant of time'. Note this meaning of the verb **pono** in the passive.

l. 8. **accidit.** Link this, the main verb of the sentence, with the previous clauses which have been made main ones, by a connecting adverb or phrase ; e.g. 'at this juncture' or 'just then'.

ll. 8–9. **quod . . . existimavimus,** '(a deed) which, as it seemed worthy of mention, we did not think it was to-be-(=should be) passed over'.

ll. 10–11. **per manus . . . glaebas,** 'lumps of fat and pitch passed (to him) from hand to hand (**per manus**)'.

l. 12. **scorpione.** The **scorpio** is said to have been a quick-firing engine that shot bolts or arrows at point-blank range (Rice Holmes).

l. 12. **ab latere dextro,** 'in his . . .'.

l. 13. **ex proximis** goes with **unus.**

l. 13. **iacentem,** 'as he lay'.

ll. 14–15. **alteri** is dat. dependent upon **successit** and **exanimato** agrees with it. The 'skeleton' of the sentence is 'a third took the place of the second'. We may say, however, 'when the second . . . , his place was taken by a third, and the third's by a fourth'.

l. 16. **prius** goes with **quam** in l. 17 and means 'until'.

CHAPTER 26

l. 2. **consilium ceperunt.** We should normally expect the genitive of the gerund **profugiendi** after this phrase. As, however, it is equivalent in meaning, to 'they decided', the use of the infinitive is understandable.

ll. 4–5. **conati... sperabant** *lit.*, 'having tried they hoped'. But the perfect participle is really equivalent to the protasis of a conditional clause : ' if they made the attempt, they hoped . . .'.

l. 4. **non magna iactura,** 'with no great loss' i.e. 'with little loss'.

ll. 5–8. **quod . . . aberant . . .'tardabat.** The use of the indicative shows that these reasons are given by Caesar : they do not exist in the minds of the Gauls : otherwise the subjunctive would have been used.

ll. 6–7. **quae . . . intercedebat,** 'which lay between (them) without-a-break'. **ad insequendum,** 'in the pursuit'.

l. 10. **proiectae,** 'flinging themselves'. Note : (i) the passive here has a reflexive sense. (ii) the Latin perfect participle is more natural in English as a present.

ll. 11–12. **hostibus ad supplicium,** 'to the enemy for punishment' is usually rendered by 'to the tender mercies of the enemy'.

ll. 12–13. **quos ... impediret,** 'whom the weakness of their nature and their strength (=their naturally weak physique) hindered from taking flight'.

ll. 15–16. **conclamare et significare,** 'to scream and to gesticulate'.

l. 17. **perterriti.** Supply **sunt.**

CHAPTER 27

ll. 1–2. **derectisque ... instituerat,** 'and having set in order[1] the works which he had decided to construct'. Some editors read **perfectisque . . . .** 'having completed . . .'.

ll. 3–4. **non ... arbitratus est,** '(Caesar) thought it was a not useless (=a very useful) opportunity for carrying out his design'.

l. 4. **paulo incautius,** 'a little more carelessly (than usual)'.

ll. 5–6. **suos . . . versari,** 'to go about their work rather listlessly'. **languidius,** comparative adverb, **(languide).**

l. 6. **quid ... vellet,** 'what he wanted to be done'. i.e. 'his intentions'.

ll. 7–8. **legionibus ... expeditis,** 'when the legions had secretly got ready for action outside the camp within the mantlets'.
This passage of which the reading is doubtful is much disputed. The meaning, however, is clear. Caesar wished to make a surprise attack : his legionaries were therefore concealed as best they could be within the lines of mantlets or sheds that lined the ramp.

l. 8. **aliquando,** 'at last'.

ll. 9–10. **eis qui ... ascendissent,** 'to those who should be first to climb the wall'. The pluperfect subjunctive (in direct speech, future-perfect indic.) is used because it is virtually in indirect speech.

l. 12. **compleverunt,** 'occupied'.

[1] After the incidents mentioned in Ch. 24, 25.

CHAPTER 28

ll. 1–2. **muro . . . deiecti,** 'because they had been driven from the wall and their towers'. **deiecti** gives the reason why they were **perterriti.**

ll. 3–4. **hoc animo . . . depugnarent,** 'with this intention that if a move were made against them from any direction (by the enemy), they would draw up their battle-line and fight it out'.

Note : (i) **veniretur**—impersonal passive : in this case the English translation is closer to the Latin. (ii) **qua ex parte**; **qua** comes from **qui, quae, quod,** the indefinite adj., 'any' after, **si, nisi, num, ne.** (iii) **instructa acie** : this abl. absol. becomes a finite verb in the active in the translation : *lit.,* 'the line having been drawn up'. See the note on Ch. 1, ll. 12–13.

ll. 5–6. **toto muro,** 'all along the wall'. With **totus, omnis,** and **medius,** the abl. of place where is generally used without the preposition **in.**

l. 6. **circumfundi.** Supply **omnes** as the subject and note that the Latin passive is often equivalent to the intransitive use of an English transitive verb : 'that all were pouring round on every side'.

l. 8. **continenti impetu,** 'in an unbroken stream'.

l. 9. **cum . . . premerent,** 'while the outlet of the gates (being) narrow, they themselves pressed on themselves', i.e. 'while they trampled upon each other at the narrow gates'.

l. 10. **egressa** *lit.,* 'having got out of', = 'that had got clear from'.

l. 11. **studeret.** The subjunctive is due to the relative clause being adverbial, for **qui** (= **ut is**) introduces a result or consecutive clause.

l. 12. **Cenabi,** 'of (= at) Cenabum'.

l. 12. **aetate** goes closely with **confectis** ; 'worn out by age' = 'the aged'.

Caesar obviously made no attempt to stop this indiscriminate massacre—he merely finds excuses for his soldiers' behaviour—namely the slaughter of their fellow-citizens at Cenabum and their hardships in the siege, (**labore operis**). In any case we have plenty of evidence that he could be cold-blooded and ruthless, if he thought it expedient to his policy.

l. 17. **quos**, ' them ', relative connection again.

l. 17. **multa nocte**, ' late at night '.

l. 18. **qua**, ' any ', (for which see the note on ll. 3–4 above), goes with **seditio**.

ll. 18–19. **ex eorum . . . vulgi**, *lit.*, ' from their-thronging together and the pity of the host '. i.e. ' from the pity his army might feel for them as they came thronging in '.

l. 19. **ut** introduces the result clause : ' in such a way that'.

ll. 20–1. **procul . . . civitatum**, ' by stationing his friends . . . .'.

ll. 21–2. **(ut) disparandos . . . curaret**, '(that) he saw-to (them) to-be-parted and to-be-conducted to their friends ', i.e. ' he had them parted and . . . '.

ll. 22–3. **quae . . . obvenerat** ; order for translation : **in eam partem castrorum quae obvenerat cuique civitati ab initio.** Note that the antecedent of **quae** (**partem**) has been attracted into the relative clause and put in the same case as the relative : **in eam** is then dropped : it must of course be supplied in English.

CHAPTER 29

ll. 2–3. **ne . . . ne.** Translate the second **ne** as **neve** which is what we should normally have expected Caesar to write.

l. 3. **non virtute. . . .** From here until the end of the chapter, we have reported speech (Oratio Obliqua). Remember two points : (i) all subordinate clauses will have their verbs in the subjunctive. (ii) strict application of the rules of sequence does not occur in the historians : so we shall find perfect and present subj., although the sequence is historic.

l. 5. **cuius rei.** **rei** can be ignored in translation.

ll. 6–7. **errare si qui . . . exspectent,** 'if any expected . . , (they) were wrong ', i.e. ' all those who expected . . . were wrong '.

l. 6. **omnes,** ' nothing but '.

ll. 7–8. **sibi . . . defendi,** ' that Avaricum be defended had never pleased him ', i.e. ' he had never agreed with the defence of Avaricum '.

l. 8. **cuius rei :** again **rei** can be omitted.

l. 8. **testes ipsos,** i.e. **ipsos testes,** ' themselves (as) wit-nesses '.

ll. 9–11. **sed factum (esse) . . . acciperetur,** ' but it had hap-pened that this disaster was received owing to the folly of the B. and the excessive complaisance of the rest ', i.e. ' the cause of their experiencing this disaster was the . . . '.

ll. 9–10. **imprudentia, obsequentia** are ablatives of cause.

l. 12. **sanaturum.** Supply **esse** to give the future infin. active.

ll. 12–13. **nam quae . . . dissentirent.** Take this relative clause after **(se) adiuncturum (esse) sua diligentia has civi-tates.** It will be noticed that the last word, the antecedent of the relative, has been inserted inside the relative clause— an order which seems most unnatural to us.

l. 14. **unum . . . Galliae,** ' one purpose of (i.e. for) the whole of Gaul '.

l. 15. **cuius consensui** ' the unanimity of which ' is dat. because **obsistere** takes that case.

l. 16. **effectum habere,** a stronger expression for **effe-cisse.**

ll. 17–18. **aequum esse ab eis impetrari,** ' it was right, he said, that it be obtained from them ', i.e. ' that they should be prevailed upon '.

l. 18. **quo facilius.** **quo** replaces **ut** in purpose clauses that contain a comparative.

CHAPTER 30

ll. 1–2. **et maxime quod,** 'and especially because '.

ll. 2–3. **tanto . . . incommodo** ; this abl. absol. could be concessive here, 'although such a great disaster . . . '.

ll. 3–4. **neque . . . fugerat,** 'and had not gone away into hiding and avoided . . . '. The **neque** negatives both verbs. Note **fugio,** 'I flee ', used here as a transitive verb, 'flee from ', 'shun ', 'avoid '.

ll. 4–5. **plusque . . . existimabatur,** *lit.,* 'he was considered to foresee in his mind and to presage the more ', i.e. 'he was given all the more credit for his foresight and prescience '.

l. 5. **re integra,** abl. absol., 'the thing (being) whole ', i.e. 'while things were going well '.

ll. 5–6. **incendendum . . . deserendum.** Note the gerundives, 'that A. be burnt, and afterwards be abandoned ', i.e. 'the burning of A., and afterwards its abandonment '.

l. 7. **ut,** 'as '.

l. 8. **ex contrario,** 'on the contrary '.

l. 9. **incommodo accepto,** 'in consequence of the disaster he had sustained '. **in dies,** 'daily ', is regularly found with comparatives or words of a comparative idea.

ll. 9–11. **simul . . . civitatibus,** *lit.,* 'at the same time they came into the hope, because of his assurance, about the remaining tribes to-be-won over ', i.e. 'because of . . . , they began to entertain the hope of winning over . . . '.

l. 10. **adfirmatione,** abl. of cause.

ll. 13–14. **insueti . . . existimarent,** 'that (although) unaccustomed to toil, they thought all things which were ordered (were) to-be-submitted to by them ', i.e. 'they ought to submit to every order '. **imperarentur.** The subjunctive is due to the influence of **existimarent. insueti laboris,** 'unused to manual labour '. **laboris** is an objective genitive.

Digging is an essential but rather unromantic part of a

soldier's discipline that could never have appealed to the Gallic warriors. Now, however, schooled by defeat, they decide to imitate the camp discipline of the Romans.

CHAPTER 31

l. 1. **nec minus quam**, ' not less than ' = ' just as much as '.

l. 2. **animo laborabat ut**, ' worked in purpose to ', = ' did his best to '.

ll. 3–4. **huic rei**, ' for this purpose '.

ll. 4–5. **quorum quisque ... posset**, ' each of whom could '. **posset**, subjunctive, because the relative pronoun introduces an adverbial clause of result (consecutive).

ll. 6–7. **qui ... curat**, ' he saw-to (those) who ..., to-be-armed and clothed ', i.e. ' he had those ... armed and clothed '.

Note two things : (i) the antecedent of **qui** has to be supplied in English. (ii) the relative clause precedes—an order which is most unnatural for us.

l. 8. **imperat.** Note that this verb can mean *de*mand as well as *com*mand, and that the dative associated with it will then be translated ' from '.

l. 9. **quem et quam ante diem**, ' what (number) and before what date ', i.e. ' fixing the number and the date he wanted them ... '.

ll. 11–12. **his rebus**, ' by these measures '. **id quod ... deperierat**, ' that which had perished at A.,' i.e. ' the losses at A.'.

ll. 14–15. **amicus erat appellatus.** ' Friend ' was a title of prestige given by the Romans to local chieftains and princes who had rendered or were intended to render loyal service to Roman interests.

CHAPTER 32

l. 1. **Avarici**, locative case.

l. 3. **ex**, ' after '.

ll. 4–9. **iam ... subveniat.** Note the structure of this

period : abl. absol., **cum** clause with two verbs, subordinate clause, main clause with dependent indirect command. Translate literally and then try this suggestion : make the abl. absol. a main verb, insert ' and ' before **cum** which should be dropped and then finally put ' when ' before **legati principes.**

l. 6. **sive,** ' (to see) whether '.

l. 8. **oratum,** supine in the acc. case to express purpose.

ll. 8–9. **maxime . . . tempore,** ' at a most critical time '.

ll. 9–23. **summo esse . . . .** From here until the end of the chapter, we have indirect speech (Oratio Obliqua). See the note on Ch. 29, l. 3.

l. 10. **rem,** ' the situation ', subject of **esse.**

l. 10. **quod,** ' because '. **cum,** ' although '.

l. 10. **singuli** ' one at a time '.

l. 10. **antiquitus,** adverb, ' of old '.

l. 11. **annum,** acc. of duration of time, ' for one year '.

l. 11–2. **consuessent,** = **consuevissent.**[1]

ll. 12–13. **duo . . . dicat,** ' two (people) were holding office and each of them said he had been elected by the laws (=legally) '.

l. 15. **antiquissima . . . natum,** *lit.,* ' born from a very old family ', i.e. ' scion of . . . '. **familia,** abl. of origin.

ll. 16–17. **magnae cognationis,** ' of high connections '.

l. 17. **proximo,** ' previous '.

l. 20. **suas . . . clientelas,** *lit.,* ' of each of them (there were) his own retainers ', i.e. ' each was supported by his own retainers '. See the Introduction p. xxii.

l. 20. **quod si,** ' but if '.

ll. 21–2. **fore uti . . . confligat,** *lit.,* ' it would be that one half came to blows with the other half of the tribe ', i.e. ' one half would come . . . '.

---

[1] This replaces **consueverant** of direct speech : hence the pluperfect subj., although in every other case Caesar uses primary tenses.

fore ut + present or imperfect subjunctive, is an alternative form for the future infin. active or passive.

l. 22. **id ne accidat,** ' that it should not happen ' is the subject of **positum (esse)** which means ' depended '. Translate the **ne** clause by : ' Its prevention '.

CHAPTER 33

l. 2. **non ignorans,** *lit.,* ' not being ignorant ', =' being fully aware '. Translate the present participle by a finite verb, ' he was fully aware ' and insert ' and ' before **ne tanta.**

ll. 4–6. **ne tanta ... civitas ... descenderet,** ' lest a tribe so great and so united to Rome should have recourse ', i.e. ' to ' prevent so important a tribe so closely connected to Rome having recourse '.

l. 6. **ad vim atque arma,** *lit.,* ' to violence and arms ', i.e. ' to armed violence '—an excellent example of an hendiadys. See Ch. 23, ll. 12–13.

ll. 6–8. **atque (ne) ea pars ... arcesseret,** ' and to prevent that party sending for '.

l. 7. **quae . . . confideret,** ' which had less confidence in itself '.

l. 8. **huic rei . . . existimavit,** ' he thought that attention-should-be-given to this first (prae) ', i.e. ' that he ought to give his attention . . . '.

l. 9. **quod,** ' because '.

l. 9. **legibus,** ' in accordance with the laws '.

l. 10. **liceret.** The subj. is used because Caesar is giving the reasons in his own mind—virtual Oratio Obliqua, ' because (as he thought) . . . '. See the note on Ch. 20, ll. 2–3.

l. 11. **quid . . . deminuisse,** ' to have diminished anything of their rights or laws ', =' to have slighted in any way their rights or laws '.

l. 13. **quos inter,** =inter quos, i.e. **eos inter quos.**

l. 13. **esset.** The subj. is used because the clause is virtually subordinate in indirect speech. Translate as though we had **erat.**

ll. 13–14. **ad se Decetiam,** we say, ' to him at Decetia'. The latter is the modern Décize.

ll. 15–17. **paucis . . . renuntiatum.** Begin with **fratrem renuntiatum (esse) a fratre. paucis clam convocatis** is abl. absol. **alio . . . oportuerit,** *lit.,* ' in a place and at a time different from (what) it ought to have been ', i.e. ' at a place and a time that were unconstitutional '.

l. 17. **cum,** ' although '.

ll. 17–18. **cum . . . vetarent.** Order for translation : **cum leges non solum vetarent duo** (*acc.*) **ex una familia creari magistratus** (*as* magistrates) **utroque vivo.**
The last two words are abl. absol., ' both (being) alive ', i.e. ' in the lifetime of both '.

ll. 20–2. **qui esset creatus. qui** introduces an adverbial clause of reason here : hence the subj.: ' inasmuch as he '.

l. 21. **intermissis magistratibus,** *lit.,* ' the magistrates having been left off ', i.e. ' when the magistrates were not in office '.

CHAPTER 34

l. 1. **cohortatus.** This perfect participle has dependent upon it the following lines as far as **disponeret.** Make it a main verb and insert ' and then ' before **exercitum,** l. 7.

l. 2. **obliviscerentur.** Remember that this verb is followed by the genitive.

ll. 4–5. **eaque . . . exspectarent,** ' and to expect from him those rewards which they had earned, once the conquest of Gaul was complete ' (**Gallia devicta,** abl. absol.).

ll. 6–7. **quae . . . disponeret,** ' that he might distribute them at-different-points to protect (**in praesidiis**) his corn supply '. **quae** which refers only to **peditum milia X** introduces an adverbial clause of purpose.

ll. 8-9. **in Senones . . . ducendas,** 'to-be-led (i.e. to lead) against . . .'.

l. 9. **sex ipse** . . . (while) he himself . . .'. See Ch. 6, l. 8.

ll. 9-10. **ad oppidum Gergoviam,** 'to the town of Gergovia'. The latter is identified with a mountain about 4 miles south of Clermont.

l. 10. **secundum flumen Elaver,** 'along the river Allier' i.e. upstream.

l. 11. **illi** is dative.

l. 13. **ab altera fluminis parte,** '*on* the other side of the river', i.e. on the left bank. Caesar was on the north of the Allier, Vercingetorix on the south.

CHAPTER 35

l. 1. **cum . . . exercitus,** *lit.,* 'when each army had gone forth on each side'. The meaning of this sentence is obscure, as is shown by the fact that a group of MSS. has another reading : H. J. Edwards in the Loeb edition renders : ' when the two armies had drawn apart'.

ll. 1-2. **in conspectu . . . e regione castris,** 'in sight of and almost opposite (each other's) camp'.

l. 3. **dispositis exploratoribus,** i.e. by Vercingetorix.

ll. 4-5. **erat . . . res,** 'Caesar's position was fraught with great difficulties'.

l. 5. **maiorem . . . partem,** 'for the greater part of the summer', acc. of duration of time.

l. 6. **quod,** 'because'.

l. 6. **ante autumnum.** The river Allier is swollen in the spring and summer by the snows that melt on the Cevennes.

l. 8. **castris positis.** Make this abl. absol. a main verb in the active: 'he pitched camp'. 'And' will have to be inserted before **postero die.**

l. 8. **e regione unius eorum pontium,** 'opposite one of those bridges'.

l. 9. **quos . . . curaverat.** See Ch. 31, ll. 6-7.

l. 12. **apertis**[1] . . . **cohortibus,** ' opening out some cohorts '. In this way the four legions would give the appearance of being six, the number with which he began his march.

ll. 13–14. **quam longissime possent.** See the note on Ch. 8, ll. 11–12.

ll. 14–15. **cum . . . perventum (esse),** ' when from the time of day he had reckoned that they had reached camp '. Note (i) **cum** + pluperfect indicative for the more usual subj. (ii) **perventum (esse),** the infin. of the impersonal passive **perventum est,** ' they reached '.

l. 16. **pars inferior,** ' the lower end ', i.e. of the piles under the water.

l. 17. **pontem,** probably at Varennes, about 48 miles from Gergovia.

l. 19. **reliquas copias,** i.e. the four legions which had marched on the other bank. They must have returned by night.

ll. 20–1. **magnis itineribus,** ' by forced marches '. The Roman legionary averaged about 15 to 20 miles a day although on occasion he could do up to 30 miles, ' a forced march '. We may assume that the forces of Vercingetorix could do the same.

l. 21. **antecessit,** i.e. to Gergovia.

CHAPTER 36

l. 1. **quintis castris,** ' on the fifth day '. It will be seen how this meaning is obtained, if it is remembered that at the end of each day, the Roman army made an encampment.

l. 3. **posita,** *lit.,* ' placed ', i.e. ' situated '.

ll. 5–6. **de . . . constituit quam,** *lit.,* ' he determined that it should not be done about a blockade until ', i.e. ' that he should do nothing about . . . '.

[1] **Apertis** is Deiter's emendation for the MS. reading **captis** which is meaningless.

l. 8. **mediocribus circum se intervallis,** ' at moderate intervals (from one another) around him '.

ll. 9–10. **omnibus . . . occupatis.** The tribal contingents of the Gauls were encamped along the higher slopes of the southern side of the mountain and on the heights of Risolle which is linked by a saddle to the plateau on which the town of Gergovia was situated. **iugum,** therefore, includes the range of the mountain and the heights of Risolle. (See the map.)

l. 10. **qua dispici poterat,** ' where a good view could be obtained '.

ll. 13–15. **seu . . . videretur,** ' in case anything seemed to-be-communicated or to-be-arranged ', i.e. ' in case there seemed anything to communicate . . . '.

ll. 15–17. **neque . . . quin . . . periclitaretur,** ' and he let practically no day pass but that he tested (i.e. without testing) '.

l. 16. **interiectis sagittariis,** ' with archers placed between (the lines of cavalry) '. Their task was not only to support their own cavalry but also to impede the effectiveness of the enemy's horse.

ll. 16–17. **quid . . . suorum,** *lit.*, ' what in each of his followers (there) was of spirit and valour '. For the gen. **animi, virtutis,** see the note on Ch. 5, ll. 13–14.

ll. 18–19. **collis . . . circumcisus.** This is La Roche Blanche. **egregie munitus,** i.e. by nature, ' excellently fortified ' = ' with excellent natural fortifications '.

l. 20. **et** means ' both ' here and can be ignored in translation.

ll. 20–1. **aquae . . . libera,** ' from . . . '. The abls. are abls. of separation. The occupation of this hill by Caesar's men prevented the Gauls from getting supplies of water from the Auzon brook.

l. 21. **prohibituri videbantur,** ' they seemed about-to-cut off ', ' it seemed that they would cut off '.

l. 21. **hostes,** acc. plural.

l. 24. **prius quam . . . posset.** Note : (i) the subjunctive in the temporal clause because there is an additional idea of prevention. (ii) **veniri,** the infinitive of the impersonal passive : **venitur =**' they came '. ' Before they could come . . . '.

l. 25. **deiecto praesidio.** Translate by a main verb in the active.

l. 26. **fossam.** These two ditches were discovered by Colonel Stoffel who gives as their measurements not 12 ft. broad, in each case, but 6 ft. wide and 4 ft. deep.

ll. 26–7. **a maioribus . . . ad minora,** i.e. from the camp half-a-mile from the village of Orcet to the camp on La Roche Blanche.

ll. 27–8. **tuto . . . incursu,** ' safely as far as a sudden attack on the part of the enemy was concerned '. For the gen. **hostium,** see the note on Ch. 37, l. 12.

l. 28. **etiam singuli,** nom. pl., ' (the soldiers) even one at a time '.

CHAPTER 37

l. 1. **dum geruntur.** dum in the meaning ' while ', is very commonly used with the present indicative, without regard to the tense appropriate to the context.

l. 1. **ad Gergoviam,** ' at or near Gergovia '.

ll. 2–3. **cui . . . demonstravimus,** i.e. in Ch. 33.

l. 6. **amplissima familia,** abl. of origin, with **nati,** *lit.,* ' born from a most distinguished family '.

ll. 7–8. **hortaturque ut meminerint,** ' and encouraged (them) to remember '.

ll. 8–16. **unam . . . .** From here to **veniant** we have indirect speech (Oratio Obliqua). Read again the note on Ch. 29, l. 3.

ll. 8–9. **unam . . . civitatem** : order for translation : **civitatem A. esse unam** (' the only one ').

ll. 10–11. **qua traducta.** This abl. absol. is equivalent to the protasis of a conditional clause, ' if this (state) were won over ', i.e. to the national cause.

l. 12. **esse . . . adfectum** : **se adfectum esse non nullo** (=some) **beneficio Caesaris.**

Caesaris is a good example of the subjective genitive. The translation ' of ' is inadequate in English : hence we must say ' on-the-part-of Caesar '. See the note on Ch. 5, l. 13.

ll. 13–14. **sic tamen ut . . . obtinuerit,** ' yet in such a way that he had won his cause with him most justly '.

l. 14. **sed . . . tribuere.** Supply **se** as the subject of **tribuere** ; *lit.*, ' he assigned more (i.e. he had a greater obligation to) the common liberty '.

ll. 14–16. **cur ... Aedui ... veniant,** ' why should the Aedui come ?' This question (here indirect) had a subjunctive verb in the direct form.

l. 16. **disceptatorem,** ' (as) an umpire ', i.e. ' to give a decision '. Take this with **de suo iure et de legibus.**

l. 17. **et . . . et ;** the first **et** means ' both ' and can be ignored.

ll. 18–19. **cum . . . profiterentur,** ' when they offered that they would be even chiefs of (be the first to carry out) that plan '.

l. 21. **placuit ut,** ' it pleased that ', =' it was decided that '.

l. 22. **decem illis milibus** is dative, dependent upon **praeficeretur.** For these troops, see Ch. 34.

l. 22–3. **quae mitterentur ;** the relative clause is adverbial (purpose), ' which were to be sent '.

l. 23. **atque ... curaret,** ' and (that) he see-to them to-be-led ', ' the leading of them '.

ll. 24–5. **reliqua . . . constituunt,** ' they decided in what way it pleased (them) the remaining things to be done ', i.e. ' they decided upon the way in which they should carry out the rest of their plan '.

CHAPTER 38

l. 3. **lacrimans.** The Romans and Gauls did not consider the shedding of tears as unmanly.

l. 6. **insimulati proditionis,** ' accused of treachery '.

l. 7. **indicta causa,** abl. absol., ' their case not-said ', = ' without being given a hearing '.

ll. 9–10. **prohibeor . . . pronuntiare,** ' I am prevented from declaring '. Note the infinitive which is usually found after **prohibeo,** ' I prevent '.

l. 10. **quae gesta sunt,** ' (those things) which were done ', i.e. ' the dreadful facts '. The indicative mood shows that it is a relative clause, not an indirect question.

l. 11. **quae dici vellet,** ' the sort of thing he wanted said ', i.e. ' them to say '. **vellet** is subj. because the relative is adverbial (generic).

ll. 13–14. **quod . . . dicerentur,** ' because they were said . . . '. We prefer the impersonal construction : ' because it was said that they . . . '.

l. 17. **ut sibi consulat,** ' to have regard for them, i.e. for their safety '.

ll. 17–18. **quasi . . . res,** ' as if it were a matter of (i.e. for) consultation '.

l. 18. **ac non** ' and not (rather) '.

l. 21. **ad nos interficiendos,** ' to slay us '.

ll. 21–2. **si . . . est,** ' if there is anything in us of spirit ', i.e. ' if we have any spirit in us '. Note **quid,** ' anything ' and the partitive genitive **animi** ; for the latter see Ch. 5, ll. 13–14.

l. 22. **persequamur,** ' let us avenge '; hortative subjunctive.

ll. 24–5. **eius praesidi fiducia,** ' in reliance of (i.e. on) his protection '.

l. 25. **una** is an adverb.

ll. 27–8. **tota civitate,** ' throughout all the tribe '. See Ch. 28, ll. 5–6.

ll. 29–30. **simili ratione atque facerit,** ' in the same way *as* he had done '.

l. 30. **suas iniurias,** = ' the wrongs done to *them* ', *not* ' to him '.

CHAPTER 39

l. 1. **summo loco natus,** ' born in the highest position ', i.e. ' of very good family '.

l. 2. **summae domi potentiae,** ' of the greatest influence at home (i.e. in his own tribe) '.

l. 2. **una** is an adverb.

l. 3. **pari . . . dispari,** ablatives of quality or description. We prefer to use the genitive, ' of . . . '. Latin uses this case in the previous line.

ll. 3–5. **quem Caesar . . . traditum perduxerat,** ' whom having been introduced . . . Caesar had advanced . . . '. Say ' whom Caesar advanced . . . after he had been introduced to him by D.'.

l. 4. **ab Diviciaco.** Diviciacus was a chieftain of the Aedui, and a protégé and close friend of Caesar.

l. 5. **in equitum numero** means merely ' among the cavalry '.

l. 6. **nominatim ab eo evocati,** ' invited by him (i.e. Caesar) by name ', i.e. ' as a result of a personal invitation from Caesar '.

ll. 6–7. **his erat contentio,** ' to them (there) was a struggle ', =' they had a struggle '.

l. 7. **inter se,** ' with each other '.

ll. 7–8. **et in illa . . . controversia.** See Ch. 33.

l. 7. **magistratuum.** The ' of ' translation for the genitive is inadequate here : say : ' concerning the magistrates '.

ll. 13–16. **quod . . . posset,** ' he foresaw that this would be (=happen) if so many thousands of men joined . . . with the enemy whose safety (=and their safety) neither their relatives could disregard nor their tribe consider of little importance '. Note : (i) **provideat ;** subj. due to the influence of indirect speech, although the **quod** is an example of relative connection. (ii) **levi momento,** ablative of price.

CHAPTER 40

l. 1. **magna . . . Caesar,** *lit.,* ' Caesar having been affected with great anxiety by this news ' : i.e. ' Caesar became very anxious at this news ' *or* ' this news caused Caesar great anxiety '. Cf. Ch. 6, ll. 4–5.

l. 2. **quod,** ' because '.

l. 3. **nulla . . . dubitatione,** *lit.,* ' no hesitation placed between ', = ' without any hesitation '.

l. 3. **expeditas,** ' in light marching order ', i.e. without their packs which, about 45 lbs. in weight, were normally carried when the army was on the march. See Ch. 18. l. 4.

l. 5. **spatium,** ' time '.

l. 5. **tali tempore,** ' at such a crisis '.

l. 6. **quod . . . videbatur,** ' because the matter seemed to depend upon speed '. Note once again the meaning of **ponere** in the passive.

l. 7. **castris praesidio,** ' for a protection to his camps ', i.e. ' to protect his camps '. Note : (i) **praesidio,** dative of purpose. (ii) **castris** is plural in meaning here and refers to the larger and smaller camps. He could not have left either one or the other undefended.

l. 9. **paulo ante,** ' a little before ', (i.e. his orders), goes with **profugisse.** Note **paulo,** abl. of the measure of difference.

ll. 10–14. **adhortatus . . . impedit.** Note the structure of this typical Latin sentence : perfect participle of deponent (nom. case), abl. absol., two perfect participles of deponents (nom. case), abl. absol., two co-ordinate verbs.

Make **adhortatus** and **progressus** main verbs linked by ' and '. The rest of the sentence will follow naturally if we insert ' when ' before **agmen** and translate **conspicatus** as **conspicatus est.** ' Thereupon ' needs to be supplied before **immisso.**

l. 10. **necessario tempore,** ' at so urgent a time '.

l. 11. **cupidissimis omnibus,** abl. absol., ' all (being) very enthusiastic ', = ' amid universal enthusiasm '.

l. 14. **quemquam** is used as a stronger form than the more usual **quem**, ' any one at all '.

l. 16. **illi,** i.e. the Aeduans.

l. 16. **interfectos.** Supply **esse.**

l. 16. **versari,** ' to ride '.

l. 19. **mortem deprecari,** *lit.*, ' to beg off death ', i.e. ' to appeal for their lives '.

ll. 20–2. **quibus . . . patronos,** ' for whom according to the practice of the Gauls it is a crime to desert their patrons even in desperate plight '.

CHAPTER 41

l. 2. **qui docerent,** ' to report '. Note that the **qui** clause is adverbial and expresses purpose : hence the subjunctive.

ll. 2–3. **suo . . . potuisset.** Order for translation : **qui docerent quos** (those whom) **potuisset interficere iure belli conservatos (esse) beneficio suo.**

l. 4. **ad Gergoviam,** ' in the direction of Gergovia '.

ll. 5–6. **quanto . . . fuerit,** indirect question, object of **exponunt.**

l. 6. **summis copiis,** ' by the enemy in full strength '.

ll. 6–7. **oppugnata** needs **esse** to be the full form of the perfect infin. passive.

l. 7. **cum,** ' while '.

ll. 9–10. **quibus . . . permanendum,** *lit.*, ' by whom the same men, owing to the size of the camp there was to be-a-remaining on the rampart without-a-break (**perpetuo**) ', i.e. ' who without relief or a break had to remain . . . '. **isdem** is in apposition with **quibus.**

It will be remembered from Ch. 40 that Caesar had not had time to reduce the size of the camp which had been originally made for 6 legions. The two legions which had been left behind to guard the camp were, therefore, very hard pressed by this all out attack on their quarters.

ll. 10–15. **multitudine . . . apparare.** The acc. and infin. construction is continued.

l. 12. **magno usui,** predicative dative, 'a great help '.

ll. 12–13. **tormenta,** 'the artillery'. Roman war engines which were modelled on Greek ones, were obviously powerful and effective. The propelling power was obtained from arrangements of twisted ropes or cables. There was the ' **ballista** ' that shot stones, balls, and blocks of wood or metal of from 100–130 pounds and the ' **catapulta** ' which fired heavy arrows, darts, javelins or bolts horizontally or nearly so. It is believed that it had a range of 1000 yards with certain types of ammunition.

l. 13. **discessu eorum,** ' on the departure of the enemy '.

l. 14. **ceteras,** ' the rest of the gates ' ; i.e. with the exception of two (**duabus relictis portis**). There were four gates or openings, one on each side of the Roman camp. Fabius left two gates free from obstruction in order that he might make a sortie if his position became desperate.

l. 14. **pluteos.** These are breastworks to strengthen the camp defences.

l. 15. **in . . . casum,** ' for the next day and a similar event ', =' for a similar attack on the next day '.

l. 16. **summo studio militum,** 'amid the greatest enthusiasm on the part of his soldiers'. Note the translation of the genitive.

l. 17. **ante ortum solis.** Caesar marched his men some fifty miles in twenty-six hours.

CHAPTER 42

l. 1. **dum . . . geruntur.** For the tense of **geruntur**, see the note on Ch. 37, l. 1. **ad Gergoviam,** ' at *or* near Gergovia '.

ll. 2–3. **nullum . . . spatium,** ' no time for ascertaining (the truth) '.

ll. 3–4. **impellit . . . temeritas.** This sentence will run better in English if it is turned into the passive : ' some men were driven on by . . . , others by . . . '.

l. 4. **quae**, ' (a quality) which '.

ll. 5–6. **ut . . . pro re comperta.** The **ut** clause is explanatory, ' namely that they regard an idle rumour as an ascertained fact '.

l. 7. **in . . . abstrahunt.** Supply from **civium Romanorum** ' them ' as the object.

l. 8. **adiuvat . . . Convictolitavis,** *lit.,* ' Convictolitavis helped the matter tottering ', i.e. ' Convictolitavis made matters worse in a situation which was already deteriorating '.

ll. 9–10. **ut reverti pudeat,** ' that they might be ashamed to return '.

l. 11. **ex oppido Cabillono,** ' from the town of Cabillonum '. The latter is identified with Châlon-sur-Saône in Burgundy. Note that the Latin uses apposition : cf. **urbs Roma,** ' the city of Rome '.

l. 12. **idem facere,** *lit.,* ' to do the same ', i.e. ' to quit the town '.

ll. 12–13. **qui . . . constiterant.** See the note on Ch. 3, l. 4.

l. 14. **omnibus impedimentis,** abl. of separation in Latin; we say ' of '.

l. 14. **repugnantes,** acc. pl., ' (them) resisting ', i.e. ' when they offered resistance '.

CHAPTER 43

l. 3. **nihil . . . consilio,** *lit.,* ' that nothing had been done by public policy ', i.e. ' that their tribe was not responsible for what had happened '.

ll. 5–6. **sui purgandi gratia.** Note : (i) **gratia,** ' for the sake of ', which like **causa** follows its case, genitive. (ii) **sui** plural in meaning, but singular in form : hence the gerundive **purgandi** agrees with the form, not the meaning : *lit.,* ' for the sake of clearing themselves ', i.e. ' to clear themselves '.

ll. 6–7. **reciperandorum suorum causa.** Cf. the preceding note : ' to recover their own ones ', i.e. ' their kindred '.

l. 7. **capti,** ' caught ', i.e. ' dazzled '. This and the preceding perfect participle passive **contaminati** would be better as main verbs in English, with ' and ' inserted before **timore.**

l. 8. **quod,** ' because '. **ea res,** ' that matter ', i.e. the murdering of Roman citizens and the plundering of their property.

l. 11. **quae,** acc. pl. ' this '.

l. 12. **quam mitissime potest.** See Ch. 8, ll. 11–12. *Lit.,* ' as gently as possible ', i.e. ' in the most conciliatory phrases possible '.

ll. 13–14. **nihil . . . ,** acc. and infin. Supply : ' he said ' from the verb **appellat. nihil se gravius iudicare,** ' he in-no-way (**nihil**) judged more severely ', i.e. ' he made no more severe judgment '.

ll. 14–15. **de . . . benevolentia,** ' (anything) of his kindly feelings towards the Aedui '.

ll. 17–18. **quem ad modum . . . discederet . . . ,** ' (as to) how he should withdraw from-the-district-of Gergovia . . . '.

Note : (i) **discederet, contraheret,** subjunctives in indirect question, were also subjunctive in the direct form Caesar said : ' how am I to withdraw? ', **quem ad modum discedam,** deliberative subj. (ii) **ab Gergovia** means ' from the neighbourhood *or* district of Gergovia '. **Gergovia** without the preposition is the normal Latin for ' from Gergovia'.

ll. 19–20. **ne . . videretur. profectio . . . defectionis** is the subject, **similis fugae** the complement.

CHAPTER 44

ll. 1–2. **haec . . . gerendae,** *lit.,* ' to (him) pondering these matters, an opportunity of the thing to-be-carried out successfully seemed to occur ', i.e. ' as he pondered on these matters, an opportunity of successfully carrying out the withdrawal seemed to arise '. This is Caesar's assumed objective.

l. 3. **collem.** This hill marked A on the map rises to a height of 692 metres and is about 550 yds. south-west of the nearest part of the plateau of Gergovia.

l. 4. **qui . . . . tenebatur,** ' which was in the enemy's possession '.

l. 4. **qui,** ' (a hill) which '.

ll. 7–8. **constabat inter omnes,** *lit.,* ' it was agreed among all ', i.e. ' all agreed in saying '.

l. 8. **quod,** ' as '; *lit.,* ' (that) which ' of ' what '.

ll. 9–10. **dorsum . . aequum.** The iugum is probably the heights of Risolles and the **dorsum eius iugi,** is the Col des Goulles, the saddle that links the heights of Risolles to the plateau of Gergovia.

ll. 10–11. **hunc . . . oppidi,** ' (but) that it was wooded and narrow where there was access (= and afforded access) to the other side of the town ', (i.e. the western approach to the town, for the main Roman camp was on the east).

Vercingetorix was extremely nervous, now that Caesar was assured of his supplies and could think in terms of an investment, lest the Romans should capture the ridge connecting Risolles with Gergovia and thus, in preventing his men from foraging, starve the garrison into surrender. He had, therefore, concentrated all his men on the fortification of the western approach to Risolles, the only approach where an attack was possible.

l. 12. **illos,** ' the enemy '.

ll. 12–15. **nec iam aliter sentire . . . quin . . . viderentur,** ' and did not now otherwise feel but that they seemed to be practically surrounded and cut off . . . ', i.e. ' and had now no option but to believe that they would be . . . '.

ll. 12–13. **uno . . . amisissent,** ' if after the Romans had seized one hill, they (i.e. the Gauls) lost the other '. The ' one hill ' is La Roche Blanche, the other the saddle mentioned above.

l. 16. **evocatos (esse),** ' had been called away '.

CHAPTER 45

l. 2. **eo,** ' thither ', =' there ', i.e. to the west and south of the Hauteurs de Risolles, the only place where an attack on Gergovia was considered feasible. This move, as we can see later, is merely a feint to deceive the enemy.

The cavalry moved along the valley of the Auzon thence off to the left along the northern slopes of the Montagne de la Serre and thence in the direction of the pass of Opme and Risolles.

l. 2. **de media nocte,** ' just after mid-night '.

ll. 2–3. **paulo tumultuosius,** ' a little more noisily than usual '. For **paulo,** abl. of the measure of difference, see Ch. 4, l. 15.

l. 3. **omnibus locis,** ' all over the place '.

l. 4. **impedimentorum** seems here to mean ' pack-horses '.

ll. 6–7. **equitum . . . simulatione,** ' with the appearance and pretence of cavalry ', i.e. ' that they might appear as the cavalry they were pretending to be '.

l. 7. **collibus,** ' on the hills ', i.e. the northern slopes of the Montagne de la Serre.

l. 8. **qui vagarentur.** Note the subjunctive.

l. 9. **easdem regiones,** ' the same parts ', i.e. the west and south-west of the Hauteurs de Risolles. Caesar wished to give Vercingetorix the impression that a major attack was to be launched from this direction on the place which the Gallic general was fortifying.

l. 10. **ut,** ' as (was natural as) '.

l. 11. **in castra,** i.e. the larger camp, from which the movements were taking place.

ll. 11–12. **neque . . . poterat,** *lit.,* ' nor at so great a distance what of certain it was could be found out ', i.e. ' but at . . . distance, the enemy could not find out what it really meant '.

ll. 12–13. **eodem iugo** must mean ' along the same heights ',. i.e. the northern slopes of the Montagne de la Serre.

ll. 13–14. **inferiore ... occultat.** This legion followed the same route as the cavalry and muleteers, then dropped down into the valley and took up a concealed position a little to the north of the village of Chanonat, as if it was preparing for a surprise attack.

l. 14. **Gallis.** Translate this dative of the person interested as if it were a genitive depending upon **suspicio.**

l. 15. **illo ad munitionem,** ' thither (=to that spot) for the defence (=to defend it) '. Caesar's feint has succeeded. To meet the supposed attack against Risolles, Vercingetorix has concentrated all his men on this sector.

ll. 16–17. **tectis ... militaribus.** Make these two abl. absols. main verbs in the active, and insert ' and ' before **raros. tectis** is from **tego.**

l. 18. **raros,** ' in small groups '.

l. 18. **qui ... animadverterentur,** ' in order that they might be noticed from the town '. (This movement is a subsidiary feint attack, the object of which was to divert attention from the main assault which was to be launched directly from the east by the legions from the larger camp. For a fuller discussion, see Appendix A.)

l. 20. **quid fieri velit.** See Ch. 27, l. 6.

l. 22. **longius,** ' too far '.

l. 23. **quid ... proponit,** ' he stated what (of) disadvantage the inequality of the ground had ', i.e. ' the drawbacks involved in the inequality of the terrain '. **incommodi.** For the genitive, see the note on Ch. 5, ll. 13–14.

ll. 24–5. **hoc ... proeli,** ' this (he said) could be remedied only by speed ; it was a matter of a surprise, not of a pitched battle '.

ll. 25–6. **ab dextra parte,** ' on the right side ', i.e. from the east. Take this phrase after **alio ascensu** and note the common use of **ab** to denote ' place where ': cf. **a fronte, a tergo,** etc.

CHAPTER 46

l. 1. **ab planitie . . . ascensus,** ' from the level ground and from the beginning of the ascent ', i.e. ' from the level ground from which one began the ascent to Gergovia '. The level ground is situated at the foot of the east slope of the plateau.

l. 2. **recta regione,** ' in a straight line '.

ll. 2–3 **si . . . intercederent, aberat.** Note the conditional clause, **si**+imperfect subjunctive, ' if no curve intervened ' (but it did), unreal in present time, then an apodosis which is imperfect *indicative*, ' the wall was distant '. This variant is more graphic than the imperfect subjunctive, which is the normal construction.

ll. 3–4. **quidquid . . . augebat,** *lit.,* ' whatever (of) detour had been added to this (**huc**) for making the slope easier, that increased the distance of the journey '.

Note : (i) **circuitus,** partitive genitive. (ii) **accesserat :** this verb is often used as the passive of **addo.**

l. 5. **a . . . colle,** ' about half-way up the hill '.

ll. 5–6. **in . . . ferebat,** ' lengthways as the nature of the hill allowed.'

ll. 6–7. **ex . . . Galli.** Begin : **Galli praeduxerant ex . . . murum,** then, **in longitudinem . . . ferebat,** finally **qui . . . tardaret.**

Note the adverbial nature of the relative clause, (purpose).

ll. 9–10. **densissimis castris,** ' with their encampments very close to each other '.

ll. 11–12. **trinis castris,** abl. dependent upon **potiuntur. Trinis** =**tribus,** the distributive numeral being regular with words plural in form but singular in meaning.

l. 14. **ut meridie conquieverat,** ' just as he had gone to rest at mid-day ', i.e. ' while enjoying his mid-day siesta '.

CHAPTER 47

ll. 1–2. **consecutus . . . iussit.** Much has been written on the real meaning of this sentence, and as a full discussion is out of place in a school edition, it is possible to give only one interpretation, viz. the one that seems the most satisfactory in the context.

If we translate : ' having achieved what he had proposed (to himself) in his mind (i.e. his purpose), Caesar ordered a recall to be sounded ', we ask ourselves, ' what was his purpose and why did he order a recall? '

Caesar's *real* objective was to capture Gergovia and destroy the Gallic army. His *assumed* one was to cover his withdrawal from Gergovia necessitated, so he claims, by the restlessness of the Gauls, by an effective military demonstration.

Caesar's *real* reason for sounding the retreat was that he soon realized that his plan for a surprise attack had failed— the Gauls had been alerted, perhaps by king Teutomatus, and he could not run the risk of allowing his legionaries to fight a pitched battle under unfavourable conditions. The reason that Caesar wants us to accept is that he had attained his objective, i.e. a successful military demonstration which would enable him to withdraw from Gergovia without loss of face.

l. 2. **receptui cani. receptui** is a dative of work contemplated and **cani** is the infinitive of the impersonal passive ; ' the retreat to be sounded '.

l. 3. **constituit,** ' halted '. **continuo** is the emendation made by von Göler for the **concionatus** or **contionatus** that is the reading of the MSS.—readings which are meaningless. The 10th legion was a veteran one which had always given Caesar first-class service.

ll. 3–6. **ac . . . retinebantur.** The skeleton of this sentence is **milites ab tribunis legatisque retinebantur,** ' the soldiers were held back by . . . '. It would sound better, however, in the active in English and in this way the conative force of the imperfect **retinebant** could be brought out, ' the tribunes and generals tried to hold back the soldiers '.

ll. 4–5. **satis magna valles,** ' quite a large valley '.

l. 6. **ut...praeceptum,** *lit.,* ' as it had been ordered by Caesar ' =' in accordance with Caesar's orders '.

l. 7. **elati,** ' elated '.

ll. 9–10. **quod . . . possent. quod** = **ut** and introduces an adverbial clause of result.

l. 10. **neque . . . quam,** ' and they did not make an end of pursuing until ' = ' and they did not stop the pursuit until '. Note the separation of **prius** and **quam.**

ll. 12–13. **qui . . . aberant,** ' (those) who were at some distance '.

l. 16. **pectore . . . prominentes,** ' hanging over (the wall), their breasts exposed '. **passis manibus,** ' with outstretched hands ' should be taken after **obtestabantur Romanos. passis** is the perfect participle passive of **pando.**

ll. 18–19. **neu . . . abstinerent,** *lit.,* ' and-not (**neu**) as they had done at Avaricum, refrain not even from women and children '.
Note the double negative—awkward in English—' refrain not even from ' = ' to refuse quarter to '. Hence we get : ' and not to refuse quarter to even . . . '.

l. 20. **per manus demissae . . . .** Translate as if we had **demissae sunt et sese tradebant,** ' were lowered by the hands (of others) and began-to-deliver themselves up . . . '. Note the *inceptive* use of the imperfect.

ll. 21–4. **quem . . . ascenderet,** *lit.,* ' whom it was agreed to have said among his men (i.e. who, it was well known, had said . . .) that day that he was incited by the rewards at Avaricum and would not allow that anyone . . . '. **prius,** adv., i.e. ' before him '.

l. 24. **tres suos manipulares,** ' three men who belonged to his company '. Strictly a maniple was two centuries.

CHAPTER 48

ll. 1–2. **ut supra demonstravimus,** i.e. in Ch. 44, ll. 15–16.

ll. 3–5. **primo . . . contenderunt.** Note the construction : abl. absol., nom of perf. part. passive, acc. and infin., abl. absol., main verb. Make the abl. absols. main verbs in the active, inserting the necessary conjunctions 'and', 'and so', etc. The acc. and infin., 'that the town was held by the Romans', depends on the noun **nuntiis.**

ll. 5–7. **ut quisque . . . venerat, . . . augebat.** The pluperfect indic. is often found in subordinate clauses to denote repeated action, the main verb being in the imperfect. **ut =** 'as'.

l. 7. **quorum,** 'of them', relative connection again.

ll. 9–10. **tendebant,** 'had been stretching'. The use of the imperfect seems to be similar to that found in the sentence, 'I had been waiting for you a long time', **te iamdudum exspectabam.**

ll. 12–13. **erat . . . contentio,** '(there) was to the Romans neither in ground nor in numbers a fair contest', = 'the Romans had . . .'. Note **loco, numero,** ablatives of respect.

l. 13. **spatio pugnae,** 'by the long continuance of the fighting'.

CHAPTER 49

l. 1. **iniquo loco pugnari,** 'that the battle was taking place on unfavourable ground'. Note once again **pugnari,** the infin. of **pugnatur,** the impersonal passive.

l. 3. **minoribus . . . praesidio,** 'to guard the smaller camp'. See the note on Ch. 5, l. 9.

l. 5. **sub infimo . . . hostium,** 'at the foot of the hill *on* the right . . .'. See the map.

ll. 6–7. **ut . . . quo minus . . . terreret,** 'so that, if . . . , he might deter the enemy from pursuing (them) at will'. A glance at the map will make the position clear. Note that **terreo** is here followed by **quo minus,** a construction found regularly after verbs of 'hindering 'and preventing'.

CHAPTER 50

l. 1. **cum pugnaretur.** Impersonal passive again; **acerrime pugnaretur,** = 'the battle raged'.

l. 3. **ab latere nostris aperto,** '*on* the exposed flank of our men '. Note once again the Latin use of the preposition **ab** and **nostris,** dative (person interested), where we prefer the genitive.

l. 4. **ab dextra parte,** ' on the right '. See the note on Ch. 45, ll. 25–6.

ll. 4–5. **manus distinendae causa.** Caesar might have written **manum distinendi causa,** for the gerund may have a direct object when it is in the genitive. The gerundive construction, however, is frequently used as an alternative.

manus is the enemy's main forces.

l. 5. **hi,** i.e. the Aedui. Their march is indicated on the map by a dotted line.

ll. 6–7. **ac . . . animadvertebantur,** ' and although they were noticed to have their right shoulders bare '. We prefer the impersonal construction : ' it was noticed that they had . . . '. **dextris . . . exsertis** is an abl. of quality.

ll. 7–8. **quod . . . consuerat,** ' which was accustomed to be (=usually was) the badge for-those-coming-in-peace (**pacatum**) '. Some editors adopt the emendation of Heller **pactum** and translate : ' the badge agreed upon '.

ll. 8–9. **tamen . . . existimabant,** *lit.,* ' yet the soldiers believed even this to have been done by the enemy for the sake of deceiving them ', i.e. ' yet the soldiers believed that the enemy had done even this to deceive them '. Note once again **sui** can be plural in meaning though the form remains singular, hence the gerundive is singular. Cf. Ch. 43, ll. 5–6.

l. 11. **muro,** ' from the wall ', abl. of separation.

ll. 13–14. **a multitudine,** ' by superior numbers '.

l. 14. **sibi desperans,** ' despairing for himself ', i.e. ' for his own safety '.

l. 15. **manipularibus suis,** dative after **inquit.**

l. 16. **una** is an adverb.

l. 17. **vestrae quidem certe vitae,** ' for *your* lives at least '. Note : (i) **quidem.** an enclitic which emphasises the preceding word. (ii) Latin uses **vitae** sing., where we prefer the plural. The same idiom exists in French.

l. 18. **cupiditate gloriae adductus,** 'led on by the desire for glory' is in agreement with the unexpressed subject of **adduxi,** 'I' and is causal. Hence we may say : 'through my being led on . . .'. **gloriae,** objective genitive.

l. 19. **data facultate,** 'when the opportunity is given'.

l. 23. **deficiunt.** Supply 'me' as the object.

l. 24. **vos recipite** is reflexive, 'betake yourselves', 'withdraw'.

l. 25. **post paulum,** 'a little later'. It is usual to find **post paulo,** where **paulo** is an abl. of the measure of difference.

l. 25. **suis saluti fuit,** 'he was for a salvation to his men', 'he saved his men'. **saluti** is a good example of the predicative dative.

CHAPTER 51

ll. 1-2. **XLVI centurionibus amissis.** The loss of so many centurions was very serious, for they were the backbone of the Roman army, experienced men who occupied a position similar to that of sergeants and subalterns in the British army.

There were 60 centurions to a legion and their rank in relation to one another was determined by two things : (a) whether they served in the first, second, or third line, called respectively **hastati, principes, triarii** ; (b) whether they were the senior or junior centurions of their maniple. The latter included two centuries. There were thus 3 maniples in a cohort and 10 cohorts in a legion.

As Caesar always made a point of mentioning his centurions in his despatches, he obviously appreciated their quality and importance.

ll. 2-3. **intolerantius,** comparative adverb, 'too eagerly'.

l. 4. **paulo aequiore loco,** 'on ground a little more favourable', i.e. to their third position.

l. 7. **locum superiorem.** They had moved up to their first position : now they drop back to their second position, on

the lower slopes of the east side which were higher relative
to their first position in the valley. In this way they could cover
the 10th legion now in its third position and prevent the
enemy from pressing home any advantage. None of these
positions can be accurately identified.

l. 8. **infestis . . . signis**, *lit.*, ' with standards facing the
enemy ', i.e. ' ready to give battle '.

l. 9. **ab radicibus collis**, ' from the foot of the hill ', i.e. from
the foot of the slope down which the Gauls had pressed hard
on the retreating Romans.

ll. 10–11. **paulo minus septingenti**, ' a little less than seven
hundred '. Note that **minus** has no grammatical influence
on the **septingenti**.

CHAPTER 52

ll. 2–3. **quod sibi ipsi iudicavissent**, ' because (as he said)
they had decided for themselves ', i.e. without waiting for
orders. The subjunctive is that of virtual Oratio Obliqua.
See the note on Ch. 20, ll. 2–3.

ll. 3–4. **quo . . . videretur**, *lit.*, ' whither it seemed (to them)
an-advance-should-be-made or what should-be-done ', i.e.
' where, they thought, they ought to advance or what they ought
to do '.

Note the gerundives, the one impersonal **procedendum**, the
other personal **agendum**.

ll. 4–6. **neque . . . potuissent**. These two clauses are part
of the **quod** clause, ' because they had not halted . . . and
had not been able to be held back . . . '.

For the latter we might say : ' they had made it impossible
for the tribunes and generals to hold them back '.

signo . . . dato, abl. absol., equivalent to a temporal clause,
' when . . . '. **recipiendi** = **sui recipiendi**, for which see the
note on Ch. 43, ll. 5–6.

ll. 6–7. **quid . . . posset**, ' what the unfavourableness of the
ground could (do) ', = ' what could result from fighting on
unfavourable ground '.

l. 7. **ad Avaricum,** ' at *or* near Avaricum '.

l. 7. **cum,** ' when '.

ll. 7–8. **sine . . . hostibus,** abl. absol., equivalent to a concessive clause, ' although the enemy . . . '.

ll. 9–10. **ne parvum modo detrimentum accideret,** ' that even a trifling loss might not occur '.

ll. 11–18. **quanto . . . desiderare,** acc. and infinitive : hence all subordinate clauses have their verbs in the subjunctive mood.

ll. 11–14. **quanto opere . . . admiraretur , . . .** ' as much as he admired . . . ' **tanto opere . . . (se) reprehendere,** ' so much he blamed '.

l. 14. **licentiam,** ' their lack of discipline '.

ll. 14–16. **quod . . . existimarent,** ' because they believed they knew more than their commander-in-chief about . . . '.

ll. 16–18. **se desiderare,** 'he looked for '.

ll. 16–17. **nec minus . . . quam,** *lit.*, ' no less than ', i.e. ' just as much as '.

l. 16. **ab milite,** ' in his men '.

CHAPTER 53

l. 1. **ad extremam orationem,** ' at the end of his speech '.

ll. 3–4. **neu . . . tribuerent,** ' nor to attribute to the courage of the enemy what (**id quod**) the unfavourable ground had brought about '.

ll. 4–5. **eadem . . . quae,** acc. pl. neuter, ' the same as '.

l. 4. **cogitans,** *lit.*, ' thinking ', is equivalent to a concessive clause, ' though he thought '.

l. 8. **levi . . . secundo,** ' after a cavalry skirmish and that too a successful one '.

ll. 10–11. **satis . . . existimans,** ' thinking that sufficient had been done (**satis factum (esse),** =he had done enough), for the cockiness of the Gauls to-be-reduced and the spirit of his men to-be-restored ', i.e. ' to reduce . . . and to restore . . . '.

Caesar wants us to believe that he has achieved his main object, for which see the end of Ch. 43 and the beginning of Ch. 44, and can, therefore, withdraw from Gergovia without too much loss of face or prestige.

l. 12. **in Aeduos** = **in fines Aeduorum.**

ll. 12–13. **ne . . . hostibus.** Make this abl. absol. a main verb and insert ' and ' before **tertio die.**

l. 13. **ad,** ' at ' or ' by '.

l. 13. **pontes reficit.** They had been broken down by Vercingetorix.

l. 14. **eo,** ' over it '. **eo,** *lit.,* ' by means of it ' is an ablative of the instrument.

CHAPTER 54

l. 3. **profectum.** Supply **esse.**

ll. 3–4. **opus . . . civitatem,** ' it was necessary for them themselves to go before (him) for strengthening (i.e. to strengthen) the tribe (in their loyalty) '.

ll. 4–5. **etsi . . . habebat,** *lit.,* ' although he had the treachery of the Aedui detected by many things ', i.e. ' although he had plenty of evidence to detect . . . '.

l. 6. **horum discessu,** ' on their departure ', i.e. of Viridomarus and Eporedorix.

ll. 7–8. **eos . . . constituit.** Caesar usually has the infinitive after **constituit,** ' he decided ', i.e. **non eos retinere constituit.**

l. 10. **sua . . . merita,** ' his own services towards the Aedui '.

ll. 10–11. **quos . . . accepisset,** *lit.,* ' of what kind (**quos** = **quales**) and how humbled he had found them ', i.e. ' the humble position in which he had found them '.

ll. 11–13. **compulsos . . . extortis ;** these lines are explanatory of the position of the Aedui, ' driven together into towns . . . '.

l. 11–12. **multatos agris omnibus ;** we say 'deprived *of* (not '*by* ') all their lands '. **agris** is an abl. of separation.

ll. 14–15. **quam . . . deduxisset,** ' and into what fortune and into what power he had brought them ', i.e. ' and the success and power into which he . . . '.

This indirect question is the object of **exposuit** in l. 10.

l. 15. **ut,** ' with the result that '.

l. 16. **omnium temporum,** *lit.,* ' of all times ', i.e. ' of all (previous) times (in their history) '.

l. 16–7. **antecessisse,** ' to have surpassed '.

CHAPTER 55

l. 1. **Noviodunum.** This important Roman base is the modern Nevers.

l. 1. **ad,** ' by '.

l. 7. **eo,** adv., ' thither ', = ' there ', i.e. to Noviodunum.

ll. 8–13. **Litaviccum . . . missos ;** the string of acc. and infins., is explanatory of **de statu civitatis,** ' the condition of the tribe '; ' namely that L. had been received . . . , that Convictolitavis and . . . had met him, that envoys . . . '.

l. 9. **Bibracte,** locative, ' at Bibracte '.

ll. 9–10. **quod . . . auctoritatis.** The indicative mood shows that this relative clause is an addition made by Caesar, and is not part of the information gained by Eporedorix and Viridomarus.

ll. 12–13. **de pace et amicitia concilianda,** *lit.,* ' about peace and friendship to-be-procured ', i.e. ' to procure peace . . . '.

ll. 13–14. **non . . . existimaverunt,** ' they thought that so great an opportunity (was) not to-be-neglected ', i.e. ' that they should not neglect . . . '.

l. 15. **Novioduni,** ' at Noviodunum ', locative again.

ll. 15–16. **quique . . . convenerant,** ' and (those) who had gathered there (eo) for business ' (**negotiandi causa**). The antecedent which has to be supplied will be **eis** in the abl. absol. with **interfectis.**

ll. 17–18. **obsides... deducendos curaverunt,** 'they saw-to the hostages to-be-conducted ', i.e. ' they had the hostages conducted '.

l. 17. **Bibracte,** acc., ' to Bibracte '.   English, however, says ' at Bibracte '.

ll. 19–20. **ne cui . . . Romanis,** ' that it might not be of any (**cui**) use to the Romans '.   Note the predicative dative **usui.**

l. 20. **frumenti quod,** *lit.,* ' what of corn ', = ' all the corn that '.   **frumenti,** partitive gen.   **subito,** ' at once '.

l. 21. **navibus,** ' on barges '.

l. 24. **iniciendi timoris causa,** i.e. **iniciendi timorem causa.**

l. 25. **si,** ' in the hope that ' *or* ' to see if '.

ll. 27–9. **quam . . . videretur.**   The subject of **adiuvabat** is the **quod** clause, *lit.,* ' the fact that the Loire had become swollen by the snows had helped them much for this hope '.

The Latin order may be retained if we turn **adiuvabat** into the passive :   ' in this hope they were very much helped by the fact that the Loire . . . '.

CHAPTER 56

ll. 1–2. **maturandum sibi censuit,** ' decided that he must hurry '.

ll. 2–3. **si . . . periclitandum,** ' even if he had to run some risk in completing bridges '.   **si esset periclitandum** is passive in Latin and means, ' even if (some) risk had to-be-run '.

Caesar realised that if he could not find a ford over the Loire, he might be compelled to fight while he was actually engaged in throwing bridges over the river.

ll. 3–4. **ut . . . dimicaret.**   The purpose clause depends upon **maturandum** (**esse**).

priusquam . . . copiae, ' before larger forces had been collected there '.   The subjunctive **essent coactae** is due to the clause being subordinate in indirect speech.

ll. 4–10. **nam . . . timebat.**   This awkward sentence runs literally as follows : ' for that his plan changed, he should divert his route into the Province,—as he thought was to-be-done of necessity not even through fear—not only (**cum**) the dishonour and disgrace of the action and the Cevennes range placed-in-the-way and the difficulty of the roads prevented, but also (**tum**) especially because he feared greatly for Labienus separated (from him) and for those legions which he had sent together (**una**) with him '.

In a freer translation, we might say for (i) **ut commutato ... converteret,** ' as for changing his plan and diverting . . . '. (ii) **ut . . . existimabat,** ' as he thought he should not do even through fear '. (iii) **oppositus mons Cevenna,** ' the barrier of the Cevennes range '. (iv) **impediebat** might be turned into the passive : ' he was prevented not only by the dishonour and disgrace . . . '. (v) **abiuncto,** ' if he were separated (from him) '.

ll. 4–5. **in provinciam.** For the meaning of ' the Province ', see the note on Ch. 6, l. 6.

ll. 10–16. **magnis . . . perturbatis.** In this long passage, we have four abl. absols., all of which can be best translated into English by main verbs in the active : ' he completed . . . , he found . . . , etc '.

ll. 10–11. **admodum . . . itineribus,** ' very long marches by day and by night'.

ll. 12–13. **pro . . . opportuno,** ' (that was) good enough considering (**pro**) the needs of the situation '.

l. 13. **ut,** ' so that . . . '. The **ut** clause is explanatory of the preceding phrase.

l. 13. **bracchia** is nom. with **umeri,** and the adj. **liberi** agrees only with the nearer noun **umeri,** although it is to be taken with both nouns. The ford was probably close to Noviodunum.

l. 14. **ad sustinenda arma,** ' to hold up their weapons '.

l. 15. **qui . . . refringeret.** ' to break the force of the current '. Note once again the relative pronoun introducing an adverbial clause (purpose). Most commentators note that Caesar probably had two lines of cavalry, one below as well as above the infantry to rescue any soldiers who might be swept away.

ll. 18–19. **in Senones** =in fines Senonum.

CHAPTER 57

l. 3. **praesidio** ; predicative dative again. See Ch. 5, l. 9.

l. 4. **Lutetia** is the modern Paris. The latter name is derived from the tribe Parisii who are mentioned in the next line.

l. 5. **quod positum est,** ' which is placed ', i.e. ' which lies '. The island is that on which Notre Dame now stands, île de la Cité.

l. 10. **ad eum . . . evocatus,** ' had been invited to (take) that office '.

l. 11. **perpetuam esse paludem,** ' that there was a stretch of marsh '. This is generally identified with the R. Essonne which flows into the Seine about 15 miles above Paris.

ll. 12–13. **quae influeret,. . .impediret.** The subjunctive mood shows that Caesar is giving us the thoughts of Camulogenus.

CHAPTER 58

l. 1. **vineas.** The mantlets give shelter to the troops whose task it is to ' build a roadway ' (**iter munire**) across the marsh.

l. 2. **aggere,** ' with rubble '.

l. 3. **id . . . fieri,** *lit.,* ' that it was being done with too much difficulty ', i.e. ' that it was too difficult to do '.

ll. 4–5. **eodem . . . itinere,** ' by the same route by which he had come '.

l. 5. **Metiosedum.** This stronghold of the Senones was on an island on the Seine, opposite the modern town of Melun.

l. 8. **eo,** *lit.,* ' thither ' =' on them ' ; i.e. on the 50 barges which formed the temporary bridge.

ll. 7–9. **deprensis . . . perterritis oppidanis.** Again we have four abl. absols., all of which will be best rendered in English by present participles (active) for the first two and main verbs (active) for the last two : ' seizing about 50 barges . . . he put his soldiers on them and demoralised . . . '.

ll. 10–11. **sine contentione . . . potitur.** The main verb can be linked with the preceding abl. absols. by the insertion of a link phrase : ' and thus ' or ' and so ' or ' so that '.

l. 13. **secundo flumine,** ' down stream ' : along the right bank of the Seine ; the phrase means literally ' the stream following ', abl. absol.

l. 13. **ad Lutetiam,** ' in the direction of Lutetia '. Labienus is now on the north bank of the river.

l. 15. **pontes.** These are the bridges which link the île de la Cité to the north and south bank of the Seine.

l. 17. **considunt.** The enemy are on the left (i.e. south) bank of the Seine, opposite Lutetia ; Labienus is on the north bank, probably near the site of St. Germain-l'Auxerrois, so Rice Holmes conjectures.

CHAPTER 59

l. 1. **Caesar. . . discessisse audiebatur,** *lit.*, ' Caesar was heard to have retired '. Latin prefers the personal, English the *im*-personal construction : ' it was heard (i.e. becoming known) that Caesar had retired '.

l. 1. **a Gergovia.** See Ch. 43, l. 17. (ii).

l. 3. **in colloquiis,** ' in conversation ', i.e. between the Gallic cavalry of Labienus and their fellow countrymen.

ll. 3–5. **interclusum . . . contendisse,** *lit.*, ' that Caesar, cut off from marching and from the Loire, compelled through lack of corn had hastened into the province '. As the perfect participles passive **interclusum** and **coactum** are important, (they give the reason why he hastened into the province), we might render : ' Caesar, frustrated in his march and passage of the Loire, had been compelled through lack of corn to hasten . . . '.

ll. 6–7. **qui . . . infideles.** Translate this relative clause immediately after **Bellovaci**, the antecedent. **ante**, ' previously '. **per se**, ' in themselves '.

l. 9. **tanta rerum commutatione**, *lit.*, ' in so great a change of things ', i.e. ' now the situation was so greatly changed '.

ll. 9–10. **longe . . . intellegebat**, *lit.*, ' realised that a far (**longe**) different plan (was) to-be-taken by him and (=from what) he had deemed right before ' : i.e. ' that he had to form a far different plan from what . . . '.

ll. 11–13. **neque iam . . . cogitabat.** Note : (i) **neque** = ' and not '. (ii) **cogitabat**, ' he began to devise means '. (iii) the **ut** clauses are of purpose : ' not now that he should acquire anything or provoke . . . but that he should bring . . . '.

l. 13. **altera ex parte**, ' on the one side ', i.e. on his rear from the north ; the Bellovaci were north of the river. For this use of **ex**, cf. the note on **ab** in Ch. 45, ll. 25–6.

l. 14. **quae civitas = civitas quae**, ' a tribe which '.

l. 15. **alteram**, ' the other (side) ', object of **tenebat.** Camulogenus is on the south bank of the river.

ll. 15–16. ·**parato . . . exercitu**, ' with an army (that was) ready (for action) and well equipped '. **exercitu** is an instrumental abl. Hence no preposition is used. This use is common with words like ' army ', as it is naturally regarded as an instrument.

ll. 16–17. **a praesidio atque impedimentis**, i.e. the troops and baggage at Agedincum. See Ch. 57, l. 3.

ll. 18–19. **tantis . . . videbat**, *lit.*, ' such great difficulties suddenly thrown in his way; he saw that help (was) to-be-sought from the courage of his spirit ' ; i.e. ' when suddenly faced with . . . he saw that he should seek help from his own courageous spirit '.

CHAPTER 60

l. 1. **consilio**, ' council of war '. This would be attended by generals, military tribunes (of which there were six to a legion), and the senior centurions.

l. 1. **cohortatus.** Supply 'them' as the object.

l. 2. **imperasset=imperavisset.** The pluperfect subjunctive represents in reported form an original future-perfect. Labienus said : ' carry out what I shall have ordered '.

ll. 3–4. **naves . . . attribuit,** ' he assigned one each of the boats which . . . to the Roman knights '. For the latter see the note on Ch. 3, l. 5.

ll. 4–5. **prima vigilia,** ' at the end of the first watch '. See the note on Ch. 3, ll. 12–13.

l. 5. **secundo flumine,** ' down stream '.

l. 6. **se exspectari.** Translate as if you had : **se exspectare.**

l. 8. **praesidio,** predicative dative or dative of purpose, ' to guard '.

l. 10. **adverso flumine,** ' up stream '.

l. 11. **proficisci imperat.** Note that **impero** can be followed by acc. and infin. *only* when the infinitive is passive or deponent.

l. 12. **in eandem partem,** ' in the same direction '.

l. 13. **post paulo=paulo post,** ' a little later '. **paulo,** abl. of the measure of difference.

l. 14. **quo,** *lit.,* ' whither ', =' where '.

CHAPTER 61

l. 1. **eo cum esset ventum,** impersonal passive, ' when he arrived there '. See the note on Ch. 2, ll. 8–11.

l. 1. **ut,** ' just as '.

l. 4. **exercitus** here means ' infantry '.

ll. 4–5. **equitibus . . . praefecerat,** *lit.,* ' the Roman knights, whom he had put in charge of that business, directing ', i.e. ' under the direction of the Roman knights whom . . . '.

l. 6. **sub lucem,** ' just before day-break '.

ll. 7–8. **praeter . . . tumultuari,** *lit.,* ' that there was a disturbance beyond custom ', i.e. ' that there was an unusual disturbance '. **tumultuari** is used impersonally.

l. 9. **in eadem parte,** ' in the same quarter '. Refer back to the previous chapter, ll. 8–11, and the instructions given to the five cohorts.

l. 10. **paulo infra,** *lit.,* ' (by) a little below ', i.e. ' a little way down stream '.

l. 15. **Metiosedum versus,** ' in the direction of Metiosedum '. Note : (i) **versus** follows the noun it governs. (ii) as Camulogenus sent only a small force, it seems obvious that he had not been completely deceived by Labienus' stratagem.

ll. 16–17. **quae . . . processissent,** ' which was to advance as far as the boats had gone '. Note : (i) the combination of primary and historic tenses in the same sentence, **progrediatur,** primary in a relative clause expressing purpose and **processissent,** historic, the pluperfect subjunctive representing in a subordinate clause in virtual Oratio Obliqua, an original future-perfect. Camulogenus said : ' advance as far as the boats will have gone '.

See the note on Ch. 1, ll. 25–6, for the use of primary tenses after historic main verbs.

Finally note that the **naves** are the same as the **lintres** of Ch. 60, l. 11.

CHAPTER 62

l. 1. **et** means ' both ' and can be ignored in translation.

l. 1. **nostri omnes** seems to refer to the three legions with Labienus.

l. 2. **cernebatur,** ' began to come into view ', *lit.,* ' to be seen '. Note the translation of the imperfect tense.

ll. 3–4. **ut ... retinerent memoriam,** *lit.,* ' to retain the memory (of) ', = ' to remember '.

ll. 3–4. **secundissimorum proeliorum,** ' (of) their most successful battles '.

ll. 4–6. **atque ipsum Caesarem adesse existimarent,** ' and to think that Caesar himself was present in person '.

No greater tribute could be paid to Caesar's powers of leadership than that his generals often used this appeal to get the best out of their men—usually with success.

ll. 5–6. **superassent** = **superavissent.**

l. 7. **ab dextro cornu,** 'on the right wing'. Cf. Ch. 45, ll. 25–6.

l. 10. **cum,** ' although '.

l. 12. **nec ... quisquam,** 'and not one '; *lit.,* ' nor anyone '.

l. 14. **incerto ... victoriae,** *lit.,* ' the issue of victory even now (being) uncertain '. For this type of abl. absol., see the note on Ch. 1, l. 1.

We can render : ' while the issue ... was even now(=still) uncertain ', and replace **cum** before **septimae** by ' and '.

ll. 15–16. **quae ... gererentur** is indirect question, subject of **esset nuntiatum.** ' What was happening ... had been announced to the tribunes ... '.

l. 17. **legionem ostenderunt,** ' revealed (=brought up) their legion '.

l. 17. **signa intulerunt. signa** ' the standards ' is found in many military phrases—naturally, because ' the standard ' of the maniple (120 men = 2 centuries) was the rallying point of that unit. Hence **signa inferre,** *lit.,* ' to carry the standard against ', is the regular Latin for ' to charge '.

ll. 19–20. **eandem ... Camulogenus,** ' Camulogenus endured the same fate '—i.e. he too died fighting.

l. 20. **praesidio,** dative of purpose, ' on guard '.

l. 22. **collem.** This is said to be the modern Mt. Parnasse.

ll. 22–4. **neque ... potuerunt,** ' but could not '.

ll. 24–5. **quos ... texerunt,** ' (those) whom woods and hills did not protect ', i.e. ' those who did not gain the protection of woods and hills '.

CHAPTER 63

l. 2. **circummittuntur,** i.e. by the Aedui.

ll. 2–3. **quantum ... valent,** *lit.,* ' as far as they were powerful in influence, authority and money ', i.e. ' using all the power of influence ... '.

l. 5. **horum supplicio,** ' by executing them '.

l. 5. **dubitantes,** ' waverers '.

l. 7. **rationes belli gerendi,** ' his plans of (=for) conducting the campaign ', =' for the conduct of the campaign '.

ll. 7–8. **re impetrata,** 'when their wish was granted '.

l. 9. **re . . . deducta,** *lit.,* ' the matter having been brought to a dispute ', =' when the matter was disputed '.

l. 10. **Bibracte** is locative, ' at Bibracte '. The latter, the capital of the Aedui, was situated on Mont Beuvray, 12 miles west of the modern Autun.

l. 11. **multitudinis suffragiis,** ' to the votes of the gathering '.

multitudo means the ' large numbers present ' which included only the tribal leaders and perhaps some of their retainers. It does not mean the mass of their people, for they had no political rights or powers.

l. 12. **ad unum omnes,** ' all to a man '.

l. 14. **illi,** ' the two former '.

ll. 14–15. **amicitiam R. sequebantur,** ' were loyal to their friendship with Rome '.

l. 15. **aberant longius,** ' they were too far away '.

ll. 16–17. **toto. . . bello,** abl. of time, ' throughout the whole war '.

ll. 17–18. **magno . . . principatu,** *lit.,* ' the Aedui bore with great resentment that they had been cast down from (=prevented from obtaining) the leadership ', =' the Aedui were very resentful at their failure to obtain the leadership '.

ll. 20. **in se,** ' towards them '.

l. 21. **inviti,** ' unwillingly '. Latin often uses adjectives where we prefer adverbs.

ll. 21–22. **summae spei adulescentes,** ' (being) young men of the highest hopes ', =' for they were very promising young men '.

CHAPTER 64

l. 1. **ipse,** i.e. Vercingetorix.

l. 1. **imperat . . . obsides,** ' demanded hostages from the other states '. Note that this verb can mean *de*mand as well as *com*mand and that with this meaning it has acc. (direct object) and dative (indirect object), the latter meaning ' from '.

l. 2. **diemque . . . constituit.** The reading of the text (**denique ei rei constituit diem huc**) is obviously corrupt and an emendation of Hotomann has been adopted.

l. 4. **neque** = ' and not '. Hence **aut** (not **neque**) is used to link the two future infinitives.

ll. 6–8. **perfacile . . . prohibere,** *lit.,* ' to prevent the Romans from getting corn and forage (he said) was easy in-the-doing ', i.e. ' it was easy to prevent . . . '.

factu, abl. of the supine (an abl. of respect) is almost redundant here and can, therefore, be ignored in translation.

l. 8. **modo** means ' provided only '.

l. 8. **aequo** goes with **animo** to mean ' calmly '.

l. 8. **ipsi** is emphatic ' they themselves ', not somebody else.

l. 8. **frumenta.** Note the plural and its meaning, ' the standing crops '.

ll. 9–11. **qua . . . videant,** *lit.,* ' by which loss of their property they saw they were obtaining power and freedom for ever '. **qua** is the relative connection and should be translated by ' and by this '.

ll. 11–12. **Aeduis Segusiavis,** datives after **imperat.** See the note above on l. 1.

l. 12. **provinciae,** i.e. Gallia Narbonensis. See the note on Ch. 6, l. 6. So also in l. 22 below.

l. 13. **huc,** *lit.,* ' hither ', = ' to these '.

l. 15. **Allobrogibus,** ' against the Allobroges '. This people lived in the northern part of the Roman province in an area bounded by the Rhône, Isère and the lake of Geneva, an area, therefore, which corresponds roughly to what is now French Savoy.

ll. 19–21. **Allobrogas . . . sperabat. mentes,** ' temper '. **ab superiore bello.** The Allobroges, who had been originally subdued by the Romans in 121 B.C., revolted unsuccessfully in 61 B.C. It is to the latter date that ' after the late war ' refers.

CHAPTER 65

l. 1. **ad,** *lit.,* ' towards ' = ' facing ' = ' in the face of '.

ll. 1–2. **praesidia cohortium duarum et XX,** ' contingents (consisting) of 22 cohorts '. **cohortium** is a genitive of material.

ll. 2–3. **ex ipsa coacta provincia,** ' raised in the Province '. The latter is Transalpine, not Cisalpine Gaul.

l. 3. **ab Lucio Caesare legato.** Lucius Caesar was a relative of Julius Caesar and had been consul in 64 B.C.

ll. 3–4. **ad . . . opponebantur,** ' were opposed (to the enemy) at áll points'.

l. 5. **Gaio Valerio Donnotauro.** This first magistrate (**princeps**) has a Celtic name Donnotaurus and two Roman ones, Gaius Valerius which he assumed from the Gaius Valerius Flaccus who was governor of the Province in 83 B.C. and acted like all Roman governors as **patronus** to leading local men.

l. 7. **intra oppida ac muros** probably means no more than **intra muros oppidorum,**—a hendiadys. See the note on Ch. 23, l. 12.

l. 8. **crebris . . . praesidiis,** ' having placed many strong points at intervals (**dis** in **dispositis**) along the Rhône '.

l. 11. **interclusis . . . itineribus.** Make this abl. absol. a causal clause ; ' since all the roads . . . '.

l. 11. **nulla re,** ' in no way '.

ll. 13–14. **quas . . . pacaverat.** See in the Introduction the summary of Book IV of the Gallic War p. xix. Caesar is referring in particular to the Ubii and several other tribes who submitted in his German campaign. (Book IV, Chs. 16 and 18).

l. 15. **levis armaturae pedites**, 'light-armed infantry '.

l. 16. **consuerant = consueverant.** For a description of these tactics, see Gallic War, Book I, Ch. 48 where we read: '(in battle) the cavalry would retire on them (i.e. the light-armed infantry) and they (i.e. light-armed infantry) would mass to the rescue if any difficulty arose ; if any trooper fell from his horse, severely wounded, they would rally round him ; and if they had to advance further in any direction or retire more rapidly, they had acquired such speed by training that they could support themselves by the manes of the horses and keep pace with them '.

l. 16. **eorum adventu,** ' on their arrival '.

ll. 16–17. **minus =** ' not '; therefore, **minus idoneis =** ' unsuitable '.

In Book IV, Ch. 2, Caesar describes the home-bred horses of the Germans as ' inferior and misshapen '. Caesar saw that on such horses they would be at a serious disadvantage when fighting with the well-mounted Gallic cavalry.

ll. 17–18. **a tribunis . . evocatis.** For the military tribunes and Roman knights, see the notes on Ch. 17, l. 27, and Ch. 3, l. 5 respectively. The **evocati** were time-expired legionary soldiers on the reserve list who were liable for conscription in times of emergency. They had certain privileges, one of which seems to have been, the possession of a horse.

CHAPTER 66

ll. 2–3. **qui . . . imperati. impero** as a transitive verb means ' requisition '. **toti Galliae,** ' from the whole of Gaul '.

l. 3. **magno . . . numero.** This abl. absol. should be taken after **ferri posset** l. 6, and turned into the active with Vercingetorix as the subject.

l. 4. **in Sequanos,** ' into (the territory of) the Sequani '.

l. 4. **per . . . fines**, ' through the furthest (part of the) country of the L.'. ' Furthest ' means ' southernmost '.

ll. 4-5. **cum C. . . . iter faceret.** After his union with Labienus somewhere near Troyes, Caesar marched south with a view to keeping open his lines of communication with Italy and to securing an operational base in the Province (Gallia Narbonensis, now almost completely Romanised) from which he might build up a new force and embark upon this same summer[1] the task of crushing the Gallic rebellion. The revolt of his former allies, the Aedui, meant that he had to march south-east through the territory of the Lingones, cross the river Saône and thence through the territory of the Sequani towards the Province.

l. 5. **quo** regularly introduces a purpose clause which contains a comparative.

ll. 6-7. **trinis castris**, ' in three camps '. See the note on Ch. 46, ll. 11-12. The camps were sited on the slopes east of Hauteville.

l. 10. **Gallia**, ablative after **excedere**.

ll. 10-11. **id . . . satis esse.** Begin with **id esse satis sibi ad . . . .**

ll. 10-11. **ad praesentem obtinendam libertatem**, ' to win their liberty for-the-time-being '.

ll. 11-12. **ad . . . profici**, ' (but)[2] little profit was gained in-regard-to (**ad**) peace and quiet in (*lit.*, of) the future '. **profici** : present infinitive passive.

l. 13. **reversuros.** Supply **eos** (=the Romans) and **esse** (' would return ').

l. 14. **adoriantur**, indirect command, ' let them (=the Gauls) attack '. Note the primary sequence, which is continued throughout the chapter except for the last verb **perequitasset.** See the note on Ch. 29, l. 3.

l. 14. **agmine impeditos**, ' (the Romans) when hampered

---

[1] It was at this time late July or early August.

[2] For the asyndeton, see the note on Ch. 6, l. 8.

in column of route '. Vercingetorix means that the Romans
were encumbered not only by their personal packs but also
by the mules and their drivers who carried the legion's heavy
equipment (tents, etc.). In column of route the baggage
train would follow behind the legion. Vercingetorix intends
to launch a flank attack on the baggage train in the hope
that the Romans would be so anxious to reach the safety of
the Province that they would be unwilling to give up time to
saving their mules and drivers. The sacrifice of the latter
would cause the Romans to lose prestige.

l. 15. suis, ' to their comrades ', i.e. ' the baggage-drivers '.

l. 15. ferant, morentur, primary sequence again. Translate as if you had the strict sequence, ferrent, morarentur.

ll. 16–17. id . . . confidat, ' as he was sure was more likely-
to-occur '.

l. 18. usu . . . dignitate. These abls. of separation are
rendered by ' of ' in English.

l. 19. de, ' concerning '.

ll. 19–21. quin . . . dubitare. Begin, ipsos quidem non
debere dubitare quin, ' *they* at any rate . . . '. Vercingetorix is
now addressing his cavalry commanders.

ll. 19–20. progredi modo, ' so much as to stir '.

l. 21. id quo . . . animo, ' that they might act with more
spirit '.

ll. 21–2. copias omnes, ' all his infantry '.

l. 22–3. et terrori . . . futurum, ' and he would be for a
terror to ' = ' he would strike terror into . . . '.

l. 24. confirmari oportere. Supply se.

ll. 24–5. ne . . . habeat, ' that he should not be received
beneath a roof, that he should not have access to . . . '.

CHAPTER 67

ll. 1–2. probata . . . equitatu. The three abl. absolutes
will be best turned into English as main verbs, e.g. ' this was
approved . . . '.

l. 3. **acies**, ' in line of battle ' in apposition with **duae** (sc. **partes**).

l. 3. **ab**, ' on '.

ll. 3-4. **a primo agmine**, ' in front of the head of the column '.

ll. 5-6. **divisum ... iubet,** = **dividit et iubet.** See the note on Ch. 9, l. 1.

l. 6. **pugnatur,** impersonal passive, ' the battle was fought '.

l. 7. **intra legiones.** Each legion now forms a ' hollow ' square and places its baggage train within it for protection. See the note on Ch. 66, l. 14.

l. 8. **qua in parte,** ' at any place '.

l. 9. **signa inferri,** ' a charge to be made '. See the note on Ch. 62, l. 17.

l. 10. **et** means ' both ' and can be ignored.

ll. 10-11. **ad insequendum.** We say ' *in* pursuing '.

l. 12. **ab dextro latere,** ' on the right (of the Romans) '. The Germans, outflanking the enemy, occupied some high ground on the left of their cavalry which was attacking the Roman right.

l. 13. **nacti,** from **nanciscor.** The ridge is that just north of Asnières.

l. 13. **fugientes** is acc. pl. Begin with **persequuntur.**

l. 14. **usque ad flumen** ; i.e. the river Badin behind which Vercingetorix had his infantry.

ll. 16-17. **reliqui ... veriti :** order for translation, **reliqui veriti ne circumirentur. reliqui,** i.e. the rest of the Gallic cavalry.

l. 17. **omnibus locis,** ' all over the field '.

ll. 19-20. **Cotus, Convictolitavi.** For the two Aeduan chieftains and their quarrel, see Ch. 32, ll. 13-23.

l. 22. **Eporedorix** is a different man from the Eporedorix mentioned in other chapters.

l. 23. **quo duce,** abl. absol., ' under whose leadership '.

CHAPTER 68

l. 2. **ut,** ' just as '. As the Gallic infantry had not been engaged, Vercingetorix led them off just as he had posted them.

l. 3. **Alesiam.** This stronghold of the Mandubii is placed by most commentators on the plateau of Mont Auxois, about 32 miles north-west of Dijon. It appears from Chs. 69 and 71, that Alesia had already been prepared as a stronghold which Vercingetorix could use, if the occasion arose, as it did. After the failure of his flank attack on Caesar's baggage train, Vercingetorix had no alternative but to fall back on Alesia where he might hope to repeat his success at Gergovia. At any rate he could not afford to risk a pitched battle with troops now disheartened by his recent reverse and likely to disperse as Gallic troops always were, unless they were stimulated by quick victory.

This cavalry scrap[1]—for that is all that it was—, described by Caesar in this and the preceding chapters, enables us to see clearly Caesar's great qualities as a commander, his coolness and serenity, and his brilliant opportunism which enabled him to make the most out of this engagement and win a victory vastly more important in its moral effect than in its size. As Rice Holmes aptly says, ' All that Vercingetorix had achieved in six months by sustained effort was lost in a day '.

l. 3. **quod est oppidum.** Note that the relative pronoun agrees in gender not with the antecedent **Alesiam** but with the complement of the relative clause, **oppidum.**

l. 4. **celeriter** goes with **educi.**

ll. 5–7. **impedimentis deductis, duabus legionibus relictis.** These two abl. absols. may be translated as finite verbs in the active, ' Caesar withdrew . . . (and) left behind . . . '. Then translate **secutus** as **secutus est.**

ll. 6–7. **praesidio,** ' to guard (it) ', predicative dative.

---

[1] The picked Gallic infantry showed up badly, for they did nothing but fall back and failed even to conduct a defensive rearguard action.

l. 7. **quantum . . . passum,** ' as much as the time of day
(=daylight) allowed '. **passum** is from **patior.**

l. 8. **circiter . . . .** Begin a fresh sentence here.

l. 8. **ex** =' of '. The Gauls do not seem to have fought any
rearguard action.

l. 9. **ad Alesiam,** ' in-the-neighbourhood of Alesia '. See
Ch. 43, ll. 17–18. (ii).

l. 10–11. **equitatu,** abl. of respect, ' in their cavalry '.

l. 11. **qua . . . confidebant,** ' that part of the army in which
they had most confidence '.

CHAPTER 69

l. 1. **oppidum Alesia.** Latin had apposition where we
prefer ' the stronghold *of* Alesia '.

l. 1. **in colle summo,** i.e. the plateau of Mont Auxois.

ll. 1–2. **admodum edito loco,** ' in a very commanding
position '. The height of the plateau is given as 418 metres.

l. 2. **nisi obsidione,** ' except by a regular investment '.

l. 3. **radices,** acc. pl.

ll. 3–4. **duabus ex partibus,** ' on two sides ', i.e. north and
south.

ll. 3–4. **duo flumina** are the Ose and the Oserain.

l. 4. **ante id oppidum,** i.e. on the west.

l. 4. **planities,** the plain of Les Laumes.

ll. 6–7. **mediocri . . . fastigio,** *lit.,* ' a moderate interval
lying between with an equal top of height ', i.e. ' at a moderate distance and equal in height '. Caesar means that the
surrounding hills were each moderately distant from Alesia.

l. 8–9. **quae pars . . . spectabat,** ' on the side which looked to
the east '.

l. 11. **eius munitionis . . . :** order for translation : **circuitus eius munitionis quae . . . . tenebat,** ' comprised '.

l. 13. **castra . . . .** Excavations conducted during the last century showed that there were eight camps. Of the twenty-three bastions, only five have been discovered.

l. 14. **ibi,** ' on the site '.

l. 14. **quibus in castellis.** Caesar often repeats the ante-cedent in a relative clause. Ignore, therefore, **castellis** in translation.

l. 15. **ne qua . . . eruptio,** ' that-not any sortie ' = ' that no sortie '.

l. 15. **subito,** the adverb sandwiched between adjective and noun, has itself the force of an adjective.

ll. 16–17. **excubitoribus . . . praesidiis** ' with strong gar-risons of sentries '. Note : (i) the hendiadys. Cf. footnote, Ch. 23, ll. 12–13. (ii) the absence of the preposition **ab** before **excubitoribus,** the latter being an instrumental ablative. Cf. Ch. 59, ll. 15–16.

CHAPTER 70

l. 2. **intermissam collibus,** ' lying between hills '.

l. 4. **ab utrisque contenditur.** See the note on Ch. 2, l. 11. and translate, ' both sides fought '.

ll. 5–6. **pro castris.** These are the camps of the infantry, marked on the map as A, D. The camps of the cavalry were situated in the plain.

l. 6. **ne qua subito irruptio . . . .** See the note on Ch. 69, l. 15.

l. 7. **nostris.** Translate this dative as a genitive dependent upon **animus.**

ll. 8–9. **ipsi multitudine,** ' themselves by their numbers ', = ' by sheer numbers '.

ll. 9–10. **angustioribus . . . relictis,** ' as the gates had been left too narrow '. The gates are those in the **maceria** or ' rough wall '.

l. 14. **non minus . . .** Begin with **Galli qui . . .**

ll. 15–16. **veniri . . . existimantes,** ' believing that the enemy were coming at them at once '. Note **veniri,** the infinitive of the impersonal passive **venitur,** ' (the enemy) were coming'. Cf. Ch. 2, l. 11.

l. 18. **portas,** i.e. of the town.

CHAPTER 71

ll. 1–2. **prius quam . . . perficiantur,** ' before the entrenchments *could* be completed '.
Temporal clauses with the secondary element of purpose or anticipation have their verbs in the subjunctive mood.

ll. 2–3. **consilium capit dimittere.** See the note on Ch. 26, l. 2.

l. 4. **omnes,** acc. pl., object of **cogant.** The latter is plural because Caesar wishes to emphasise the combined efforts of all, not their individual role as in the verb **quisque adeat.**

ll. 6–7. **ut . . . habeant,** ' to have regard for his safety '.

ll. 7–8. **neu . . . dedant,** ' and not to surrender to the foe for torture one who had done such great service for the common liberty '.

ll. 7–8. **se . . . meritum,** *lit.,* ' him having deserved best for the . . . '.

l. 9. **quod si,** ' but if '.

ll. 9–10. **milia . . . LXXX,** *lit.,* ' 80 chosen thousands of men ', i.e. ' 80,000 chosen men '. Many commentators believe that Caesar has deliberately exaggerated the number. All we know, for certain, is that Alesia was large enough to contain so many.

l. 10. **interitura.** Supply **esse** to give the future infinitive active, ' were destined to perish '.

l. 11. **ratione inita,** *lit.,* ' a calculation having been entered upon ', =' after a calculation had been made '.

l. 13. **parcendo,** *lit.,* ' by sparing ', i.e. ' by economy '.

l. 16. **capitis poenam,** ' penalty of death '.

ll. 20–1. **his rationibus,** ' by these measures '.

CHAPTER 72

l. 2. **haec . . . munitionis**, ' kinds of entrenchment like this '.

l. 3. **pedum XX**, i.e. wide.

ll. 3–5. **ut . . . distarent**, ' (in such a way) that the bottom of that ditch extended just as much as the edges at the top of the ditch were apart '. This is a clumsy sentence, but Caesar seems anxious to make his meaing clear. Trenches were usually dug in a V shape, not as here with perpendicular sides—an operation which must have imposed a tremendous amount of work on the Roman soldiers.

This trench, 20 ft. wide, was made only across the plain of Les Laumes.

l. 6. **id hoc consilio . . .**, ' this (he did) with this purpose ; since he had of necessity enclosed so vast an area, and the whole of the works could not easily be surrounded by a circle of troops . . . '.

The subjunctives are used because they give the thoughts that are in Caesar's mind i.e. they are in virtual Oratio Obliqua.

ll. 8–11. **ne . . . advolaret . . . possent.** For the change in the number of the verb from singular to plural, see the note on Ch. 71, l. 4.

ll. 10–11. **in nostros . . . destinatos**, ' at our men (while) busily employed in their work '.

l. 11. **hoc . . . spatio**, ' behind this interval ', i.e. of 400 yards.

l. 12. **eadem altitudine**, ' of the same depth ', i.e. as each other. We do not know how deep they were.

l. 13. **interiorem**, ' the inner one ', i.e. the one nearer the town. This one was continued right round Alesia. The outer one was dug only in the plain of Les Laumes.

ll. 13–14. **campestribus . . . locis**, ' where the ground was level with or lay below the plain '.

l. 14. **ex flumine.** Caesar could get water from the Rabutin and the Oserain, to the north and south of the town respectively.

l. 15. **aggerem ac vallum,** 'a rampart and palisade', of which the combined height is 12 ft.

ll. 16–18. **grandibus . . . tardarent,** 'with huge fraises projecting at the junctions of the screens and rampart to delay the ascent of the enemy'.

The **cervi** were pointed stakes (obviously like stag's antlers in shape) which were inserted where the screen and the rampart were joined.

ll. 18–19. **toto opere,** 'all around the siege-works'.

ll. 19–20. **quae . . . distarent ;** the subjunctive is one of result (consecutive), *lit.,* 'so that they were distant', = 'to be distant'.

CHAPTER 73

l. 1. **erat . . . .** Order for translation : **erat eodem tempore necesse materiari . . . .**

l. 2. **deminutis . . . progrediebantur,** 'thus our forces which had to go a considerable distance from the camp were greatly diminished'.

ll. 6–7. **quare . . . putavit,** 'wherefore Caesar thought that he should add further to these siege-works'.

l. 7. **quo** introduces the purpose clause, because it contains a comparative.

ll. 8–10. **truncis . . . cacuminibus,** abl. absol. Translate as main verbs in the passive.

l. 9. **horum** depends upon **cacuminibus,** 'their ends'.

ll. 10–11. **perpetuae . . . ducebantur,** 'continuous trenches were dug 5 ft. deep'. Caesar cannot mean that these trenches were continuous all round the town—the labour would have been enormous—but continuous only in places where they were necessary.

l. 11. **huc**, ' into them ', i.e. into the trenches.

l. 11. **stipites**, i.e. the trunks *or* branches.

l. 12. **ab infimo**, ' at the bottom '.

l. 12. **demissi et. . . revincti.** Supply **sunt** and ' and ' before **ab ramis**.

ll. 12–13. **ab ramis eminebant**, ' they projected from the bough-ends ', i.e. ' the bough-ends projected '.

ll. 13–16. **quini . . . appellabant**, ' there were five rows (of trunks) connnected with each other and interlaced : (those) who entered (the trenches) got entangled on the very sharp points ; these they called grave-stones '.

Note : (i) **quo . . . intraverant**, *lit.*, ' whither ' (=into which =into them). Cf. **huc** in l. 11. The pluperfect indicative is similar to that used in **cum** ' whenever ' clauses. (ii) **cippos** means ' grave ' or ' boundary stone ' and shows that the Roman soldiers had the usual grim sense of humour common to all fighting men.

ll. 16–18. **ante . . . fastigio**, ' in front of these in diagonal rows arranged in a figure of five, pits 3 ft. in depth were dug, the slope (becoming) gradually narrower to the bottom '. For the last phrase we might say, ' gradually narrowing as they sloped . . . '.

A **quincunx** is :•:.

l. 19. **huc**, ' into these '.

l. 19. **teretes . . . praeusti**, ' tapering stakes with the thickness of a thigh (i.e. as thick as . . .), sharpened at the top and burnt to a point '.

ll. 21–3. **simul . . . exculcabantur**, ' at the same time to make (all) firm and secure, 1 ft. from the bottom of each pit was trodden down with earth '.

Note : **causa**, ' for the sake of ', preceded by the genitive, *lit.*, ' for the sake of making . . . '.

ll. 25–6. **ternos . . . distabant**, ' were 3 ft. apart '.

l. 28. **ferreis . . . infixis**, ' with iron hooks attached '.

l. 29. **omnibus locis,** ' all over the ground '.   Cf. Chap. 1, l. 13.

l. 30. **quos . . . nominabant,** ' they called these " spurs " '.

CHAPTER 74

ll. 1–2. **regiones . . . natura,** ' following the ground the most level he could as-the-nature-of-the-locality-allowed (**pro loci natura**) '.

ll. 2–3. **XIIII . . . complexus,** *lit.,* ' having encompassed 14 miles ', i.e. with a compass of 14 miles .

l. 4. **diversas . . . hostem,** ' facing the opposite way (*lit.,* turned away from these) to ward off (*lit.,* against) the enemy from without '.

After the completion of the lines of contravallation, Caesar began similar lines of circumvallation to prevent the Gallic army of relief from breaking through to their besieged countrymen.   These lines followed the heights of Flavigny, Pevenal and Bussy and the intervening valleys and enclosed a circuit of at least 10 English miles.

l. 5. **ne . . . accidat,** ' not even by vastly superior numbers, should it turn out so '.

accidat.   Strict sequence would demand the imperfect subjunctive **accideret.**   The text, however, is corrupt, having two words **eius discessu** which cannot be satisfactorily explained nor emended.

ll. 7–8. **ne . . . cogatur,** ' that he might not be compelled to make dangerous forays from camp ', *lit.,* ' to leave the camp with danger '.

l. 9. **habere convectum,** ' to have, collected '.   Note the punctuation.

CHAPTER 75

ll. 2–4. **non omnes eos qui . . . possent, convocandos statuunt,** ' decided that not all those who . . . (were) to-be-called up ', i.e. ' decided that they should not call up all . . . '.

l. 3. **ut,** ' as '.

ll. 4–5. **sed . . . imperandum,** ' but that a fixed number (was) to-be-requisitioned from each (chieftain) from his tribe ', i.e. ' but that they should requisition . . . '.

ll. 5–7. **ne tanta . . . possent.** On previous occasions, the Gallic chieftains had been unable to organise supplies for large tribal contingents. Hence their decision at this crisis was a wise one.

l. 8. **clientibus,** i.e. dependent tribes. This dependence might involve liability to render military service or to pay tribute. Otherwise the client tribes possessed independence in their internal affairs.

l. 8. **Ambluaretis.** As the name of this tribe is not found elsewhere, commentators are tempted to adopt the proposal of Glück and read **Ambivaretis,** identifying them with the Ambibareti who are mentioned in Ch. 90. We are not very much wiser, as the position of the latter is unknown.

l. 15. **Senonibus.** As the **Senones** have already been mentioned, editors emend to **sena Andibus** or **Suessionibus.**

l. 18. **Lexoviis.** As the Lexovii are placed by other authorities at the mouth of the Seine, commentators have been encouraged to put this tribe among the maritime states whom Caesar mentions later. In doing so, they are especially influenced by the fact that the **Lemovices** whom Caesar does include among such tribes have already been mentioned and a second tribe of **Lemovices** on the coast is not found elsewhere in Caesar or in any other writer. Hence the following solution which many editors find attractive : read **Lexovii** in line 23 ; for **Lexoviis** in l. 18, read **Lemovicibus** : finally **totidem Lemovicibus** in l. 14 is removed as redundant.

ll. 19–20. **XXX universis civitatibus,** ' 30,000 in all from the tribes '.

l. 22. **quo sunt in numero,** ' in their number '.

l. 24. **numerum,** ' their quota '.

l. 25. **suo nomine,** ' on their own account '.

ll. 26–7. **neque . . . obtemperaturos,** ' and they would not obey *anyone's* command '.

l. 28. **pro eius hospitio,** ' in consideration of their friendship with him '. **una** is an adverb.

CHAPTER 76

ll. 1–3. **huius ... Caesar.** Note : (i)**opera,** abl. of the 1st declension noun, is dependent upon **erat usus.** (ii) the latter should be translated as ' had found '. (iii) **fideli, utili** are in agreement with **opera. ut antea demonstravimus,** i.e. in Book IV, Ch. 21.

l. 3. **quibus ... pro meritis,** ' for these services '. **ille,** i.e. Caesar.

ll. 3–4. **civitatem eius,** i.e. the Atrebates.

l. 4. **immunem.** The services from which Caesar released the Atrebates were probably the vital ones of providing corn and supplies to the Roman army. They may also have been tribute or taxes, paid either to the Romans or to another tribe.

l. 4. **iura legesque reddiderat,** i.e. he had restored their independence. The Atrebates may have been subject to some other tribe, as Caesar made the Morini subject to the Atrebates.

l. 5. **ipsi,** i.e. to Commius.

ll. 6–7. **libertatis ... reciperandae.** We should say, ' to assert . . . , to recover . . . ; *lit.,* ' of their freedom to-be-asserted . . . '.

l. 8. **moverentur.** The subject is the ' Gauls '.

ll. 10–11. **coactis ... CCXL.** Translate by a ' when ' clause with the verb retained in the passive. The numbers do not agree with those given in Ch. 75 which are 288,000.

l. 12. **numerus inibatur,** ' a return was made '.

ll. 16–17. **quorum . . . administraretur,** =**ut eorum consilio . . .**

l. 17. **ad Alesiam.** See the note on Ch. 41, l. 4.

ll. 18–20. **qui ... arbitraretur,** consecutive subjunctive.

l. 19. **aspectum modo,** ' the mere sight '.

l. 20. **ancipiti proelio** ' in an engagement on two fronts '.

ll. 20–2. **cum . . . cernerentur,** ' since a battle would be fought (on the inside) in a sortie from the town, (while) on the outside such vast forces of cavalry and infantry would be in sight (=visible) '.

CHAPTER 77

l. 1. **ei qui . . . obsidebantur** is the subject of the main verb **consultabant.** In English it would be better to translate the abl. absols. first, possibly by ' when ' clauses, then the subject **ei . . . obsidebantur,** then **inscii** with its dependent question **quid . . . gereretur,** and finally **concilio coacto** as a main verb, ' called a council and '. For the gender of **dies,** see the note on Ch. 3, l. 1.

l. 1. **Alesiae,** locative, ' in Alesia '.

l. 4. **consultabant,** ' began to discuss '.

l. 7. **non . . . videtur,** *lit.,* ' the speech of Critognatus does not seem to-be-passed over', i.e. ' I do not think I should pass over '.

l. 9. **summo . . . ortus loco,** *lit.,* ' sprung from the highest position ', ='of the highest family '.

ll. 9–10. **magnae . . . auctoritatis,** *lit.,* ' considered (to be) of great influence '.

l. 10. **inquit** is used in Latin only in direct speech. It is never placed first.

Practically all the speeches given in Caesar's narrative are short and in Indirect Speech and, as is the practice among all other ancient historians, aim only at giving the main sense or meaning of what was said. This long speech of Critognatus, in direct speech, has, therefore, been unnecessarily suspect. It seems reasonable to infer that Caesar was as much impressed by what was said in this proposal as his original audience was. An account, therefore, could easily be obtained from prisoners who had been at the council of war.

ll. 12–13. **neque hos . . . censeo** ' and I do not think that they are to-be-regarded (=should be regarded) as citizens nor summoned to the council '.

ll. 13–14. **cum his mihi res sit,** 'let my business be with those'.

ll. 17–18. **qui . . . reperiuntur,** '(men) are more easily found to offer themselves . . .'.

ll. 17–19. **qui offerant, ferant,** consecutive subjunctives.

l. 20. **tantum . . . potest,** 'such power has the authority (of those who hold this opinion) with me'.

ll. 24–6. **quid . . . existimatis :** order for translation ; **quid existimatis fore animi nostris propinquis . . . , LXXX milibus hominum interfectis in uno loco,** 'what do you think will be the courage of our kinsmen . . .?

quid animi. animi is a partitive genitive. Translate as though you had **quem . . . animum.**

l. 26. **in,** 'over'.

l. 29. **nec** = **et nolite.**

l. 31. **quod,** 'because'.

ll. 33–4. **in illis . . . munitionibus,** i.e. the circumvallation of Ch. 74.

l. 34. **animine causa,** 'for the sake of amusement', 'to amuse themselves'. **-ne** is the interrogative enclitic.

ll. 35–6. **omni . . . praesepto.** Translate by a 'since' (causal) clause.

l. 36. **his . . . testibus,** 'use these men (i.e. the Romans) as witnesses (i.e. to prove)'.

l. 38. **quid ergo mei consili est,** 'what, then, is my counsel?'. **consili** is partitive genitive.

ll. 39–40. **nequaquam . . . Teutonum,** 'in the war in no way equal (to this) of (=with) the Cimbri and the Teutones'. The latter were German tribes who had invaded and plundered Gaul, and had only been stopped and utterly destroyed at the frontiers of Italy by a great Roman general, Marius, in battles fought in 102 and 101 B.C.

Teutonum has the original **-um** ending of the gen. pl. of the 2nd declension—a form which is met with so often in poetry.

l. 43. **neque** = 'but not'.

l. 43. **cuius rei.** We say 'for this'.

ll. 44–5. **tamen . . . iudicarem**, ' yet I should judge it a most glorious thing for the sake of freedom that it be established and handed down to posterity '.

l. 46. **nam . . . fuit**, ' for what was to that war (=for what did that war have) like (to this) '.

l. 50. **nisi**, ' except '.

ll. 51–3. **quos . . . servitutem** : order for translation : **considere in agris civitatibusque horum quos cognoverunt esse nobiles fama potentesque bello atque iniungere aeternam servitutem his.**

l. 54. **neque . . . condicione**, ' for on no other terms '.

l. 55. **quod si**, ' but if '.

l. 56. **finitimam Galliam**, i.e. the Roman Province.

ll. 57–8. **securibus subiecta**, ' subdued beneath the axes '. The latter were strictly the **fasces** or axe bound in a bundle of rods, borne by the lictors who attended Rome's most important magistrates. The axe and the rods were symbols of the magistrates' power to execute and to flog. In this passage, the word is used metaphorically for ' Roman supremacy '.

CHAPTER 78

ll. 1–2. **valetudine aut aetate**, ' by reason of their health or age '; abl. of cause.

ll. 3–4. **quam descendant**, ' than have recourse to '.

l. 4. **illo . . .** : Oratio Obliqua ; ' yet they must employ that plan at that time if . . . '. The **potius** goes with the **quam** in l. 6.

ll. 6–7. **quam... subeundam condicionem**, '(rather) than that they should submit to conditions '. Note the gerundive construction.

ll. 10–11. **ut se . . . receptos . . . iuvarent.** See the note on Ch. 9, ll. 20–1, (ii).

l. 12. **recipi prohibebat**, ' prevented (them) from being admitted '. Their fate is left to the reader's imagination.

CHAPTER 79

ll. 2–3. **ad Alesiam,** ' in the neighbourhood of Alesia '.

l. 3. **colle exteriore** is identified with the hill of Mussy-la-Fosse, west of Alesia.

l. 6. **omnem eam planitiem,** i.e. the plain of Les Laumes.

ll. 8–9. **pedestres copias ... abditas ... constituunt.** See the note on Ch. 9, ll. 20–1, (ii)., and translate, ' they withdrew and posted their infantry '.

l. 13. **proximam fossam.** See Ch. 72, ll. 3–5.

CHAPTER 80

ll. 1–2. **ad ... munitionum,** ' on both parts of the lines of entrenchments ', i.e. facing both ways, the town and the relieving forces.

l. 2. **si usus veniat,** ' should the need arise '.

l. 5. **summum undique iugum.** See Ch. 69, l. 1.

l. 6. **intenti,** adj. for adverb, ' eagerly '.

ll. 9–10. **qui ... succurrerent ... sustinerent.** Note the mood. **suis cedentibus,** ' to their men giving way ', i.e. ' if they gave way '.

l. 11. **excedebant,** the inceptive imperfect, ' began to withdraw '.

l. 12. **cum,** ' as '. **suos ... esse.** ' that their men were better in the battle ', i.e. ' were getting the better of the fighting '.

l. 14. **et** means ' both '.

l. 16. **quod,** ' because '.

ll. 17. **res gerebatur,** ' the fighting was taking place '. **neque ... factum,** ' and nothing done honourably or shamefully ', i.e. ' and no deed of honour or shame '.

l. 18. **utrosque,** ' both sides ', object of **excitabat,** which is singular although it has two subjects, **cupiditas, timor.** To retain the Latin order, we can turn into the passive.

l. 21. **Germani,** i.e. the German cavalry.

l. 25. **sui ... facultatem,** ' an opportunity of rallying ', *lit.,* ' of themselves to-be-rallied '.

l. 26. **ab Alesia,** must mean ' from Alesia ', in spite of what is said in the note on Ch. 43, ll. 17–18, (ii).

l. 26. **maesti,** adj. for adv., ' sadly '.

CHAPTER 81

l. 1. **uno ... intermisso,** ' after an interval of (only) one day '.

hoc spatio refers to **uno ... intermisso** and means literally ' in this interval '. Translate by ' during which ' and omit **atque.**

ll. 1–2. **magno ... effecto.** Make this abl. absol. a main verb in the active with **Galli** as the subject.

l. 2. **harpagonum.** These grappling hooks were to be used for pulling down the **pluteus** and **pinnae** on the Roman **agger.**

l. 4. **qua ... possent,** ' in order that by this intimation (those) who ... could learn ... '.

l. 6. **crates proicere,** ' to fling down hurdles ', i.e. into the trenches. The infin. as also **proturbare** and **administrare** depend upon **parant** = ' they prepared ', i.e. ' they began '.

l. 9. **clamore exaudito,** ' hearing the shout in the distance '.

l. 11. **educit,** ' led (his forces) out '.

l. 11. **ut** ' as '.

ll. 11–12. **ut ... attributus,** ' as to each man his position had been assigned ', i.e. ' each to his appointed position '.

ll. 12–13. **fundis librilibus,** ' with one pounder slings ', i.e. with slings capable of throwing stones of one pound.

If, however, we punctuate, **fundis, librilibus sudibusque,** we get, ' with slings, one pounders, and stakes '. The ' one pounders ' are the stones of that weight propelled probably by engines.

l. 14. **glandibus.** These bullets of lead or clay were used in slings.

l. 16. **M. Antonius.** This is Mark Antony, best known to English readers in Shakespeare's play *Julius Caesar*. He had joined Caesar in Gaul in 54 B.C.

ll. 17–18. **ad defendendum,** ' for defence '.

ll. 18–20. **qua . . . summittebant.** The order—relative clause preceding the main clause—is typical of Latin but difficult for English students. Translate : **summittebant deductos ex ulterioribus castellis auxilio eis qua ex parte intellexerant nostros premi.**

Finally note **summittebant deductos . . . ,** ' kept sending up men withdrawn . . . '' i.e. ' withdrew men from . . . and kept sending them up '. **qua ex parte :** ' wherever '.

CHAPTER 82

l. 2. **plus . . . proficiebant,** ' they did more execution owing to the large quantity of their missiles '.

ll. 3–4. **se induebant,** ' they got entangled ', *lit.,* ' put themselves on '.

l. 4. **delati,** ' falling '.

l. 5–6. **pilis muralibus,** ' by heavy javelins '. These would probably be fired by artillery from the walls.

ll. 6–7. **multis . . . perrupta.** Make these abl. absolutes main verbs and insert ' but ' before **nulla** and ' and ' before **cum.**

l. 8. **ab . . . eruptione,** ' on their exposed (i.e. right) flank by a sortie from the camp above them '. The latter is the Roman camp on the heights to the south of Alesia.

ll. 9–10. **interiores,** ' the inner garrison '.

l. 11. **priores fossas,** ' the nearer ditches '. For a discussion on what these were, see Appendix B.

l. 12. **diutius . . . .** Insert ' but ' before **diutius.**

suos, ' their allies ', i.e. the relieving forces.

ll. 12–14. **prius . . . quam . . . appropinquarent,** ' before they could get near . . . '. For the subj., see the note on Ch. 36, l. 24.

CHAPTER 83

l. 2. **locorum peritos,** ' men who knew the country well '.

l. 3. **superiorum castrorum,** ' of the upper camps ', i.e. the camps to the north of Alesia.

l. 4. **erat . . . collis,** ' on the north there was a hill '. The latter is Mont Réa.

l. 5. **opere circumplecti,** ' to include within their lines '.

ll. 6–7. **necessario . . . fecerant,** ' of necessity they had made their camp on what was practically .unfavourable ground, i.e. it was gently sloping '.

ll. 10–11. **ex omni numero . . . earum civitatum,** = **ex omnibus eis civitatibus.**

ll. 12–13. **quid . . . constituunt.** Order for translation : constituunt inter se quid placeat agi-que quo pacto.

quid placeat agi, *lit.,* ' what it pleased (them) to be done ', i.e. ' what should be done '.

l. 14. **cum . . . videatur,** ' (at the time) when it was seen to be mid-day '. **videatur :** the subjunctive is used because the clause is virtually in indirect speech.

l. 18. **sub lucem,** ' just before dawn '.

l. 19. **ex nocturno labore,** ' after their night's work '.

CHAPTER 84

l. 2. **musculos.** These were huts to protect the Gauls as they were filling up Caesar's trenches.

l. 3. **falces.** See the note on Ch. 22, l. 5.

l. 4. **pugnatur.** The Latin impersonal passive is best rendered here impersonally also in English : ' fighting went on '.

l. 4. **uno tempore,** ' at one and the same time '.

ll. 5–6. **quae . . . concurritur** : ' what part was seen least strong, hither there was a rush ', i.e. ' troops were rushed to that part which was seen (to be) least strong '.

l. 6. **manus,** ' the main body '.

ll. 6–7. **tantis munitionibus,** probably abl. absol., ' the lines (being) so extensive '.

ll. 7–8. **nec . . . occurrit,** *lit.,* ' nor easily met (the enemy) at several points (at once) ' : i.e. ' and could not meet . . . '.

Latin often states the *fact* where English prefers to mention the *possibility.*

l. 8. **multum . . . clamor,** ' the shouting was greatly responsible for demoralising our men '.

l. 9. **pugnantibus.** We prefer the genitive, ' of (them) fighting ', i.e. ' of the men in the fighting line '.

ll. 9–10. **quod . . . constare,** ' because they saw that their own danger depended on the safety of others '.

Caesar seems to mean that those in the lines facing Alesia realised that their own danger or escape from it depended on the safety and success of their comrades who were holding the lines behind them and opposite the relieving forces.

CHAPTER 85

l. 1. **idoneum locum.** All commentators agree in identifying this with the hill of Flavigny.

ll. 1–2. **quaque ex parte,** ' in every sector '.

l. 2. **summittit.** Supply ' men in support ' as the object.

l. 3. **utrisque . . . occurrit,** *lit.,* ' it comes to the mind to both sides '; i.e. ' both sides realised '.

l. 4. **quo . . . conveniat,** *lit.,* ' at which it was fitting that it be fought most '; i.e. ' at which they should make a supreme effort '.

l. 5. **de omni salute,** ' of any safety at all '.

l. 6. **si rem obtinuerint,** ' if they won the day '.

ll. 7–8. **maxime laboratur ad,** ' the greatest struggle was at '.

l. 8. **quo,** ' to which '.

l. 8. **missum.** Supply **esse.**

ll. 9–10. **iniquum . . . momentum,** ' the unfavourable slope of the ground downwards exercised great influence '.

l. 10. **alii . . . alii,** ' some (Gauls) . . . others '.

l. 11. **testudine facta.** The ' tortoise ' was an arrangement whereby assaulting parties advanced, each soldier carrying his shield above his head and over or underlapping that of his neighbour in the ranks.

l. 12. **agger . . . coiectus,** ' earth thrown by the whole body onto the defences '. **et** means ' both ' and can be ignored.

l. 13. **ea quae,** ' the contrivances which '. Caesar is referring to the defensive work he describes in Ch. 73.

CHAPTER 86

l. 1. **Labienum.** He was in the infantry camp on Bussy Hill.

l. 2. **subsidio laborantibus.** See the note on Ch. 5, l. 9.

l. 3. **sustinere,** used as here without an object means ' hold out '.

l. 4. **eruptione,** abl. of manner, ' by means of a sally '.

l. 4. **id . . . ne faciat,** ' he was not to do so, unless of necessity '.

l. 5. **ipsi adit reliquos.** To address and hearten his men, Caesar rode down from his position on Flavigny hill between the Roman defence works on to the plain where Vercingetorix was delivering his supporting attack with his forces.

l. 7. **interiores,** ' the enemy within Alesia '. They now abandon their attack on the plain, wheel left, cross the Oserain, and attack the Roman lines at the foot of Flavigny hill.

l. 9. **loca praerupta,** ' the steep parts ', i.e. of Mont Flavigny.

l. 9. **ex ascensu,** ' on the climb ', i.e. ' as they climbed '.

CHAPTER 87

l. 1. **Brutum adulescentem**, 'the young Brutus', i.e. Decimus Brutus, destined later to be among Caesar's murderers. Caesar seems to have been very attached to him. He is not to be confused with the more famous Brutus, best known to English readers from Shakespeare's play *Julius Caesar*.

l. 2. **post** is an adverb, 'afterwards'.

l. 5. **eo quo**, *lit.*, 'thither whither', i.e. 'to the place to which'.

l. 7. **circumire**, i.e. 'to ride round on the outside'. T. Rice Holmes seems to be right in assuming that the cavalry who were ordered to ride round the circumvallation were stationed at Grésigny about a mile north-east of Labienus' position. The order probably reached them by means of a trooper who could have ridden by the space between the contravallation and the circumvallation. Otherwise cavalry stationed near Caesar's position would have had to ride round the outer lines by the east and thus have taken too long to have had any decisive effect on the battle.

l. 10. **XI cohortibus.** The MSS. have XL. This number, equivalent to $\frac{2}{5}$ of the total Roman forces, cannot be correct, for it is too great for mere reinforcements, and in any case a group of 15,000 men could not manoeuvre in such conditions.

ll. 12–13. **quid . . . existimet,** 'what he thought should be done'.

CHAPTER 88

l. 1. **ex colore vestitus.** Caesar was wearing the scarlet cloak of the commander-in-chief.

ll. 1–2. **quo insigni,** 'which (abl. after **uti**) . . . (as) a distinguishing mark'.

ll. 3–4. **ut . . . cernebantur,** 'as these slopes and low lying ground could be seen from the higher positions '.

The latter are the positions occupied by the enemy on Mont Réa. The former are the slopes of Flavigny hill from which Caesar is bringing up reserves of cavalry and infantry.

At this moment while Vercingetorix is attacking north and
south, and Cassivellauus is desperately throwing in picked
troops on Mont Réa, where two-fifths of the Roman army has
been concentrated, the 170,000 Gauls on the plain, admittedly
not first-class troops, seem strangely inactive.   If they had
launched a vigorous attack north-west of Flavigny hill, it
seems doubtful whether the Roman line, which must have
been dangerously thin in many places, could have repelled
them.   Perhaps the Aedui were only half-hearted, if not
actually treacherous, and there may have been much inter-
tribal jealousy among the chieftains.

l. 6. **excipit,** ' there follows '.   The verb is used intrans-
itively.

ll. 7–8. **rem gerunt.**   Cf. the English slang :   ' did their
stuff '.
The Romans discarded their javelins which they normally
threw before engaging the enemy at close quarters, because
the enemy were on higher ground.   Note finally the absence
of conjunctions or connecting particles (asyndeton) in the
description of the battle—a common literary device which
adds vigour and freshness to the narrative.

l. 8. **equitatus,** i.e. Roman cavalry.   See Ch. 87, l. 7.

ll. 16–17. **a munitionibus,** ' from the (attack on the Roman)
lines '.

l. 18. **quod nisi,** ' now if '.

ll. 18–19. **crebris . . . labore,** ' by constant reinforcing and
their day-long effort '.   **totius diei** is a limiting or defining
genitive.

l. 20. **deleri potuissent,** ' might have been destroyed '.
The use of the subjunctive with **possum** in a conditional
clause unreal in past time, instead of the indicative which is
often found, seems to suggest that the possibility is more
remote.

l. 20. **de media nocte.**   See the note on Ch. 45, l. 2.

l. 20. **missus.**   Supply **est.**

CHAPTER 89

ll. 3–4. **quoniam . . . cedendum,** ' since they had to give in to fortune '.

ll. 4–5. **ad . . . offerre,** ' he offered himself to them for either course '.

l. 8. **eo,** ' thither ', i.e. ' there '.

l. 10. **si,** ' (to see) if '.

ll. 11–12. **ex reliquis . . . distribuit,** ' from the rest of the captives he distributed one apiece to each man in all the army (**toto exercitui**) by way of booty ', **(praedae nomine).**

Note **toto,** used as the dative of **totus,** instead of the more usual **toti.**

The soldiers would not, of course, retain the prisoners as slaves, but sell them to the dealers who accompanied the armies and in addition to supplying their needs, disposed of the booty for them—a job that was nearly always profitable and occasionally dangerous.

CHAPTER 90

l. 1. **in Aeduos.** See the note on Ch. 5, l. 3.

l. 2. **recipit** here means ' received-the-submission-of '.

ll. 6–7. **et equitatu,** ' and (some) cavalry '.

l. 7. **in Sequanos.** Ch. 5, l. 3.

ll. 10–11. **ne quam ... calamitatem accipiant,** ' that they (i.e. the Remi) should suffer no hurt '. The Remi had remained loyal to Rome throughout the campaign.

l. 14. **Cabilloni** is the locative case of **Cabillonum,** identified with Châlon-sur-Saône.

l. 15. **Matiscone,** locative of **Matisco,** identified with Mâcon.

l. 16. **Bibracte,** locative. As has already been explained in the note on Ch. 1, l. 1, Caesar usually spent the winter in north Italy, not only to perform his duties as governor, but also to keep a watchful eye on politics in Rome. His decision to winter in Bibracte suggests that he feared there might be another Gallic rising.

l. 17. **his litteris cognitis**, ' these things being learned by-means-of-a-despatch '.

ll. 17–18. **dierum . . . supplicatio redditur**, *lit.*, ' a public thanksgiving of 20 days was given (to the gods) '. Translate, however, ' a public . . . was held '. Days of thanksgiving were treated as part-holidays from legal and other official business.

APPENDIX A

Chapter 45, ll. 18–19.

Raros milites qui ex oppido animadverterentur ex maioribus castris in minora traducit.

The reading **qui** is found in the better group of MSS. and is adopted by the Oxford Classical text. Another group has **ne**, a reading which has a long tradition of support. The translation, ' that they should not be noticed from the town ', was explained by Stoffel, Holmes and other scholars as follows : the main attack was to come from the smaller camp into which the main body of troops has been moved in small parties to avoid observation. The map on p. 184 shows the probable positions of the Xth and XIIIth legions which moved up to support the retreating Romans. The same map also shows the direction of the attack, if delivered directly from the south.

After considerable thought and an exchange of views with M. le Père André Noche who has made an intensive study of the terrain and is an ardent supporter of the new theory which was first developed by the French scholars P. F. Fournier and others between 1928 and 1933, I have been convinced that the new theory based on the reading **qui** is to be preferred.

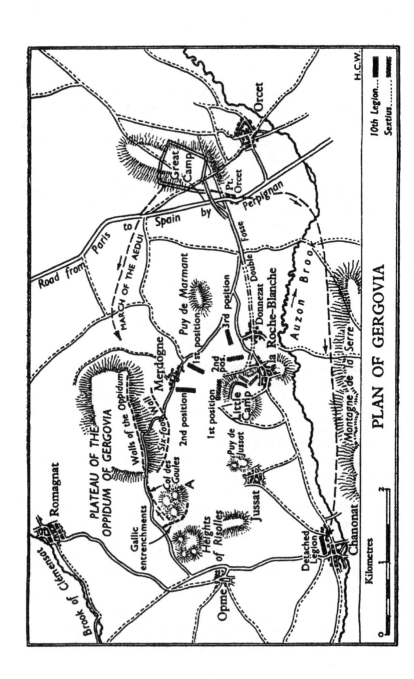

PLAN OF GERGOVIA

Kilometres

10th Legion ......
Sextius ....

H.C.W.

Brook of Clémensat

Romagnat

PLATEAU OF THE
OPPIDUM OF GERGOVIA

Gallic
entrenchments

Walls of the Oppidum

Six-foot Wall

Col des
Goules

A

Opme

Heights
of Rigolles

Jussat

Puy de Jussat

Chanonat

Detached
Legion

Merdogne

2nd position

2nd position

1st position

1st position

3rd position

2nd
pos.

Little
Camp

Puy de Marmant

1st position

Donnezat

la Roche-Blanche

Montagne de la Serre

Auzon Broo

Double Fosse

Road from Paris to Spain by Perpignan

MARCH OF THE AEDUI

Great Camp

Pt.
Orcet

Orcet

The reasons which have most influenced me are as follows :
the movement of over 10,000 troops from the larger to the
smaller camps must have been ; (i) long, tiring and prodigal
of time in an attack which had to rely on speed and surprise
to be effective, (ii) complicated, in view of the dimensions of
the smaller camp, (iii) impossible to conceal from observation,
for the whole terrain is completely dominated by any observer
on the plateau.   Other reasons in support are : (i) the
distance 1200 paces from the smaller camp in a direct line
to the top of the plateau, is much too long, (ii) there seems to
be little ' dead ground ' which would enable such a large body
of troops to carry out the manoeuvres preliminary to a sudden
attack from the south, (iii) the phrase **ad alteram partem
oppidi** (Ch. 48) can now have its full meaning ' the west '
as opposed to ' the east '.

For a further discussion, see also *J.R.S.* Vol. XXIII,
pp. 239–241.

APPENDIX B

priores fossas.   There has been much dispute among
commentators as to the meaning of these two words.   Here is
a summary of the arguments.   Some have identified the
priores fossas with the 20 ft. trench which is described in Ch.
72, ll. 2–3.   Three objections have been made : (i) in Ch. 79
Caesar called this **proximam fossam** and there seems to be no
reason why he should not have used the same term here. (ii)
the garrison had already filled up this trench, Ch. 79, ll. 13–4.
(iii) the use of the plural.

Other commentators believe that Caesar is referring to the
20 ft. trench and the nearer of the two parallel 15 ft. trenches.
Again there are three objections : (1) the distance of 400 yds.
between the two trenches makes the use of **priores** seem
strange.   (2) this theory assumes without any authority that
the garrison successfully crossed the system of subsidiary

defences.   (3) If they had done so, why did Caesar definitely say that they did not get near the entrenchments?

Rice Holmes' suggestion seems to me to be the best : the **priores fossas** refer to the small trenches which Caesar calls **cippi,** Ch. 73, l. 15.

MM. Debeauvais, André Noche and other French scholars make a clear distinction between the two 15 ft. parallel trenches and the trench at the palisade proper.   In this case the zone of subsidiary defences will lie between these two trenches and the main defence lines of rampart, palisade and towers.   This theory certainly enables us to give a clear meaning to the phrase **priores fossas,** for they will now be the two parallel trenches across the plain of Les Laumes.

In conclusion, we may add that at least two commentators make **priores** nominative to denote the front rank of the besieged, the idea being that they were to fill up the ditches while the rest brought up the tools and implements necessary for attacking the contravallation proper.

VOCABULARY

*(In the following vocabulary, only irregular verbs have their
principal parts given. Otherwise the figures (1), (2), (3),
(4), following a verb denote that it is a regular example of
that conjugation. No conjugation number is given in the
case of -io verbs like capio. Numbers after meanings refer
to Chapters.)*

a *or* ab, *prep. with abl.*, by, from ; **ab tergo**, in the rear.
abdo, -ere, -didi, -ditum (3), put away, hide.
abeo, -ire, -ii, -itum, go away, depart.
abicio, -ere, -ieci, -iectum, throw away.
abiungo, -ere, -nxi, -nctum (3), separate, detach.
abscido, -ere, -di, -sum (3), cut off *or* away.
absens, -ntis, absent.
abstineo, -ere, -ui, -tentum (2), refrain from ; spare (ch. 47).
abstraho, -ere, -xi, -ctum (3), drag *or* carry off.
absum, -esse, afui, am away, absent, distant.
abundo (1), abound.
ac, *conj.*, and ; *after* alius, than, from.
accedo, -ere, -cessi, -cessum (3), approach ; am added.
accelero (1), hasten.
accido, -ere, -cidi (3), happen.
accipio, -ere, -cepi, -ceptum, receive ; suffer (*disaster*).
acclivis, -e, sloping.
Acco, -onis, *m.*, Acco (*chieftain of the Senones*).
accuso (1), accuse, reproach.
acerbe, *adv.*, *comparat.*, **acerbius**, too bitterly *or* keenly.
acerbitas, -atis, *f.*, suffering, hardship.
acerbus, -a, -um, bitter, harsh, cruel.
acies, -ei, *f.*, line of battle ; battle.
acriter, *adv.*, vigorously, fiercely ; *comparat*, **acrius**, *superlat.*,
    acerrime.

acutus, -a, -um, sharp.

ad, *prep. with acc.,* to, towards ; at, near ; for.

adaequo (1), equal, make equal to.

addo, -ere, -didi, -ditum (3), add.

adduco, -ere, -xi, -ctum, bring up (ch. **87**) ; persuade, induce.

adeo, -ire, -ii, -itum, approach ; attack (ch. **83**).

adeo, *adv.,* to such an extent, so.

adfero, -ferre, -tuli, allatum, bring ; occasion, cause.

adficio, -ere, -feci, -fectum, affect, treat.

adfingo, -ere, -nxi, -ctum (3), add on, invent.

adfirmatio, -onis, *f.,* declaration, assertion.

adhibeo (2), apply, use ; summon (chs. **77, 83**).

adhortor (1 *dep.*), exhort, encourage.

adicio, -ere, -ieci, -iectum, throw to, add.

adigo, -ere, -egi, -actum (3), drive to ; bind (*with an oath* (ch. **67**)).

adimo, -ere, -emi, emptum (3), take away.

aditus, -us, *m.,* approach, access.

adiudico (1), assign *or* adjudge to.

adiungo, -ere, -nxi, -nctum (3), attach to ; win over to one's side (chs. **29, 30, 31**).

adiuvo, -are, -iuvi, -iutum (1), aid, help.

admaturo (1), hasten.

administro (1), carry out, perform, execute.

admiror (1 *dep.*), admire, marvel at.

admitto, -ere, -misi, -missum (3), admit ; commit (*a crime*).

admodum, *adv.,* very, very much.

adorior, -iri, -ortus, (4 *dep.*), attack.

adquiro, -ere, -quisivi, -quisitum (3), gain, acquire.

adsum, -esse, adfui, am present ; stand by (*with dat.* (ch. **62**)).

adulescens, -ntis, *m.,* young man, youth ; *as adj.,* young.

adventus, -us, *m.,* arrival.

adversarius, -i, *m.,* political opponent.

adversus, -a, -um, adverse ; **res adversae** (ch **30.**), disasters, reverses.

advoco (1), call to, summon.

advolo (1), fly to *or* against, *or* upon ; dart upon.

aedificium, -i, *n.,* building, homestead ; granary.

Aeduus, -i, *m.,* Aeduan ; *in pl.,* the Aedui.

aequus, -a, -um, equal, level (ch. **44**), calm (ch. **64**).

aestas, -atis, *f.,* summer.

aestimo (1), value, estimate.

aetas, -atis, *f.,* age.

aeternus, -a, -um, everlasting, perpetual.

Agedincum, -i, *n.,* Agedincum (*capital of the Senones, now Sens*).

ager, -gri, *m.,* land, country, territory.

agger, -eris, *m.,* earth, rubble , earthwork.

agito (1), discuss ; discuss heatedly (ch. **2**).

agmen, -inis, *n.,* line of march, column.

ago, -ere, egi, actum (3), do, act ; bring up ; treat, discuss (ch. **36**).

alacer, -cris, -cre, eager, alert.

Alesia, -ae, *f.,* Alesia (*stronghold of the Mandubii, now Alise Ste. Reine*).

alieno (1), estrange, alienate.

alienus, -a, -um, of *or* belonging to another.

aliquando, *adv.,* one day ; at last (ch. **77**).

aliquis, -qua, -quid, some *or* any one.

aliter, *adv.,* otherwise.

alius, -a, -ud, other, another ; **alii ... alii ... ,** some ... others ; **alius atque,** other than, different from (ch. **33**).

allicio, -ere, -lexi, -lectum, entice, allure.

Allobroges, -um, *m. pl., acc. in* **-as** (ch. **64**), the Allobroges (*Gallic tribe*).

alo, -ere, -ui, -itum (3), (nourish) ; foment (ch. **32**) ; foster, cherish (ch. **33**).

alter, -era, -erum, one *or* the other (*of two*) ; second.

alternus, -a, -um, alternate.

altitudo, -inis, *f.,* depth, height.

altus, -a, -um, deep, high.

Ambarri, -orum, *m. pl.,* the Ambarri (*Gallic tribe*).

Ambiani, -orum, *m. pl.,* the Ambiani (*Gallic tribe*).

Ambibareti, -orum, *m. pl.,* the Ambibareti (*Gallic tribe*).

Ambibarii, -orum, *m. pl.,* the Ambibarii (*Gallic tribe*).

Ambluareti, -orum, *m. pl.,* the Ambluareti (*Gallic tribe*).

amicitia, -ae, *f.,* friendship.

amicus, -i, *m.,* friend.

amitto, -ere, -misi, -missum (3), lose.

amplitudo, -inis, *f.,* greatness, splendour, powerful position (ch. **54**).

amplius, *comparat. adv.,* more.

amplus, -a, -um, large, grand, splendid.

an, *interrog. particle,* or, whether.

anceps, -cipitis, (two-headed), double.

Andi, -orum (*or* **Andes, -ium**), *m. pl.,* the Andi (*Gallic tribe*).

anfractus, -us, *m.,* bend, curve.

angustiae, -arum, *f. pl.,* narrowness, difficulty.

angustus, -a, -um, narrow.

animadverto, -ere, -ti, -sum (3), notice, observe.

animus, -i, *m.,* mind, spirit, temper, courage.

annus, -i, *m.,* year.

ante, *adv., and prep. with acc.,* before.

antea, *adv.,* before, formerly.

antecedo, -ere, -cessi, -cessum (3), go before (ch. **12**), move ahead (ch. **35**) ; surpass (ch. **54**).

anteverto, -ere, -ti, -sum (3), prefer ; adopt (ch. **7**).

antiquitus, *adv.,* of old.

antiquus, -a, -um, old, ancient ; former.

Antistius, -i, *m.,* Gaius Antistius Reginus (*a general of Caesar*).

Antonius, -i, *m.,* Marcus Antonius.

aperte, *adv.,* openly.

apertus, -a, -um, open, exposed.

apparo (1), prepare.

appello (1), call ; address ; approach, greet (ch. **54**).

appello, -ere, -puli, -pulsum (3) drive to ; *of ships,* put in (ch. **60**).

appeto, -ere, -ivi *or* **-ii, -itum** (3), aim at ; *intrans.,* draw near (ch. **82**).

approbo (1), approve.

appropinquo (1), approach, draw near (*often with dat.*).

aptus, -a, -um, fitting, suitable.

apud, *prep. with acc.,* near, with ; at (ch. **75**).

aqua, -ae, *f.*, water.
Aquitania, -ae, *f.*, Aquitania.
Arar, -aris, *m.*, the Arar (*now R. Saône*).
arbitrium, -i, *n.*, judgment, will.
arbitror (1 *dep.*), think, consider.
arbor, -oris, *f.*, tree.
arcesso, -ere, -ivi, (-ii), -itum (3), send for, summon.
arduus, -a, -um, difficult.
Arecomici, *see* Volcae.
Aremoricus, -a, -um, Aremorican.
argentum, -i, *n.*, silver.
aridus, -a, -um, dry.
aries, -etis, *m.*, ram, a battering ram.
Aristius, -i, *m.*, Marcus Aristius (*military tribune*).
arma, -orum, *n. pl.*, arms, equipment.
armatura, -ae, *f.*, armour, equipment.
armo (1), arm, equip.
arroganter, *adv.*, arrogantly.
arrogantia, -ae, *f.*, arrogance, presumption.
arte, *adv.*, closely, tightly.
artificium, -i, *n.*, strategy.
artus, -a, -um, close, thick, dense.
Arvernus, -a, -um, Arvernian ; *as noun in pl.*, the Arveni.
arx, arcis, *f.*, citadel.
ascendo, -ere, -di, -nsum (3), climb, mount.
ascensus, -us, *m.*, ascent ; means of ascent (ch. 85).
aspectus, -us, *m.*, sight, appearance.
assiduus, -a, -um, constant, continual.
at, *conj.*, but.
atque, *conj.*, and, and moreover.
Atrebas, -atis, one of the Atrebates ; *in pl.*, the Atrebates (*Gallic tribe*).
attingo, -ere, -tigi, -tactum (3), border upon ; reach.
attribuo, -ere, -ui, -utum (3), assign ; allot to.
auctoritas, -atis, *f.*, influence, authority.
audacia, -ae, *f.*, boldness.
audacter, *adv.*, boldly.
audeo, -ere, ausus (2 *semi-dep.*), dare, venture.

audio (4), hear.

auditio, -onis, *f.,* hear-say, report.

augeo, -ere, -xi, -ctum (2), increase ; *in pass.,* spread (ch. **63**).

Aulercus, -i, *m.,* an Aulercan ; *in pl.,* the Aulerci (*Gallic tribe*).

auris, -is, *f.,* ear.

aut, *conj.,* or ; **aut . . . aut,** either . . . or.

autem, *conj.,* but, however ; moreover.

autumnus, -i, *m.,* autumn.

auxilior (1 *dep.*), help.

auxilium, -i, *n.,* help, aid ; *in pl.,* reinforcements.

Avaricensis, -e, of Avaricum.

Avaricum, -i, *n.,* Avaricum (*now Bourges*).

avaritia, -ae, *f.,* greed, avarice.

aveho, -ere, -xi, -ctum (3), carry off.

averto, -ere, -ti, -sum (3), turn away.

Basilus, -i, *m.,* Lucius Minucius Basilus (*Roman officer*).

bello (1), make war ; campaign.

Bellovaci, -orum, *m., pl.,* the Bellovaci (*Gallic tribe*).

bellum, -i, *n.,* war.

bene, *adv.,* well ; successfully.

beneficium, -i, *n.,* kindness, favour.

benevolentia, -ae, *f.,* goodwill, kindness.

Bibracte, -is, *n.,* Bibracte (*capital of the Aedui*).

biduum, -i, *n.,* space of two days.

bini, -ae, -a, two each.

bis, *adv.,* twice.

Bituriges, -um, *m. pl.,* the Bituriges (*Gallic tribe*).

Blanovii, -orum, *m. pl.,* the Blannovii (*Gallic tribe, clients of the Aedui*).

Boii, -orum, *m. pl.,* the Boii (*Gallic tribe*).

bona, -orum, *n. pl.,* property, goods.

bonus, -a, -um, good.

bracchium, -i, *n.,* arm.

Brannovices, -um, *m. pl.,* the Brannovices (*a division of the Aulerci*).

breviter, *adv.,* briefly.

Britannia, -ae, *f.,* Britain.
Brutus, -i, *m.,* Decimus Junius Brutus (*Roman general*).

C.=Gaius.
Cabillonum, -i, *n.,* Cabillonum (*town of the Aedui*).
Caburus, -i, *m.,* Caburus (*chieftain of the Helvii*).
cacumen, -inis, *n.,* point, top.
cadaver, -eris, *n.,* corpse, body.
Cadurcus, -i, *m.,* a Cadurcan ; *in pl.,* the Cadurci (*Gallic tribe*).
caedes, -is, *f.,* slaughter, massacre.
caerimonia, -ae, *f.,* rite, ceremony.
Caesar, -aris, *m.,* (i) Gaius Julius Caesar. (ii) Lucius Caesar (*a relative of* (i)).
calamitas, -atis, *f.,* disaster, calamity, misfortune.
Caletes, -um, *m. pl.,* the Caletes (*Gallic tribe*).
campester, -tris, -tre, on level ground.
campus, -i, *m.,* plain.
Camulogenus, -i, *m.,* Camulogenus (*chieftain of the Aulerci*).
Caninius, -i, *m.,* Gaius Caninius Rebilus (*Roman general*).
cano, -ere, cecini, cantum (3), (sing) ; sound (*on the trumpet*).
capillus, -i, *m.,* hair.
capio, -ere, cepi, captum, take, seize, reach ; take up (*arms*) ; form (*plans*) ; captivate (ch. 31).
captivus, -i, *m.,* captive, prisoner.
caput, -itis, *n.,* head, person.
careo (2), am without (*with abl.*).
Carnutes, -um, *m. pl.,* the Carnutes (*Gallic tribe*).
caro, carnis, *f.,* flesh.
carrus, -i, *m.,* cart.
carus, -a, -um, dear, precious.
cassis, -idis, *f.,* helmet.
castellum, -i, *n.,* fort, bastion.
castra, -orum, *n. pl.,* camp.
casus, -us, *m.,* (fall) ; chance, fate ; *in pl.,* eventualities (chs. 65, 79).
causa, -ae, *f.,* pretext, cause, reason; *abl.,* **causa,** for the sake of.
Cavarillus, -i, *m.,* Cavarillus (*chieftain of the Aedui*).

caveo, -ere, cavi, cautum (2), am on my guard ; take care.

cedo, -ere, cessi, cessum (3), yield ; give ground.

celer, -eris, -ere, quick, speedy.

celeritas, -atis, *f.*, quickness, speed.

celeriter, *adv.*, quickly.

celo (1), hide, conceal.

Celtillus, -i, *m.*, Celtillus (*father of Vercingetorix*).

Cenabensis, -e, of Cenabum.

Cenabenses, -ium, *m. pl.*, the people of Cenabum.

Cenabum, -i, *n.*, Cenabum (*now Orléans*).

Cenomani, -orum, *m. pl.*, the Cenomani (*a division of the Aulerci*).

censeo, -ere, -ui, censum (2), think, advocate (chs. 30, 75, 77) ; decide (ch. 56).

centum, a hundred.

centurio, -onis, *m.*, centurion.

cerno, -ere, crevi, cretum (3), perceive.

certe, *adv.*, at least, at any rate.

certus, -a, -um, fixed, definite ; **certiorem, -es, facere,** to inform ; **certior, -es, fieri,** be informed.

cervus, -i, *m.*, (stag) ; forked stake.

ceteri, -ae, -a, remaining, the other, rest of.

Cevenna, -ae, *f.*, the Cevennes.

cibus, -i, *m.*, food.

Cicero, -onis, *m.*, Q. Tullius Cicero (*Roman general*).

Cimbri, -orum, *m. pl.*, the Cimbri (*Gallic tribe*).

cingo, -ere, -nxi, -nctum (3), surround, gird.

cippus, -i, *m.*, gravestone.

circiter, *adv.*, about.

circuitus, -us, *m.*, (a going round) ; detour (ch. 45) ; perimeter (ch. 69) ; circumference (ch. 83).

circum, *prep with acc.*, around.

circumcido, -ere, -cidi, -cisum (3), cut away ; *in perf. part. pass.*, **circumcisus,** scarped, steep.

circumdo, -are, -dedi, -datum (1), put round, surround.

circumeo, -ire, -ivi, (-ii), -itum, go round, surround.

circumfundo, -ere, -fudi, -fusum (3), (pour round) ; surround (ch. 74) ; *in pass.*, pour round (ch. 28).

circummitto, -ere, -misi, -missum (3), send round.

circumplector, -i, -plexus (3 *dep.*), include.

circumsisto, -ere, -stiti (3), surround.

circumvallo (1), invest.

circumveho, -ere, -xi, -ctum (3), carry around ; *in pass.*, ride round.

circumvenio, -ire, -veni, -ventum (4), surround.

Cita, *see* Fuflus.

civis, -is, *c.*, citizen.

civitas, -atis, *f.*, citizenship ; state, tribe.

clam, *adv.*, secretly.

clamor, -oris, *m.*, shouting, shout, cry.

clandestinus, -a, -um, secret.

claudo, -ere, -si, -sum, shut.

cliens, -ntis, dependent, retainer.

clientula, -ae, *f.*, retainers.

clivus, -i, *m.*, slope.

Clodius, -i, *m.*, Publius Clodius Pulcher.

coacervo (1), heap up ; *in pass.*, mass *or* herd together.

coagmento (1), fasten *or* cement together.

coemo, -ere, -emi, -emptum (3), buy up.

coepi, -isse, *defect.*, began.

cogito (1), think ; devise means (ch. 59).

cognatio, -onis, *f.*, relationship.

cognosco, -ere, -gnovi, -gnitum (3), get to know, learn, ascertain.

cogo, -ere, coegi, coactum (3), collect, assemble ; compel.

cohors, -rtis, *f.*, cohort.

cohortor (1 *dep.*), exhort, encourage.

coicio, -ere, -ieci, -iectum, throw, hurl ; **in fugam coicere**, to put to flight.

collaudo (1), praise highly, commend.

colligo, -ere, -legi, -lectum (3), collect; rally.

collis, -is, *m.*, hill, slope.

colloco (1), place, post, station.

colloquium, -i, *n.*, conference ; conversation, gossip (ch. 59).

colloquor, -i, -locutus (3 *dep.*), speak with, confer, converse.

color, -oris, *m.*, colour.

comitia, -orum, *n. pl.*, elections.

commeatus, -us, _m._, supplies.

commeo (1), go to and fro.

comminus, _adv._, hand to hand ; at close quarters.

commissura, -ae, _f._, junction.

committo, -ere, -misi, -missum (3), commit (ch. 4) ; allow (ch. 47); **proelium committere,** to join battle.

Commius, -i, _m._, Commius (_chieftain of the Atrebates_).

commodum, -i, _n._, advantage ; opportunity (ch. 55).

commodus, -a, -um, suitable, advantageous.

commoror (1 _dep._), stay.

communico (1), (make common) ; impart (ch. 63).

communis, -e, common, in common.

commutatio, -onis, _f._, change.

commuto (1), change.

comparo (1), make ready, prepare.

compello, -ere, -puli, -pulsum (3), drive together, collect.

compendium, -i, _n._, profit.

comperio, -ire, -peri, -pertum (4), ascertain.

complector, -i, -plexus (3 _dep._), embrace, include.

compleo, -ere, -plevi, -pletum (2), fill ; man (ch. 12) ; occupy (ch. 72) ; make up (ch. 75).

complures, -a, several, many.

comprehendo, -ere, -di, -sum (3), seize, capture.

concedo, -ere, -cessi, -cessum (3), concede, give in.

concessus, -us, _m., only in abl. sing._, permission, leave.

concido, -ere, -di (3), fall.

concilio (1), win over.

concilium, -i, _n._, council, meeting.

concito (1), rouse ; bring up (ch. 42).

conclamo (1), raise a shout ; cry aloud.

Conconnetodumnus, -i, _m._, Conconnetodumnus (_chieftain of the Carnutes_).

concrepo, -are, -ui, -itum (1), with **armis** (ch. 22), clash their arms together.

concurro, -ere, -(cu)curri, -cursum (3), hasten, rush.

concurso (1), run hither and thither.

concursus, -us, _m._, running together ; pace (ch. 48) ; onset (ch. 62).

condemno (1), condemn.

condicio, -onis, *f.*, condition, terms.

conduco, -ere, -xi, -ctum (3), hire.

confectus, -a, -um, worn out.

confero, -ferre, -tuli, collatum, bring together, collect; pile up (ch. 18).

confertus, -a, -um, crowded, dense, compact.

confestim, *adv.*, immediately, straitway.

conficio, -ere, -feci, -fectum, finish, perform.

confido, -ere, -fisus (3 *semi-dep.*), trust in (*with dat. or abl.*).

confio, -fieri, am done *or* carried out.

confirmo (1), strengthen, encourage; bind by oath (ch. 66).

confligo, -ere, -flixi, -flictum (3), fight, struggle.

confluo, -ere, -xi (3), flock together.

confundo, -ere, -fudi, -fusum (3), crowd together; confusus, assembled, herded together.

congredior, -i, -gressus, (*dep.*), meet (*in battle*); fight.

coniectura, -ae, *f.*, guess.

coniungo, -ere, -nxi, -nctum (3), join together, unite.

coniunx, -iugis, *c.*, husband, wife.

coniuro (1), take an oath.

conor (1 *dep.*), try.

conquiesco, -ere, -quievi, -quietum (3), rest, take a siesta.

conquiro, -ere, -quisivi, -quisitum (3), search out, collect.

consanguineus, -i, *m.*, blood relation.

consensio, -onis, *f.*, agreement, unanimity.

consensus, -us, *m.*, agreement, unanimity.

consequor, -i -secutus (3), follow up, reach, gain.

conservo (1), save, preserve.

consido, -ere, -sedi, -sessum (3), take up a position; establish oneself; settle down; settle (ch. 77).

consilium, -i, *n.*, plan, counsel, policy, design; consilium inire, to form a plan; consilium capere, to form a plan.

consisto, -ere, -stiti, -stitum (3), take up a position, stand fast (ch. 28); halt; settle down (chs. 3, 42); get a footing (ch. 37); consistere in, depend upon.

consobrinus, -i, *m.*, cousin.

consolor (1 *dep.*), comfort, console.

conspectus, -us, *m.,* sight.

conspicio, -ere, -spexi, -spectum, catch sight of ; notice.

conspicor (1 *dep.*), catch sight of, descry.

constantia, -ae, *f.,* firmness, resolution.

consternatus, -a, -um, alarmed.

constat, -are, -stitit, (1), *impersonal,* it is certain.

constituo, -ere, -ui, -utum (3), post, set up ; halt (chs. 45, 47) ; form (*line of battle* (ch. 67)) ; arrange, decide.

consto, -are, -stiti (1), stand firm ; remain unchanged (ch.35).

consuesco, -ere, -suevi, -suetum (3), grow accustomed ; *in perfect tenses,* am wont, am accustomed.

consuetudo, -inis, *f.,* custom.

consulo, -ere, -ui, -sultum (3), consult ; *with dat.,* consult the interests *or* safety of ; have regard for (chs. 8, 12).

consulto (1), deliberate, consult together.

consulto, *adv.,* on purpose, deliberately.

consultum, -i, *n.,* decree.

consumo, -ere, -sumpsi, -sumptum (3), spend, consume ; destroy.

contabulo (1), furnish with stories.

contaminatus, -a, -um, tainted.

contego, -ere, -texi, -tectum (3), cover up, conceal.

contendo, -ere, -di, -tum (3), hasten ; fight ; urge (ch. 63).

contentio, -onis, *f.,* struggle, rivalry ; fighting, action (ch. 52) ; contest (ch. 58).

contentus, -a, -um, content, satisfied.

contexo, -ere, -texui, -textum (3), weave *or* bind together.

continens, -ntis, continuous, persistent.

continentia, -ae, *f.,* moderation, self-control (ch. 52).

contineo, -ere, -ui, -tentum (2), keep in *or* in check ; keep in its place (ch. 22).

contingo, -ere, -tigi, -tactum (3), reach, extend to.

continuo, *adv.,* forthwith.

continuus, -a, -um, successive, continuous.

contio, -onis, *f.,* assembly ; parade (ch. 52) ; harangue (ch. 53).

contra, *prep. with acc.,* against ; contrary to ; *adv.,* on the contrary.

contraho, -ere, -xi, -ctum (3), get together; reduce in size (ch. 40); concentrate (ch. 43).

contrarius, -a, -um, opposite.

controversia, -ae, *f.*, dispute.

contumelia, -ae, *f.*, insult.

conveho, -ere, -vexi, -vectum (3), bring together.

convenio, -ire, -veni, -ventum (4), come together, meet: muster (ch. 66); am agreed upon; *impersonal*, it is fitting.

conventus, -us, *m., in pl.*, the assizes.

converto, -ere, -ti, -sum (3), change, turn.

Convictolitavis, -is, *m.*, Convictolitavis (*chieftain of the Aedui*).

convoco (1), call together, summon.

coorior, -iri, -ortus (4 *dep.*), rise.

copia, -ae, *f.*, plenty, supply; *in pl.*, forces, troops.

corium, -i, *n.*, hide.

cornu, -us, *n.*, (horn); wing (*of an army*).

corona, -ae, *f.*, circle, ring.

corpus, -oris, *n.*, body.

corrumpo, -ere, -rupi, -ruptum (3), spoil, destroy.

cotidianus, -a, -um, daily.

cotidie, *adv.*, daily.

Cotuatus, -i, *m.*, Cotuatus (*chieftain of the Carnutes*).

Cotus, -i, *m.*, Cotus (*chieftain of the Aedui*).

crassitudo, -inis, *f.*, thickness.

crates, -is, *f.*, hurdle, fascine.

creber, -bra, -brum, frequent.

crebro, *adv.*, frequently.

creo (1), create, appoint, elect.

cresco, -ere, crevi, cretum (3), grow; swell (*of a river*).

Critognatus, -i, *m.*, Critognatus (*chieftain of the Arverni*).

cruciatus, -us, *m.*, torture.

crudelitas, -atis, *f.*, cruelty.

crudeliter, *adv.*, cruelly.

cum, *prep. with abl.*, with.

cum, *conj.*, when, since, although; whenever; **cum...** tum, both ... and.

cunctus, -a, -um, all together, all.

cuneatim, *adv.,* in wedge formation.

cuniculus, -i, *m.,* (rabbit) ; mine.

cupiditas, -atis, *f.,* desire ; hot-headed conduct (ch. 52).

cupidus, -a, -um, desirous, eager for.

cur, *conj.,* why.

Curiosolites, -um, *m., pl.,* the Curiosolites (*Gallic tribe*).

cura, -ae, *f.,* care.

curo (1), take measures, see to.

curro, -ere, cucurri, cursum (3), run, hasten.

cursus, -us, *m.,* running, course.

custodia, -ae, *f.,* watching, guard ; *in pl.,* guards, sentinels.

custos, -odis, *c.,* guard.

de, *prep. with abl.,* from ; about, concerning, of ; *in time expressions,* about, at.

debeo (2), owe, ought.

decem, ten.

decerno, -ere, -crevi, -cretum, decide upon, decree.

decerto (1), fight to the end (ch. 77).

Decetia, -ae, *f.,* Decetia (*town of the Aedui*).

decimus, -a, -um, tenth.

declivia, -ium, *n. pl.,* slopes.

declivitas, -atis, *f.,* downward slope.

decretum, -i, *n.,* decree.

deditio, -onis, *f.,* surrender.

dedo, -ere, -didi, -ditum (3), give up, surrender.

deduco, -ere, -duxi, -ductum (3), lead down *or* away ; win over (ch. 37) ; withdraw (ch. 87).

defatigo (1), exhaust.

defectio, -onis, *f.,* revolt.

defendo, -ere, -di, -sum (3), ward off, defend.

defensio, -onis, *f.,* defence.

defensor, -oris, *m.,* defender.

defero, -ferre, -tuli, -latum, bring down ; report ; confer (*power,* (ch. 4)) ; *in pass.,* am borne, fall.

defessus,-a, -um, worn out.

deficio, -ere, -feci, -fectum, fail, lose (*heart* (ch. 30)) ; revolt (ch. 39).

definio (4), define, fix.

deformis, -e, misshapen, unsightly (ch. 23).

deicio, -ere, -ieci, -ectum, hurl down, dislodge.

deinceps, *adv.*, successively, each in turn.

deleo, -ere, -evi, -etum (2), destroy.

delibero (1), deliberate, consider.

delibro (1), peel.

delictum, -i, *n.*, offence.

deligo, -ere, -legi, -lectum (3), choose, pick off (ch. 14).

deminuo, -ere, -ui, -utum (3), diminish.

demissus, -a, -um, low-lying.

demitto, -ere, -misi, -missum (3), let down, lower; *reflexive*, descend (ch. 28), lose heart (ch. 29).

demonstro (1), point out, show.

denique, *adv.*, at last, finally.

densus, -a, -um, thick, close, dense.

depello, -ere, -puli, -pulsum (3), drive away.

depereo, -ire, -ii, perish, am lost.

depono, -ere, -posui, -positum (3), lay down; lodge (ch. 63).

depopulor (1 *dep.*), lay waste; **depopulatus** *in pass. sense* (ch. 77).

deposco, -ere, -poposci (3), demand.

deprecor (1 *dep.*) deprecate, beg off.

deprendo, -ere, -di, -sum (3), catch, seize upon.

depugno (1), fight bitterly.

derectus, -a, -um, straight, perpendicular.

derigo, -ere, -rexi, -rectum (3), direct, get into position.

derivo (1), divert, draw off.

descendo, -ere, -di, -sum (3), (come down); have recourse to.

deseco, -are, -ui, -ctum, (1), cut off.

desero, -ere, -rui, -rtum (3), desert, abandon.

desidero (1), miss, lose; *in pass.*, am wanting.

desisto, -ere, -stiti, -stitum (3), desist, cease from (*often with abl.*).

despectus, -us, *m.*, view, prospect.

despero (1), despair; despair of (chs. 80, 88); despair of victory (ch. 86).

despicio, -ere, -spexi, -spectum, look down on, despise.

destino (1), secure, fasten.

destringo, -ere, -strinxi, -strictum (3), draw, unsheathe.

detineo, -ere, -ui, -tentum (2), delay, hinder.

detracto (1), avoid, shirk.

detraho, -ere, -traxi, -tractum (3), take off.

detrimentosus, -a, -um, ruinous.

detrimentum, -i, *n.,* loss.

deturbo (1), dislodge.

deuro, -ere, -ussi, -ustum (3), burn down.

devexus, -a, -um, sloping ; *in neut. pl.,* low-lying ground.

devinco, -ere, -vici, -victum (3), conquer, subdue.

dexter, -(e)ra, -(e)rum, on the right, right.

dico, -ere, dixi, dictum (3), say, speak.

dies, -ei, *m. or f.,* day, time.

differo, -ferre, distuli, dilatum, put off.

difficilis, -e, difficult.

difficilius, *comparat. adv.,* with some difficulty.

difficultas, -atis, *f.,* difficulty.

digitus, -i, *m.,* finger.

dignitas, -atis, *f.,* honour, prestige (chs. **30, 54, 66**) ; authority (ch. **77**).

dignus, -a, -um, worthy, deserving ; *often with abl.*

dilectus, -us, *m.,* levy.

diligenter, *adv.,* carefully.

diligentia, -ae, *f.,* care, zeal ; energy (ch. **32**).

dimicatio, -onis, *f.,* contest, struggle.

dimico (1), fight.

dimitto, -ere, -misi, -missum (3), send (*in different directions*) ; dismiss ; give up (chs. **17, 52**).

directus, -a, -um, straight, perpendicular.

diripio, -ere, -ripui, -reptum, plunder, seize.

discedo, -ere, -cessi, -cessum (3), depart ; abandon (ch. **33**).

disceptator, -oris, *m.,* judge, umpire.

discerno, -ere, -crevi, -cretum (3), distinguish.

discessus, -us, *m.,* departure.

discludo, -ere, -si, -sum (3), separate.

disco, -ere, didici (3), learn.

discutio, -ere, -cussi, -cussum (3), break up ; dash aside.
dispar, -paris, unequal, different.
disparo (1), separate.
dispersus, -a, -um, dispersed, scattered.
dispicio, -ere, -spexi, -spectum, look around.
dispono, -ere, -posui, -positum (3), place at intervals ; post (ch. 65) ; arrange.
dissensio, -onis, f., dispute, quarrel, disagreement.
dissentio, -ire, -sensi, -sensum (4), differ, disagree.
dissero, -ere, -serui, -sertum (3), spread or scatter about.
dissuadeo, -ere, -si, -sum (2), dissuade.
distineo, -ere, -ui, -tentum (2), keep apart or off ; hinder (ch. 37), separate ; distract (ch. 50) ; string out (ch. 84).
disto (1), stand apart, am distant.
distraho, -ere, -traxi, -tractum (3), pull or drag apart.
distribuo, -ere, -ui, -utum (3), distribute, assign.
diu, adv., for a long time ; comparat., diutius.
diurnus, -a, -um, by day.
diversus, -a, -um, different, separate.
Diviciacus, -i, m., Diviciacus (chieftain of the Aedui).
divido, -ere, -visi, -visum (3), divide.
do, dare, dedi, datum (1), give.
doceo, -ere, -cui, -ctum (2), teach, inform.
documentum, -i, n., lesson, proof.
doleo (2), am grieved or resentful.
dolor, -oris, m., grief, pain.
domus, -us, f., house, home ; loc., domi, at home.
Donnotaurus, -i, m., Gaius Valerius Donnotaurus (chieftain of the Helvii).
dono (1), give, present.
donum, -i, n., gift.
dorsus, -i, m., (back) ; slope or crest.
dubitatio, -onis, f., doubt, hesitation.
dubito (1), hesitate, doubt.
dubius, -a, -um, doubtful, uncertain.
ducenti, -ae, -a, two hundred.
duco, -ere, -xi, -ctum (3), lead ; make or construct.
ductus, -us, m., guidance, leadership.

dum, *conj.,* while, as long as, until.

duo, -ae, -a, two.

duodecimus, -a, -um, twelfth.

duodeni, -ae, -a, twelve each.

duplex, -icis, two-fold, double.

durus, -a, -um, hard, difficult ; severe, inclement (*of weather*).

dux, ducis, *c.,* leader.

e *or* **ex,** *prep. with abl.,* out of ; from ; **ex nivibus,** in consequence of the snows.

Eburovices, -um, *m. pl.,* the Eburovices (*part of the Aulerci*).

editus, -a, -um, high, lofty (ch. 69).

edoceo, -ere, -ui, -doctum (2), teach, inform, point out.

educo, -ere, -xi, -ctum (3), lead out.

effarcio, -ire, -, -fartum (4), stuff, fill out.

effero, -ere, extuli, elatum, lift up ; *in pass.,* be noised abroad, divulged ; am elated (ch. 47).

efficio, -ere, -feci, -fectum, produce, bring about ; accomplish.

effodio, -ere, -fodi, -fossum, dig out ; put out (*of eyes*).

egens, -ntis, needy.

ego, mei, I.

egredior, -i, -gressus, go out *or* forth ; leave.

egregie, *adv.,* excellently, admirably.

eicio, -ere, -ieci, -iectum, cast out ; fling (ch. 47) ; **se eicere,** to rush forth.

Elaver, -eris, *m.,* the river Elaver.

Eleuteti, -orum, *m. pl.,* the Eleuteti (*Gallic tribe*).

elicio, -ere, -licui (3), entice out.

emineo (2), project, stick out.

eminus, *adv.,* from *or* at a distance.

enim, *conj.,* for ; **neque enim,** for indeed . . . not.

eo, *adv.,* thither; there.

eo, ire, ivi, itum, go.

eodem, *adv.,* to the same place.

Eporedorix, -igis, *m.* (i), Eporedorix (*prominent Aeduan*). (ii) Eporedorix (*Aeduan chieftain* (ch. 67)).

eques, -itis, *m.,* horseman ; *in pl.,* cavalry.

equester, -tris, -tre, of cavalry ; cavalry (*as adj.*).

equitatus, -us, *m.*, cavalry

equus, -i, *m.*, horse.

ergo, *adv.*, then, therefore.

eripio, -ere, -ripui, -reptum, snatch *or* carry away ; **se eripere** to save oneself, to escape.

erro (1), (wander) ; am mistaken, err.

eruptio, -onis *f.*, sally, raid.

et, and ; also, even ; **et . . . et,** both . . . and.

etiam, *conj.*, even, also.

etsi, *conj.*, although.

eventus, -us, *m.*, outcome, result.

evoco (1), invite.

evocatus, -i, *m.*, a veteran called up for service.

evolo (1), fly *or* rush out.

ex, *see* **e.**

exanimo (1), kill.

exaudio (4), hear.

excedo, -ere, -cessi, -cessum (3), depart.

excepto (1), catch up.

excido, -ere, -cidi, -cisum (3), cut through ; break open (ch. 50).

excipio, -ere, -cepi, -ceptum, take up (*a shout*) ; catch up, intercept (ch. 28) ; take prisoner (ch. 20) ; receive ; cover (ch. 51).

excito (1) incite, arouse.

excludo, -ere, -si, -sum (3), shut off, prevent.

excrucio (1), torture, torment.

excubitor, -oris, *m.*, sentry.

excubo, -are, -ui, -itum (1), am on guard ; bivouac (ch. 24).

exculco (1), tread down.

exemplum, -i, *n.*, precedent.

exeo, -ire, -ii (-ivi), -itum, go out, *or* forth.

exerceo (2), exercise ; *in pass.*, am busy with, *or* engaged (ch. 77).

exercitus, -us, *m.*, army : infantry.

exigue, *adv.*, scarcely, barely.

exiguus, -a, -um, scanty, small.

existimo (1), think, consider.

exitus, -us, *m.,* way out, passage (ch. **28**) ; outcome, result.

expedio (4), get ready ; secure (ch. **36**).

expeditus, -a, -um, unencumbered; *in masc. pl.,* light-armed troops.

expello, -ere, -puli, -pulsum (3), drive out, expel.

experior (4 *dep.*), make trial of ; attempt.

expleo, -ere, -plevi, -pletum (2), make good (ch. **31**) ; fill up (ch. **79**).

explorator, -oris, *m.,* scout ; *in pl.,* patrols (ch. **11**).

exploro (1), ascertain ; *in perf. part. pass.,* **exploratus,** assured.

expono, -ere, -posui, -positum (3), explain ; relate.

exposco, -ere, -poposci (3), demand.

exprimo, -ere, -pressi, -pressum (3), raise, express.

expugnatio, -onis, *f.,* capture by storm, storming.

expugno (1), carry by storm ; reduce by blockade (ch. **69**); subdue (ch. **10**).

exscensus, -us, *m.,* ascent.

exsero, -ere, -rui, -rtum (3), bare.

exsisto, -ere, -stiti (3), stand forth ; arise (ch. **84**).

exspecto (1), await, expect.

exspolio (1), deprive.

exstruo, -ere, -xi, -ctum (3), build, construct.

exterior, -ius, outer.

exterritus, -a, -um, frightened, alarmed.

extorqueo, -ere, -si, -tum (2), wrest *or* force from.

extra, *prep with acc.,* beyond.

extremus, -a, -um, last, furthest ; extreme (ch. **17**).

exuo, -ere, -ui, -utum (3), strip.

Fabius, -i, *m.,* (i) Gaius Fabius (*Roman general*).   (ii) Lucius Fabius (*Roman centurion*).

facile, *adv.,* easily.

facilis, -e, easy.

facinus, -oris, *n.,* deed, crime.

facio, -ere, feci, factum, do, make.

facultas, -atis, *f.,* opportunity ; *in pl.,* means.

fallo, -ere, fefelli, falsum (3), deceive.

falx, -cis, *f.,* (sickle) ; a hook.

fama, -ae, *f.,* report ; reputation.

fames, -is, *f.,* hunger.

familia, -ae, *f.,* family ; **matres familiae,** matrons.

familiaris, -e, domestic, private.

familiaris, -is, *c.,* friend, comrade.

fastigium, -i, *n.,* (top) ; height, slope.

fatigo (1), weary.

fax, facis, *f.,* torch.

femina, -ae, *f.,* woman, female.

femur, -oris, *and* **-inis,** *n.,* thigh.

fere, *adv.,* nearly, almost.

fero, ferre, tuli, latum, bear, carry ; endure, suffer.

ferraria, -ae, *f.,* iron mine.

ferreus, -a, -um, of iron.

fertilis, -e, fertile.

fervefactus, -a, -um, made hot.

fidelis, -e, loyal.

fides, -ei, *f.,* faith, loyalty ; pledged word (ch. **2**) ; protection
(ch. **5**).

fiducia, -ae, *f.,* confidence.

filius, -i, *m.,* son.

finis, -is, *m. and f.,* end : *m. pl.,* territories.

finitimus, -a, -um, neighbouring ; *as a noun,* a neighbour.

fio, fieri, factus, am made, done ; become (*used as passive of*
facio).

firmus, -a, -um, strong, firm.

fleo, -ere, flevi, fletum (2), weep.

florens, -ntis, influential, powerful.

flos, floris, *m.,* flower.

flumen, -inis, *n.,* river, stream.

fodio, -ere, fodi, fossum, dig.

foris, *adv.,* outside, from without.

forma, -ae, *f.,* shape.

fortis, -e, brave, strong, vigorous.

fortuito, *adv.,* by chance.

fortuna, -ae, *f.,* chance, fate, fortune.

forum, -i, *n.,* forum, market-place.

fossa, -ae, *f.,* ditch, trench.

frater, -tris, *m.*, brother.

fraus, -dis, *f.*, treachery, deceit.

frequens, -ntis, thronging ; in large numbers (ch. **63**).

frigus, -oris, *n.*, cold.

frons, -ntis, *f.*, front, forehead.

fructus, -us, *m.*, fruit.

frumentarius, -a, -um, of corn ; **res frumentaria,** the supply of corn.

frumentatio, -onis, *f.*, foraging for corn.

frumentor (1 *dep.*), forage.

frumentum, -i, *n.*, corn.

frustra, *adv.*, in vain.

Fufius, Gaius Fufius Cita (*Roman knight*).

fuga, -ae, *f.*, flight.

fugio, -ere, fugi, fly, flee, shun.

fugo (1), put to flight, rout.

fumo (1), smoke.

funda, -ae, *f.*, sling.

fundo, -ere, fudi, fusum (3), pour ; rout.

fungor, -i, functus (3 *dep.*), perform (*often with abl.*)

furor, -oris, *m.*, madness, rage.

Gabuli, -orum, *m. pl.*, the Gabuli (*Gallic tribe*).

Gaius, -i, *m.*, Gaius (*Roman praenomen*).

Gallia, -ae, *f.*, Gaul.

Gallicus, -a, -um, Gallic, of the Gauls.

Gallus, -i, *m.*, a Gaul.

generatim, *adv.*, by families, by tribes.

genus, -eris, *n.*, race, birth, kind.

Gergovia, -ae, *f.*, Gergovia.

Germani, -orum, *m. pl.*, the Germans.

Germania, -ae, *f.*, Germany.

gero, -ere, gessi, gestum (3), do ; hold (*magistracy*) ; carry on, conduct (*war*) ; fight ; get to work ; *in pass.*, happen.

gladius, -i, *m.*, sword.

glaeba, -ae, *f.*, clod ; piece *or* lump.

glans, -ndis, *f.*, (acorn) ; bullet *or* slug.

gloria, -ae, *f.*, renown, glory.

Gnaeus, -i, *m.*, Gnaeus (*Roman praenomen*).

Gobannitio, -onis, *m.*, Gobannitio (*uncle of Vercingetorix*).

Gorgobina, -ae, *f.*, Gorgobina (*Gallic town*).

grandis, -e, great, tall.

gratia, -ae, *f.*, influence, popularity.

gratulatio, -onis, *f.*, congratulation.

gravis, -e, heavy ; serious, disagreeable.

graviter, *adv.*, heavily, severely : *comparat.*, more severely, too hard (ch. 67).

Gutruatus, -i, *m.*, Gutruatus (*chieftain of the Carnutes*).

habeo (2), have, hold ; regard, consider.

haesito (1), stick fast.

hamus, -i, *m.*, hook.

harpago, -onis, *m.*, grappling-hook.

Helveticus, -a, -um, of *or* with the Helvetii.

Helvetii, -orum, *m. pl.*, the Helvetii.

Helvii, -orum, *m. pl.*, the Helvii (*Gallic tribe*).

hiberna, -orum, *n. pl.*, winter quarters.

hibernus, -a, -um, wintry.

hic, haec, hoc, this ; he, she, it ; they.

hic, *adv.*, here.

hiemo (1), winter.

hiems, hiemis, *f.*, winter.

Hispania, -ae, *f.*, Spain.

homo, -inis, *c.*, man.

honestus, -a, -um, honourable, good.

honor, -oris, *m.*, honour, office.

hora, -ae, *f.*, hour.

horribilis, -e, horrible, terrifying.

hortor (1 *dep.*), encourage, exhort.

hospitium, -i, *n.*, hospitality.

hostis, -is, *c.*, enemy.

huc, *adv.*, hither, here.

humilis, -e, humbled ; inferior.

iaceo (2), lie, am fallen.

iacio, -ere, ieci, iactum, throw.

iacto (1), throw.

iactura, -ae, *f.*, sacrifice, loss.

iam, *adv.*, by now, already.

ibi, *adv.*, there.

ictus, -us, *m.*, blow.

idem, eadem, idem, same.

idoneus, -a, -um, suitable, convenient.

ignis, -is, *m.*, fire.

ignominia, -ae, *f.*, shame, disgrace.

ignoro (1), am ignorant of.

ignosco, -ere, -gnovi, -gnotum (3), pardon (*with dat.*).

ille, -a, -ud, that ; he, she, it, they.

illic, *adv.*, there.

illo, *adv.*, to that place, there.

imbecillitas, -atis, *f.*, weakness.

imber, -bris, *m.*, rain.

imitor (1 *dep.*), imitate.

immitto, -ere, -misi, -missum (3), send against.

immunis, -e, free from tax.

impedimentum, -i, *n.*, hindrance ; *in pl.*, baggage.

impedio (4), hinder.

impeditus, -a, -um, hindered ; impassable, troublesome (ch. 19).

impello, -ere, -puli, -pulsum (3), drive on, impel.

imperator, -oris, *m.*, commander-in-chief.

imperitus, -a, -um, unskilled, inexperienced.

imperium, -i, *n.*, command, power, rule.

impero (1), command, order (*with dat.*) ; requisition.

impetro (1), obtain.

impetus, -us, *m.*, attack, onset ; impetum facere, to charge.

implico, -are, -avi(-ui), -atum, (-itum) (1), tie *or* weave together.

impono, -ere, -posui, -positum (3), put upon, impose.

improvisus, -a, -um, unforeseen ; de improviso, unexpectedly.

imprudentia, -ae, *f.*, imprudence, want of foresight.

in, *prep. with acc.*, into, to, against ; *with abl.*, in, on, among.

inanis, -e, empty, groundless.

incaute, *adv.*, carelessly.

incendium, -i, *n.*, conflagration, fire.

incendo, -ere, -di, -sum (3), set on fire, burn ; inflame.

incertus, -a, -um, uncertain.

incido, -ere, -di (3), befall, occur, happen.

incipio, -ere, -cepi, -ceptum, begin.

incito (1), spur on, excite, madden (ch. 28) ; row (*of boats* (ch. 60)).

incolumis, -e, safe, unharmed.

incommodum, -i, *n.*, inconvenience ; disaster ; trouble (ch. 33).

incumbo, -ere, -cubui, -cubitum (3), (lie upon) ; devote myself to (ch. 76).

incursus, -us, *m.*, attack.

inde, *adv.*, thence, from this place ; thereupon, then.

indicium, -i, *m.*, information.

indico, -ere, -xi, -ctum (3), proclaim ; convene (chs. 1, 63, 75).

indictus, -a, -um, unsaid.

indigne, *adv.*, unworthily, undeservingly.

indignitas, -atis, *f.*, disgrace, dishonour.

indignor (1 *dep.*), am indignant ; resent.

indignus, -a, -um, unworthy of (*with abl.*).

indiligens, -ntis, careless, remiss.

indiligentia, -ae, *f.*, remissness, apathy.

indulgentia, -ae, *f.*, indulgence, kindness.

indulgeo, -ere, -si, -tum (2), indulge ; *with dat.* (ch. 40).

induo, -ere, -ui, -utum (3), put on.

industrie, *adv.*, jealously.

ineo, -ire, -ii, -itum, enter ; **rationem inire**, to form a calculation.

infamia, -ae, *f.*, discredit, scandal.

infans, -ntis, infant.

infectus, -a, -um, not done ; **re infecta**, without accomplishing their object.

inferior, -ius, lower.

infero, -ferre, -tuli, illatum, carry against ; inflict (chs. 54, 77) ; **signa inferre**, to attack ; instil (ch. 8) ; **bellum inferre**, to make war upon.

infestus, -a, -um, hostile.

inficio, -ere, -feci, -fectum, stain.

infidelis, -e, unfaithful, disloyal.

infigo, -ere, -xi, -xum (3), fix on *or* in.

infimus, -a, -um, lowest : *also as noun*, the bottom.

infirmitas, -atis, *f.*, weakness.

infirmus, -a, -um, weak.

influo, -ere, -xi, -xum (3), flow *or* drain into.

infodio, -ere, -fodi, -fossum (3), dig in, bury.

infra, *adv.*, below.

ingratus, -a, -um, displeasing, unwelcome.

inicio, -ere, -ieci, -ectum, put *or* strike in ; put on board (ch. 58) ; inspire (ch. 55).

iniquitas, -atis, *f.*, injustice ; inequality (ch. 19).

iniquus, -a, -um, unequal, unfavourable.

initium, -i, *n.*, beginning.

iniungo, -ere, -nxi, -nctum (3), impose upon.

iniuria, -ae, *f.*, injustice ; *in pl.*, wrongs.

inlustris, -e, illustrious. famous.

innascor, -i, -natus (3 *dep.*), am born *or* innate in.

inopia, -ae, *f.*, scarcity, lack.

inopinans, -ntis, off one's guard, not expecting.

inprimis, *adv.*, above all, especially.

inquam, -is, -it (*defect. verb*), say.

inscientia, -ae, *f.*, ignorance.

inscius, -a, -um, ignorant ; not knowing (ch. 77).

insequor, -i, -secutus (3 *dep.*), follow up, pursue.

insidiae, -arum, *f. pl.*, ambush, deceit, trap (ch. 73).

insigne, -is, *n.*, badge (chs. 45, 50) ; distinguishing mark (ch. 88).

insimulo (1), accuse.

inspecto (1), look on *or* in.

instituo, -ere, -ui, -utum (3), begin, set about ; determine (ch. 1) ; arrange (ch. 71) ; devise (ch. 72) ; establish (*precedent* (ch. 77)).

institutum, -i, *n.*, practice, usage.

insto, -are, -stiti (1), press on ; threaten.

instruo, -ere, -xi, -ctum (3), draw up.

insuetus, -a, -um, unaccustomed to (*with gen.*).

insula, -ae, *f.,* island.

insuper, *adv.,* on the top, besides.

integer, -gra, -grum, unimpaired, fresh ; intact (ch. **35**).

intego, -ere, -xi, -ctum (3), cover over, protect.

intellego, -ere, -xi, -ctum (3), perceive, understand.

intentus, -a, -um, eager.

inter, *prep. with acc.,* among, between.

intercedo, -ere, -cessi, -cessum (3), intervene, lie between.

intercludo, -ere, -clusi, -clusum (3), cut *or* shut off.

interdico, -ere, -xi, -ctum (3), forbid (*with dat.*).

interdiu, *adv.,* by day.

interea, *adv.,* meanwhile.

intereo, -ire, -ii, -itum, perish.

interest, *see* **intersum.**

interficio, -ere, -feci, -fectum, kill, slay.

intericio, -ere, -ieci, -iectum, throw between ; *in pass.,* take part in ; lie between.

interim, *adv.,* meanwhile.

interior, -ius, inner.

intermitto, -ere, -misi, -missum (3), leave off, discontinue ; leave incomplete (ch. **71**).

interpono, -ere, -posui, -positum (3), put between ; issue (ch. **34**) ; *in pass.,* come between.

interrogo (1), question.

interrumpo, -ere, -rupi, -ruptum (3), break down.

interscindo, -ere, -scidi, -scissum (3), cut out (ch. **24**).

intersum, -esse, -fui, am between ; take part in (*dat.*) ; *imperson.,* **interest,** it makes a difference.

intervallum, -i, *n.,* interval, distance.

intervenio, -ire, -veni, -ventum (4), come between, appear.

intoleranter, *adv.,* eagerly, relentlessly.

intra, *prep. with acc.,* within, inside.

intro (1), enter.

intromitto, -ere, -misi, -missum (3), send in.

introrsus, *adv.,* inwards.

inutilis, -e, useless ; incapacitated (ch. **78**).

invenio, -ire, -veni, -ventum (4), come upon, find.

invicem, *adv.*, in turn.

invidia, -ae, *f.*, envy.

invitus, -a, -um, unwilling.

ipse, -a, -um, self ; himself, themselves, *etc.*

iracundia, -ae, *f.*, anger, passion.

irrumpo, -ere, -rupi, -ruptum (3), burst in.

irruptio, -onis, *f.*, attack, assault.

is, ea, id, that ; he, she, it, they.

iste, -a, -ud, this, that (*of yours*).

ita, *adv.*, so, thus.

Italia, -ae, *f.*, Italy.

itaque, *conj.*, and so.

item, *adv.*, likewise.

iter, itineris, *n.*, march ; route, road ; **ex itinere**, en route.

iubeo, -ere, iussi, iussum (2), order.

iudico (1), judge, decide.

iugum, -i, *n.*, ridge ; range (ch. 36).

iumentum, -i, *n.*, pack animal.

iungo, -ere, -nxi, -nctum (3), join.

iunior, -oris, younger.

ius, iuris, *n.*, right, law.

ius iurandum, iuris iurandi, *n.*, oath.

iussus, -us, *m.*, *only in abl.*, by the command.

iustus, -a, -um, just, proper, regular.

iuvo, -are, iuvi, iutum (1), help, aid, assist.

Labienus, -i, *m.*, Titus Labienus (*Roman general*).

labor, -oris, *m.*, toil.

laboro (1), am in difficulties *or* hard pressed.

labrum, -i, *n.*, lip, edge.

lacesso, -ere, -ivi (-ii), -itum (3), provoke, harass.

lacrimo (1), weep.

laetitia, -ae, *f.*, joy, rejoicing.

languide, *adv.*, feebly, listlessly.

lapis, -idis, *m.*, stone.

laqueus, -i, *m.*, noose.

late, *adv.*, widely.

latro, -onis, *m.*, bandit.

latus, -eris, *n.*, side, flank.

latus, -a, -um, broad, wide.

laus, laudis, *f.*, praise, honour, renown.

legatio, -onis, *f.*, embassy, deputation.

legatus, -i, *m.*, (i) envoy ; (ii) general.

legio, -onis, *f.*, legion.

legionarius, -a, -um, legionary.

Lemovices, -um, *m. pl.*, the Lemovices (*Gallic tribe*).

lenis, -e, gentle.

leniter, *adv.*, gently.

levis, -e, light, slight.

levitas, -atis, *f.*, fickleness.

lex, legis, *f.*, a law.

Lexovii, -orum, *m. pl.*, the Lexovii (*Gallic tribe*).

liber, -era, -erum, free ; unrestricted (ch. 36).

libere, *adv.*, freely.

liberi, -orum, *m. pl.*, children.

libertas, -atis, *f.*, freedom.

librilis, -e, weighing a pound.

licentia, -ae, *f.*, licence.

licet (2), *impers.*, it is allowed.

Liger, -eris, *m.*, Liger (*river Loire*).

lilium, -i, *n.*, lily (*military technical term*).

linea, -ae, *f.*, line.

Lingones, -um, *m. pl.*, the Lingones (*a Gallic tribe*).

linter, -tris, *m.*, boat.

Litaviccus, -i, *m.*, Litaviccus (*Aeduan chieftain*).

littera, -ae, *f.*, letter (*of alphabet*) ; *in pl.*, letter, dispatch.

locus, -i, *m.*, *pl.*, loci *or* loca ; place, post, position ; ground ; room (ch. 37).

longe, *adv.*, far, by far ; **longius,** farther, longer ; **longissime,** farthest.

longinquus, -a, -um, far distant.

longitudo, -inis, *f.*, length.

longurius, -i, *m.*, long pole.

longus, -a, -um, long.

lorica, -ae, *f.*, (breastplate) ; breastwork.

Lucius, -i, *m.*, Lucius (*Roman praenomen*).

Lucterius, -i, *m.,* Lucterius (*chieftain of the Cadurci*).

Lutetia, -ae, *f.,* Lutetia.

lux, lucis, *f.,* light ; **prima luce,** at dawn.

maceria, -ae, *f.,* rough wall.

maestus, -a, -um, sad, melancholy.

magis, *adv.,* more.

magistratus, -us, *m.,* magistrate, magistracy.

magnitudo, -inis, *f.,* greatness; severity (ch. **4**).

magnopere, *adv.,* greatly ; *comparat.,* **magis,** *superlat.,* **maxime.**

magnus, -a, -um, big, great ; *comparat.,* **maior** ; *superlat.,* **maximus.**

maiestas, -atis, *f.,* greatness, dignity.

maiores, -um, *m. pl.,* ancestors.

malo, malle, malui, prefer.

malus, -i, *m.,* beam, scaffolding.

mandatum, -i, *n.,* order, command, charge ; instruction (ch. **71**).

mando (1), entrust, enjoin upon ; **se fugae mandare,** to turn to flight.

Mandubii, -orum, *m. pl.,* the Mandubii (*Gallic tribe*).

mane, *adv.,* in the morning.

maneo, -ere, mansi, mansum (2), remain.

manipularis, -is, *m.,* a member of a maniple *or* company.

manus, -us, *f.,* band (*of soldiers*) ; force.

Marcus, -i, *m.,* Marcus (*Roman praenomen*).

Mars, -rtis, *m.,* Mars (*Roman god of war*).

materfamilias, matrisfamiliae, *f.,* matron.

materia, -ae, (**ēs, -eī**), *f.,* timber.

materior (1 *dep.*), fetch *or* collect timber.

Matisco, -onis, *f.,* Matisco (*stronghold of the Aedui*).

mature, *adv.,* early; **maturius** (ch. **10**), too early.

maturo (1), hasten.

mediocris, -e, slight, fair, moderate.

Mediomatrici, -orum, *m. pl.,* the Mediomatrici (*Gallic tribe*).

medius, -a, -um, middle, mid, midst of.

memini, -isse, *defect. verb,* remember.

memoria, -ae, *f.*, memory.

mendacium, -i, *n.*, lie.

mens, -ntis, *f.*, mind.

mereo (2), earn, deserve ; serve (*as a soldier* (ch. 17)).

mereor (2 *dep.*), earn, deserve.

meridies, -ei, *f.*, midday, noon.

meritum, -i, *n.*, good deed, service.

-met, *emphasising suffix with personal pronouns.*

metior (4 *dep.*), measure out.

Metiosedum, -i, *n.*, Metiosedum (*town of the Senones*).

metus, -us, *m.*, fear.

meus, -a, -um, my, mine.

miles, -itis, *m.*, soldier.

militaris, -e, military, of soldiers ; **res militaris,** the art of war, warfare.

militia, -ae, *f.*, military service, warfare.

mille, a thousand ; *n. pl.*, **milia, -ium,** thousands.

minime, *adv.*, least.

minor, -us, smaller, less.

Minucius, -i, *m.*, Lucius Minucius Basilus (*Roman general*).

minuo, -ere, -ui, -utum (3), lessen, diminish.

minus, *adv.*, less.

miror (1 *dep.*,) wonder (*at*).

misericordia, -ae, *f.*, pity, compassion.

miseror (1 *dep.*), pity.

mite, *adv.*, gently.

mitto, -ere, misi, missum (3), send ; throw (*of missiles*).

moderor (1 *dep.*), manage, control.

modestia, -ae, *f.*, orderly conduct, good discipline (ch. 52).

modo, *adv.*, only, lately ; merely (ch. 66).

modus, -i, *m.*, way, manner ; kind.

moenia, -ium, *n. pl.*, walls.

mollio (4), soften ; loosen, break.

mollitia, -ae, *f.*, softness, irresolution.

momentum, -i, *n.*, weight, importance.

moneo (2), advise, warn.

mons, -ntis, *m.*, mountain, hill.

Morini, -orum, *m. pl.*, the Morini (*Gallic tribe*).

moror (1 *dep.*), stop, halt, delay.

mors, -rtis, *f.*, death.

mos, moris, *m.*, manner, habit, custom.

motus, -us, *m.*, disturbance ; rising (chs. **43, 59**).

moveo, -ere, movi, motum (2), move, influence ; strike (*camp*).

mulier, -eris, *f.*, woman.

mulio, -onis, *f.*, muleteer.

multitudo, -inis, *f.*, great number ; host.

multo (1), deprive (*of*), (*with abl.*).

multum, *adv.*, much, greatly.

multus, -a, -um, much ; *in pl.*, many.

mulus, -i, *m.*, mule.

munio (4), fortify, protect.

munitio, -onis, *f.*, defence works, lines (ch. **74**).

munus, -eris, *n.*, function, office, duty ; service.

muralis, -e, thrown from walls.

murus, -i, *m.*, wall.

musculus, -i, *m.*, pent-house, shed.

muto (1), change.

nam, *conj.*, for.

namque, *i.e.* **nam.**

nanciscor, -i, nactus *or* **nanctus** (3 *dep.*), get, gain ; find.

Narbo, -onis, *m.*, Narbo (*Narbonne*).

nascor, -i, natus (3 *dep.*), am born.

natio, -onis, *f.*, nation.

natura, -ae, *f.*, nature.

navis, -is, *f.*, ship.

ne, *enclitic, to denote a question.*

ne, *conj.*, in order that . . . not, lest.

ne . . . quidem, not even.

nec, neque, *conj.*, neither, nor.

necessario, *adv.*, of necessity.

necessarius, -a, -um, necessary, critical ; **res necessariae,** necessaries, (ch. **66**).

necesse, *indeclin.*, necessary.

necessitas, -atis, *f.*, need ; necessity.

neco (1), kill, slay.

necubi, *adv.*, lest anywhere.

nefarius, -a, -um, criminal, wicked.

nefas, *indecl. n.*, sin, crime.

neglego, -ere, -lexi, -lectum (3), neglect, disregard.

negotior (1 *dep.*), do business *or* trade.

negotium, -i, *n.*, business ; operation (ch. 62).

nemo, -inem, *m. or f.*, no-one.

nequaquam, *adv.*, by no means.

neque, *see* nec.

Nervii, -orum, *m. pl.*, the Nervii (*Gallic tribe*).

neu, *conj.*, and not, neither, nor.

neuter, -tra, -trum, neither (*of two*) ; *in pl.*, neither side.

neve, *see* neu.

nihil, *indecl.*, nothing.

nihilominus, *adv.*, nevertheless.

nimis, *adv.*, too much, excessively.

nimius, -a, -um, too great, excessive.

nisi, *conj.*, unless, except.

Nitiobriges, -um, *m. pl.*, Nitiobriges (*Gallic tribe*).

nitor, -i, nisus *or* nixus (3 *dep.*), strive, exert myself.

nix, nivis, *f.*, snow.

nobilis, -e, noble.

nobilitas, -atis, *f.*, nobility.

noctu, *adv.*, by *or* at night.

nocturnus, -a, -um, in *or* of the night, by night.

nolo, nolle, nolui, am unwilling, not wish.

nomen, -inis, *n.*, name.

nominatim, *adv.*, by name.

nomino (1), name, nominate.

non, *adv.*, not.

nondum, *adv.*, not yet.

non nullus, -a, -um, some.

non numquam, *adv.*, sometimes.

nos, nostrum, we.

nosco, -ere, novi, notum (3), learn ; *in perfect*, I know.

nosmet, *emphatic form of* nos.

noster, -tra, -trum, our ; nostri, our men, troops.

notus, -a, -um, known.

Noviodunum, -i, *n.,* Noviodunum, (i) *a town of the Aedui.* (ii) *a town of the Bituriges.*

novitas, -atis, *f.,* newness ; suddenness (ch. 58).

novus, -a, -um, new ; **novissimum,** newest, last, rear ; **novissimum agmen,** the rearguard.

nox, noctis, *f.,* night.

nudatus, -a, -um, naked.

nudo (1), strip ; leave bare (*of defenders*).

nudus, -a, -um bare, naked.

nullus, -a, -um. none, no.

numerus, -i, *m.,* number, quantity.

numquam, *adv.,* never.

nuntio (1), announce, tell.

nuntius, -i, *m.,* message ; messenger.

nuper, *adv.,* lately.

nusquam, *adv.,* nowhere.

ob, *prep with acc.,* on account of.

obicio, -ere, -ieci, -iectum, throw in the way of.

obliquus, -a, -um, sloping, slanting.

obliviscor, -i, oblitus (3 *dep.*), forget (*with gen.*).

obsecro (1), implore, beseech.

obsequentia, -ae, *f.,* subservience, deference.

observo (1), watch, observe.

obses, -idis, *c.,* hostage.

obsessio, -onis, *f.,* blockade.

obsideo, -ere, -sedi, -sessum (2), besiege, blockade.

obsidio, -onis, *f.,* siege, blockade.

obsisto, -ere, -stiti, -stitum (3), resist (*with dat.*).

obstruo, -ere, -struxi, -structum (3), block up, barricade.

obtempero (1), obey (*with dat.*).

obtestor (1 *dep.*), entreat, adjure.

obtineo, -ere, -tinui, -tentum (2), hold, retain (ch. 33) ; win (chs. 37, 66).

obvenio, -ire, -veni, -ventum (4), am assigned to (chs. 28, 81).

obviam, *adv.,* in the way ; **obviam ire** *or* **venire,** to go *or* come to meet (*with dat.*). Similarly, **obviam proficisci** (ch. 12).

occasio, -onis, *f.*, opportunity.

occasus, -us, *m.*, setting.

occido, -ere, -cidi, -cisum (3), kill.

occulte, *adv.*, secretly.

occulto (1), hide, conceal.

occultus, -a, -um, hidden, secret; **in occulto** (ch. 27), in secret, in hiding.

occupatus, -a, -um, occupied in, busy.

occupo (1), occupy, seize.

occurro, -ere, -curri, -cursum (3), *with dat.*, meet (ch. 88); counteract, match (ch. 22).

Oceanus, -i, *m.*, the Ocean (*Atlantic*).

octavus, -a, -um, eighth.

octingenti, -ae, -a, eight hundred.

octo, eight.

octoginta, eighty.

octoni, -ae, -a, eight each.

oculus, -i, *m.*, eye.

offero, -ferre, obtuli, oblatum, offer; put in his way (ch. 87).

Ollovico, -onis, *m.*, Ollovico (*father of Teutomatus*).

omitto, -ere, -misi, -missum (3), leave alone; throw away, discard (ch. 88).

omnino, *adv.*, at all, in all, altogether.

omnis, -e, all, every.

opera, -ae, *f.*, trouble, services (ch. 76), agency.

opinio, -onis, *f.*, opinion; reputation (chs. 59, 83); expectation (ch. 56).

oportet (2), *imperson.*, it is proper, it behoves: ought.

oppidanus, -i, *m.*, townsman; *as adj.*, of a town.

oppidum, -i, *n.*, town, stronghold.

oppono, -ere, -posui, -positum (3), put in the way; oppose.

opportunitas, -atis, *f.*, opportunity.

opportunus, -a, -um, suitable, convenient.

opprimo, -ere, -pressi, -pressum (3), overwhelm; surprise (ch. 46).

oppugnatio, -onis, *f.*, attack, assault; operations (ch. 29).

oppugno (1), attack.

(ops), opis, *f.*, *no nom. or dat. sing.*, aid, help ; *in pl.*, resources ;
  summis opibus, with their utmost efforts.

optime, *adv.*, very well, best.

optimus, *superlat. of* bonus.

opus, operis, *n.*, fortification *or* siege works.

opus, *indecl. n.*, needful, necessary.

oratio, -onis, *f.*, speech.

orbis, -is, *m.*, circle ; orbis terrarum, the whole world.

ordo, -inis, *m.*, row, rank.

orior, -iri, ortus (4 *dep.*), rise, spring from ; oriente sole, at
  sunrise.

ornamentum, -i, *n.*, ornament, honour.

orno (1), adorn, honour.

oro (1), ask, beseech.

ortus, -us, *m.*, rising.

Osismi, -orum, *m. pl.*, the Osismi (*Gallic tribe*).

ostendo, -ere, -di, -tum (3), show ; se ostendere (chs. **67, 83**),
  to make a demonstration.

ostentatio, -onis, *f.*, show, display.

ostento (1), show, parade.

otium, -i, *n.*, quiet.

pabulatio, -onis, *f.*, foraging.

pabulor (1 *dep.*), forage.

pabulum, -i, *n.*, forage.

paco (1), subdue.

pactum, -i, *n.*, method, fashion.

paene, *adv.*, almost.

pagus, -i, *m.*, canton.

palus, -udis, *f.*, marsh.

palustris, -e, marshy.

pando, -ere, -ndi, -ssum (3), open out ; passus, dishevelled.

par, paris, equal, like.

parce, *adv.*, sparingly.

parco, -ere, peperci, parsum (3), spare (*with dat.*).

parens, -ntis, *c.*, parent.

parento (1), avenge.

pareo (2), *with dat.*, obey.

Parisii, -orum, *m. pl.,* the Parisii (*Gallic tribe*).

paro (1), make ready, prepare.

pars, partis, *f.,* part ; a half ; side ; **pars ... pars,** some ... others ; **altera ex parte,** on the other side.

partior (4 *dep.*), divide.

parum, *adv.,* too little, insufficiently.

parvus, -a, -um, small, little.

passus, -us, *m.,* pace ; **mille passus,** a mile.

patefio, -fieri, -factus, am opened up.

patens, -ntis, open.

pateo (2), extend, stretch.

pater, -tris, *m.,* father.

patienter, *adv.,* patiently.

patior, -i, passus, *dep.,* suffer, allow.

patronus, -i, *m.,* patron.

patruus, -i, *m.,* uncle.

pauci, -ae, -a, few.

paucitas, -atis, *f.,* fewness, small numbers.

paulatim, *adv.,* little by little, gradually.

paulisper, *adv.,* for a little while.

paulum, paulo, *adv.,* a little.

pax, pacis, *f.,* peace.

pectus, -oris, *n.,* breast.

pecunia, -ae, *f.,* money ; **pecunia publica** (ch. 55), treasury.

pecus, -oris, *n.,* cattle.

pedes, -itis, *m.,* foot-soldier ; *in pl.,* infantry.

pedestris, -e, on foot : of infantry.

peditatus, -us, *m.,* infantry.

pello, -ere, pepuli, pulsum (3), drive away, rout.

penes, *prep. with acc.,* in power of ; with (ch. 21).

per, *prep. with acc.,* through, by means of.

perangustus, -a, -um, very narrow.

percipio, -ere, -cepi, -ceptum, take possession of ; seize ; perceive.

perditus, -a, -um, ruined, outcast.

perdo, -ere, -didi, -ditum (3), destroy.

perduco, -ere, -duxi, -ductum (3), lead, bring; construct (chs. 36, 72) ; bring over to (ch. 4) ; advance (ch. 39).

perequito (1), ride through.

perfacilis, -e, very easy.

perfero, -ferre, -tuli, -latum, convey ; report (chs. **1, 3**) ; endure.

perficio, -ere, -feci, -fectum, accomplish, finish.

perfidia, -ae, *f.,* treachery.

perfringo, -ere, -fregi, -fractum (3), break through.

perfuga, -ae, *m.,* deserter.

periclitor (1 *dep.*), run risk.

periculosus, -a, -um, dangerous.

periculum, -i, *n.,* danger, risk.

peritus, -a, -um, skilled.

permagnus, -a, -um, very great.

permaneo, -ere, -mansi, -mansum (2), remain, stay.

permisceo, -ere, -miscui, -mixtum (2), mix *or* mingle.

permitto, -ere, -misi, -missum (3), leave to, entrust to.

permoveo, -ere, -movi, -motum (2), influence deeply ; dismay (ch. **53**).

perpauci, -ae, -a, very few.

perpetior, -i, -pessus (*dep.*), suffer, endure.

perpetuo, *adv.,* constantly, perpetually.

perpetuus, -a, -um, unbroken ; everlasting (ch. **77**).

perrumpo, -ere, -rupi, -ruptum (3), break *or* burst through.

persequor, -i, -secutus (3 *dep.*), follow up ; avenge (ch. **38**).

perspicio, -ere, -spexi, -spectum, note, detect ; inspect (chs. **44, 68**) ; reconnoitre (ch. **36**).

persto, -are, -stiti, -statum (3), stand firm ; persist.

persuadeo, -ere, -si, -sum (2), persuade (*with dat.*).

perterreo (2), frighten, scare, alarm.

pertineo, -ere, -tinui, -tentum (2), belong to : concern (ch. **43**).

perturbo (1), confuse, disturb.

pervagor (1 *dep.*), roam, range.

pervenio, -ire, -veni, -ventum (4), come to, arrive, reach.

pes, pedis, *m.,* foot.

peto, -ere, -ivi (-ii), -itum (3), make for, seek, ask.

Petrocorii, -orum, *m. pl.,* the Petrocorii (*Gallic tribe*).

Petronius, -i, *m.,* Marcus Petronius (*Roman centurion*).

Pictones, -um, *m. pl.,* the Pictones (*Gallic tribe*).

pilum, -i, *n.,* javelin.

pinna, -ae, *f.,* pinnacle, parapet.

pix, picis, *f.,* pitch.

placeo (2), am pleasing to ; please ; **placet,** it is resolved.

planities, -ei, *f.,* plain, level ground.

plebs, plebis, *f.,* the people.

plenus, -a, -um, full.

plerique, -raeque, -raque, most.

plerumque, *adv.,* generally, for the most part.

plus, pluris, more ; *in pl.,* **plures, plura,** more, several.

pluteus, -i, *m.,* breastwork *or* screen.

poena, -ae, *f.,* penalty, punishment : **capitis poena,** the penalty of death.

polliceor (2), promise.

Pompeius, -i, *m.,* Gnaeus Pompeius.

pondus, -eris, *n.,* weight.

pono, -ere, posui, positum (3), put, place ; pitch (*of camp*) ; *in pass.,* am placed, rest, depend.

pons, pontis, *m.,* bridge.

populus, -i, *m.,* people.

porta, -ae, *f.,* gate.

posco, -ere, poposci, demand.

possum, posse, potui, am able, can.

post, *adv., and prep. with acc.,* after, behind ; afterwards.

postea, *adv.,* aferwards.

posteaquam, after, when.

posterus, -a, -um, next, following ; **posteri, -orum,** *m. pl.,* posterity.

postquam, *conj.,* after, when.

postremo, *adv.,* lastly.

postulo (1), demand.

potens, -ntis, powerful, influential.

potentia, -ae, *f.,* power, influence.

potestas, -atis, *f.,* authority, power, office.

potior (4 *dep.*), *with abl.,* gain possession of ; take.

potius, *adv.,* rather.

prae, *prep. with abl.,* before ; for (ch. **44**).

praeacutus, -a, -um, sharpened to a point.

praebeo (2), offer, afford.

praecipio, -ere, -cepi, -ceptum, take beforehand ; instruct.

praecipito (1), hurl, throw headlong.

praecipue, *adv.,* especially.

praecurro, -ere, -curri, -cursum (3), run before, anticipate.

praeda, -ae, *f.,* booty, plunder.

praedor (1 *dep.*), loot, plunder.

praeduco, -ere, -duxi, -ductum (3), mark out (ch. **46**) ; make in front (ch. **69**).

praefectus, -i, *m.,* commander (*especially of cavalry*).

praeficio, -ere, -feci, -fectum, put in command.

praemetuo, -ere (3), am anxious for (*with dat.*).

praemitto, -ere, -misi, -missum (3), send on ahead.

praemium, -i, *n.,* reward, prize ; bribe (ch. **37**).

praeoccupo (1), seize beforehand.

praeparo (1), prepare *or* get ready beforehand.

praeruptus, -a, -um, broken off, steep.

praesens, -ntis, present.

praesentia, -ae, *f.,* present ; **in praesentia,** for the present.

praesentio, -ire, -sensi, -sensum (4), perceive beforehand.

praesepio, -ire, -sepsi, -septum (4), block up beforehand.

praesertim, *adv.,* especially.

praesidium, -i, *n.,* protection, defence ; guard, garrison ; escort (ch. **1**) ; garrisoned place (ch. **8**).

praesto, -are, -stiti, -statum (1), *impersonally,* it is better.

praesum, -esse, -fui, am at head *or* in charge of (*with dat.*).

praeter, *prep. with acc.,* beyond.

praeterea, *adv.,* besides.

praetereo, -ire, -ivi (-ii), -itum, pass by *or* over ; *in pass.,* pass (ch. **77**).

praetermitto, -ere, -misi, -missum (3), omit, let slip ; pass by.

praeterquam, *adv.,* except.

praeustus, -a, -um, burnt at the end *or* to a point.

praeverto, -ere, -ti, -sum (3), forestall ; attend to first (ch. **33**).

pravus, -a, -um, mischievous, unprincipled.

premo, -ere, pressi, pressum (3), press, oppress, overwhelm.

(prex), **prece**, *f.*, *only in pl. and abl. sing.*, prayer, entreaty.

primo, *adv.*, at first.

primum, *adv.*, first ; **ubi primum**, as soon as ; **quam primum**, as soon as possible.

primus, **-a**, **-um**, first.

princeps, **-ipis**, *m.*, chieftain ; leading man ; magistrate (ch. 65).

principatus, **-us**, *m.*, chieftainship.

prior, **-us**, former, previous.

pristinus, **-a**, **-um**, former.

prius, *adv.*, before.

priusquam, *conj.*, before.

pro, *prep. with abl.*, for, on behalf of ; in front of.

probo (1), approve.

procedo, **-ere**, **-cessi**, **-cessum** (3), advance.

proclino (1), bend forwards.

procul, *adv.*, at a distance, far off.

procumbo, **-ere**, **-cubui**, **-cubitum** (3), fall forwards.

procurro, **-ere**, **-(cu)curri**, **-cursum** (3), run *or* rush forwards.

proditio, **-onis**, *f.*, treachery, treason.

prodo, **-ere**, **-didi**, **-ditum** (3), hand over, betray.

produco, **-ere**, **-xi**, **-ctum** (3), lead *or* bring forward.

proelior (1 *dep.*), fight.

proelium, **-i**, *n.*, battle, engagement.

profectio, **-onis**, *f.*, setting out, departure.

profero, **-ferre**, **-tuli**, **-latum**, bring forward ; display (ch. 48).

proficio, **-ere**, **-feci**, **-fectum**, progress.

proficiscor, **-i**, **-fectus** (3 *dep.*), set out, leave, depart.

profiteor, **-eri**, **-fessus** (2 *dep.*), profess, acknowledge.

profligo (1), put to flight, rout.

profugio, **-ere**, **-fugi**, escape *or* fly from.

progedior, **-i**, **-gressus**, (*dep.*), advance.

prohibeo (2), prevent ; cut off from.

proicio, **-ere**, **-ieci**, **-iectum**, hurl, throw, fling.

proinde, *adv.*, accordingly, therefore.

promineo (2), hang over ; stand out.

promoveo, **-ere**, **-movi**, **-motum** (2), move *or* push forward.

pronuntio (1), announce, declare.

prope, *adv., and prep. with acc.,* near, almost.

propius, *comparat. adv.,* nearer, too near.

propello, -ere, -puli, -pulsum (3), drive forward, dislodge.

propinquitas, -atis, *f.,* nearness.

propinquus, -a, -um, near ; *as noun,* relative.

propono, -ere, -posui, -positum (3), set forth, state.

propositus, -a, -um, handy for, accessible.

propter, *prep. with acc.,* on account of.

propterea, *adv.,* on that account.

propugnans, -ntis, *m.,* defender.

propugnator, -oris, *m.,* defender.

prospectus, -us, *m.,* vision, sight.

prospicio, -ere, -spexi, -spectum, provide for.

prosterno, -ere, -stravi, -stratum (3), lay low.

proterreo (2), scare, frighten away.

protinus, *adv.,.* at once, immediately.

proturbo (1), harass ; dislodge (ch. **81**).

proventus, -us, *m.,* issue, result.

provideo, -ere, -vidi, -visum (2), foresee, provide.

provincia, -ae, *f.,* a province ; *often* = **Gallia Narbonensis.**

provincialis, -e, of a province ; *as noun,* inhabitant of Gallia Narbonensis.

proximus, -a, -um, next, nearest ; last (ch. **67**).

publice, *adv.,* by public *or* state authority.

publico (1), confiscate.

publicus, -a, -um, public ; **res publica,** the state ; **in publicum,** into the open.

Publius, -i, *m.,* Publius (*a Roman praenomen*).

pudet (2) *impersonal,* is ashamed.

pugna, -ae, *f.,* battle.

pugno (1), fight.

pulcher, -chra, -chrum, beautiful, fair ; glorious.

purgo (1), clear, excuse.

puto (1), think.

qua, *adv.,* where, by which way.

quadrageni, -ae, -a, forty each.

quadraginta, forty.

quadringenti, -ae, -a, four hundred.

quaero, -ere, quaesivi, quaesitum (3), seek.

quaestio, -onis, *f.*, investigation.

quam, *adv.*, than ; *with superl.*, as . . . as possible.

quantum, *adv.*, as much as, as far as.

quantus, -a, -um, how great ; as great as.

quare, *adv.*, why, wherefore.

quartus, -a, -um, fourth.

quasi, *adv.*, as if.

quattuor, four.

quattuordecim, fourteen.

-que, *enclitic conj.*, and.

quem ad modum, how, in what manner.

queror, -i, questus (3 *dep.*), complain.

qui, quae, quod, *relat. pron.*, who, which, what, that.

qui, quae, quod, *interrog., adj.*, which? what?

quicunque, quae-, quod-, whosoever, whatever.

quid, *adv.*, how, why.

quidam, quae-, quod-, a certain one *or* thing.

quidem, *adv.*, indeed ; **ne . . . quidem,** not even.

quies, -etis, *f.*, rest.

quietus, -a, -um, quiet.

quin, *conj.*, but that ; *with* etiam *and indic.*, moreover.

quincunx, -cuncis, a group of five.

quindecim, fifteen.

quingenti, -ae, -a, five hundred.

quini, -ae, -a, five each.

quinquaginta, fifty.

quinque, five.

quintus, -a, -um, fifth.

Quintus -i, *m.*, Quintus (*Roman praenomen*).

quis, quid, *interrog. pronoun*, who? what?

quis, quid, *indefinite pronoun*, anyone, anything.

qui, quae, quod, *indefinite adj.*, any.

quisquam, quae-, quid-, any one, anything.

quisque, quae-, quid-, each.

quisquis, quidquid, whoever, whatever.

quo, *adv.*, whither.

quod, *conj.*, because ; **quod si**, but if.

quominus, *conj.*, but that ; that not.

quoniam, *conj.*, since.

quoque, *adv.*, also.

quoque versus, *adv.*, in every direction.

quot, *indeclin.*, how many.

radix, -icis, *f.*, root ; foot (*of mountain*).

ramus, -i, *m.*, bough.

rarus, -a, -um, in small bodies, here and there.

ratio, -onis, *f.*, plan, calculation ; manner, way.

Raurici, -orum, *m. pl.*, the Raurici (*Gallic tribe*).

Rebilus, *see* Caninius.

recens, -ntis, fresh ; ready for action (ch. 9).

recenseo (2), review.

receptaculum, -i, *n.*, refuge.

receptus, -us, *m.*, retreat.

recido, -ere, -cidi, -casum (3), fall *or* come upon.

recipio, -ere, -cepi, -ceptum, get back, receive ; admit (ch. 26) ; receive submission of (ch. 90) ; **se recipere**, retreat; retire, get back (ch. 88).

recipero (1), recover, regain.

recte, *adv.*, rightly, properly.

rectus, -a, -um, right, straight.

recuso (1), refuse.

reddo, -ere, -didi, -ditum (3), give back, restore.

redeo, -ire, -ii, -itum, return.

redigo, -ere, -egi, -actum (3), reduce.

redintegro (1), renew.

Redones, -um, *m. pl.*, the Redones (*Gallic tribe*).

reduco, -ere, -duxi, -ductum (3); lead back ; drag back (ch. 22) ; set back (ch. 72).

refero, -ferre, rettuli, relatum, bring back.

reficio, -ere, -feci, -fectum, repair, refresh ; **se reficere**, to rest (ch 83).

refringo, -ere, -fregi, -fractum (3), break open.

refugio, -ere, -fugi, escape.

Reginus, *see* Antistius.

regio, -onis, *f.*, district, direction; e regione, opposite (*with gen., but with dat.*, ch. 35).

regius, -a, -um, royal.

regnum, -i, *n.*, kingship (ch. 4); royal power.

relinquo, -ere, -liqui, -lictum (3), leave behind, leave.

reliquus, -a, -um, remaining, rest.

remaneo, -ere, -mansi, -mansum (2), remain.

Remi, -orum, *m. pl.*, the Remi (*Gallic tribe*).

remitto, -ere, -misi, -missum (3), send back.

remotus, -a, -um, remote.

removeo, -ere, -movi, -motum (2), remove.

remus, -i, *m.*, oar.

renuntio (1), bring back word; report back; declare elected (ch. 33).

repello, -ere, reppuli, repulsum (3), drive back; repulse.

repente, *adv.*, suddenly.

repentinus, -a, -um, sudden, unexpected.

reperio, -ire, repperi, repertum (4), find.

repleo, -ere, -plevi, -pletum (2), fill up; supply (ch. 56).

reprehendo, -ere, -di, -sum (3), blame, rebuke.

reprimo, -ere, -pressi, -pressum (3), check, suppress.

repugno (1), resist.

requiro, -ere, -quisivi, -quisitum (3), look in vain for; express regret for; say that they miss (ch. 63).

res, rei, *f.*, thing, action.

rescindo, -ere, -scidi, -scissum (3), break down.

reservo (1), keep back, keep.

resido, -ere, -sedi (3), settle down (ch. 64); remain (ch. 77).

resisto, -ere, -stiti (3), halt; *with dat.*, resist.

respicio, -ere, -spexi, -spectum, look to, regard.

respondeo, -ere, -di, -sum (2), answer.

restinguo, -ere, -nxi, -nctum (3), extinguish, put out.

restituo, -ere, -ui, -utum (3), restore.

retineo, -ere, -ui, -tentum (2), hold back, retain.

revello, -ere, -velli, -vulsum (3), tear up.

revertor, -i, -versus (3 *dep.*), return; *perfect in active form*, reverti (ch. 5).

revincio, -ire, -nxi, -nctum (4), tie, fasten.

revoco (1), call back ; withdraw.

rex, regis, *m.*, king.

Rhenus, -i, *m.*, the Rhine.

Rhodanus, -i, *m.*, the Rhone.

ripa, -ae, *f.*, bank.

rogo (1), ask.

Roma, -ae, *f.*, Rome.

Romanus, -a, -um, Roman ; *as noun*, a Roman.

rumor, -oris, *m.*, rumour, report.

rursus, *adv.*, again.

Ruteni, -orum, *m. pl.*, the Ruteni (*Gallic tribe*).

Rutilus, -i, *m.*, Marcus Sempronius Rutilus (*Roman general*).

sacerdos, -otis, *c.*, priest.

saepenumero, *adv.*, often, many times.

sagitta, -ae, *f.*, arrow.

sagittarius, -i, *m.*, archer, bowman.

saltus, -us, *m.*, wooded approach.

salus, -utis, *f.*, safety.

sancio, -ire, sanxi, sanctum (4), confirm, sanction.

sanctus, -a, -um, binding (*of an oath*) ; sacred.

sanguis, -is, *m.*, blood.

sanitas, -atis, *f.*, good sense.

sano (1), remedy.

Santoni, -orum, *m. pl.*, the Santoni (*Gallic tribe*).

sarcina, -ae, *f.*, (*soldier's*) pack.

satis, *adv.*, enough, sufficiently.

satisfacio, -ere, -feci, -factum, satisfy (*often with dat.*).

saxum, -i, *n.*, large stone, rock.

scala, -ae, *f.*, ladder.

scienter, *adv.*, skilfully, scientifically ; *comparat.*, scientius.

scientia, -ae, *f.*, skill, knowledge.

scorpio, -onis, *m.*, scorpio (*piece of artillery*).

scrobis, -is, *m.*, ditch.

se, sui, *reflex. pronoun*, himself, herself, themselves.

sebum, -i, *n.*, fat.

seco, -are, secui, sectum (1), cut.

secum, with him *or* her *or* themselves.

secundum, *prep. with acc.*, along; according to, with.

secundus, -a, -um, second; favourable; successful (ch. **59**).

securis, -is, *f.*, axe.

sed, *conj.*, but.

sedecim, sixteen.

seditio, -onis, *f.*, mutiny, sedition.

Sedulius, -i, *m.*, Sedulius (*chieftain of the Lemovices*).

Segusiavi, -orum, *m. pl.*, the Segusiavi (*Gallic tribe*).

semita, -ae, *f.*, path.

semper, *adv.*, always.

Sempronius, *see* Rutilus.

senatus, -us, *m.*, the senate.

Senones, -um, *m. pl.*, the Senones (*Gallic tribe*).

seni, -ae, -a, six each.

sententia, -ae *f,*. opinion, resolution.

sentio, -ire, sensi, sensum (4), feel.

separatim, *adv.*, separately.

separo (1), separate.

septentrio, -onis, *m.*, *in pl.*, the North.

septimus, -a, -um, seventh.

septingenti, -ae, -a, seven hundred.

septuaginta, seventy.

Sequana, -ae, *f.*, the Seine.

Sequani, -orum, *m. pl.*, the Sequani (*Gallic tribe*).

sequor, -i, secutus (3 *dep.*), follow, pursue.

servio (4), am devoted to (*with dat.*).

servitus, -utis, *f.*, slavery.

servo (1), keep, save.

servus, -i, *m.*, slave.

sescenti, -ae, -a, six hundred.

sese, *see* se.

seu, *or* sive, *conj.*, whether, or.

severitas, -atis, *f.*, severity, strictness.

sex, six.

sexaginta, sixty.

sexcenti, *see* sescenti.

Sextius, -i, *m.*, Titus Sextius (*Roman general*).

si, *conj.*, if.

sic, *adv.*, so, thus ; in such a way.

sicut, *adv.*, just as.

significatio, -onis, *f.*, behaviour (ch. 12) ; intimation (ch. 81).

significo (1), make known.

signum, -i, *n.*, sign, signal ; standard.

silentium, -i, *n.*, silence.

silva, -ae, *f.*, wood, forest.

silvestris, -e, wooded ; in the forest.

similis, -e, like ; similis atque, like as, the same as.

similitudo, -inis, *f.*, likeness.

simul, *adv.*, at the same time ; simul atque, as soon as.

simulatio, -onis, *f.*, pretence.

sincere, *adv.*, sincerely, truthfully.

sine, *prep. with abl.*, without.

singularis, -e, single (ch. 8) ; matchless (ch. 22) ; outstanding (ch. 57) ; exceptional (ch. 77).

singuli, -ae, -a, one each, each ; one at a time.

sinister, -tra, -trum, left, on the left.

situs, -us, *m.*, site, situation.

sive, *see* seu.

sol, solis, *m.*, sun.

solatium, -i, *n.*, solace, comfort.

soleo, -ere, solitus (2 *semi-dep.*), am wont *or* accustomed.

sollertia, -ae, *f.*, skill, cleverness.

sollicito (1), bribe (ch. 37) ; arouse (chs. 54, 63) ; try to win over (ch. 64).

sollicitudo, -inis, *f.*, anxiety.

solum, -i, *n.*, ground.

solum, *adv.*, only.

solus, -a, -um, alone.

sonitus, -us, *m.*, sound, noise.

sonus, -i, *m.*, sound.

spatium, -i, *n.*, distance, interval.

species, -ei, *f.*, appearance.

specto (1), look (at), face.

spero (1), hope.

spes, -ei, *f.*, hope.

spolio (1), rob ; strip.

sponte, *f., only in abl.,* of one's own accord *or* will.

stabilio (4), make firm *or* secure.

statim, *adv.,* immediately.

statio, -onis, *f.,* sentry, picket (ch. **69**).

statuo, -ere, -ui, -utum (3), settle, arrange ; determine.

status, -us, *m.,* state, condition.

stimulus, -i, *m.,* (goad) ; pointed stake (chs. **73, 82**).

stipendiarius, -a, -um, tributary ; *as noun,* a tributary.

stipendium, -i, *n.,* tribute.

stipes, -itis, *m.,* stake.

stramentum, -i, *n.,* pack-saddle.

studeo (2), attend to (*often with dat.*) ; am eager for (ch. **20**).

studium, -i, *n.,* zeal, enthusiasm.

stultitia, -ae, *f.,* folly.

sub, *prep. with acc.,* close to ; **sub lucem,** just before dawn ; **sub vesperum,** towards evening ; *with abl.,* under, beneath.

subdolus, -a, -um, deceitful ; subtle.

subeo, -ire, -ii, -itum, advance ; submit to (ch. **78**).

subicio, -ere, -ieci, -iectum, subject.

subigo, -ere, -egi, -actum (3), subdue.

subito, *adv.,* suddenly ; at once (ch. **55**).

sublevo (1), relieve, assist.

sublica, -ae, *f.,* pile.

subluo, -ere, -, -lutum (3), wash.

subsequor, -i, -secutus (3 *dep.*), follow up.

subsidium, -i, *n.,* help, succour.

subtraho, -ere, -traxi, -tractum (3), draw away from below ; undermine.

subvectio, -onis, *f.,* conveyance, transport.

subvenio, -ire, -veni, -ventum (4), come to help *or* aid, assist (*with dat.*).

succedo, -ere, -cessi, -cessum (3), come up (to) ; take the place of (*with dat.*) ; succeed.

succendo, -ere, -di, -sum (3), set fire to.

succumbo, -ere, -cubui, -cubitum (3), give way to (*with dat.*).

succurro, -ere, -curri, -cursum (3), aid, assist (*with dat.*).

sudis, -is, *f.,* stake.

sudor, -oris, *m.,* sweat, labour, toil.

sufficio, -ere, -feci, -fectum, am sufficient *or* adequate (ch. 20).

suffragium, -i, *n.*, vote.

Sulpicius, -i, *m.*, Publius Sulpicius Rufus (*Roman general*).

sum, esse, fui, am.

summa, -ae, *f.*, sum, total : summa imperi, chief command.

summitto, -ere, -misi, -missum (3), put *or* send under ; send up (*in support*).

summoveo, -ere, -movi, -motum (3), dislodge.

summus, -a, -um, highest, top (of) ; supreme, pre-eminent.

sumo, -ere, sumpsi, sumptum (3), take.

superior, -us, higher, upper ; former, earlier.

supero (1), overcome, conquer.

suppeto, -ere, -ivi (-ii), -itum (3), suffice ; last (ch. 77).

supplementum, -i, *n.*, fresh draft (*of troops*).

supplicatio, -onis, *f.*, thanksgiving.

supplicium, -i, *n.*, punishment.

supporto (1), bring up, convey.

supra, *adv., and prep with acc.*, above.

suscipio, -ere, -cepi, -ceptum, undertake.

suspicio, -onis, *f.*, suspicion.

sustento (1), support, endure.

sustineo, -ere, -tinui, -tentum (2), withstand.

suus, -a, -um, his, her, its, their own.

tabernaculum, -i, *n.*, tent.

talea, -ae, *f.*, log.

talis, -e, such, of such a kind.

tam, *adv.*, so.

tamen, *adv.*, yet, however ; after all.

tametsi, *adv.*, although.

tandem, *adv.*, at length.

tantulus, -a, -um, so small.

tantum, *adv.*, so much, so far ; tantum ... quantum, as far ... as.

tantumdem, *adv.*, just so much.

tantus, -a, -um, so great, so much.

tardo (1), delay, hinder.

tectum, -i, *n.*, roof.

tego, -ere, texi, tectum (3), cover; shelter (ch. **62**).

telum, -i, *n.,* javelin, missile.

temere, *adv.,* rashly, recklessly.

temeritas, -atis, *f.,* rashness, recklessness.

tempestas, -atis, *f.,* season, storm; opportunity (ch. **27**).

tempto (1), try, attempt; test (ch. **73**).

tempus, -oris, *n.,* time, season; weather.

tendo, -ere, tetendi, tensum *or* **tentum** (3), stretch out; pitch (*of tents*).

tenebrae, -arum, *f. pl.,* darkness.

teneo, -ere, tenui, tentum (2), hold, occupy.

tenuitas, -atis, *f.,* scarcity, poverty.

teres, -etis, smooth.

tergum, -i, *n.,* back, rear.

terni, -ae, -a, three each *or* apiece.

terra, -ae, *f.,* earth, ground; land.

terreo (2), frighten, scare.

territo (1), frighten, terrify.

terror, -oris, *m.,* alarm, panic.

tertius, -a, -um, third.

testis, -is, *c.,* witness.

testudo, -inis, *f.,* (tortoise); mantlet; locked shields formation (ch. **85**).

tertius decimus, -a, -um, thirteenth.

Teutomatus, -i, *m.,* Teutomatus (*Gallic chieftain*).

Teutoni, -orum, *m. pl.,* the Teutoni (*German people*).

timeo (2), fear, am afraid.

timor, -oris, *m.,* fear.

Titus, -i, *m.,* Titus (*Roman praenomen*).

tolero (1), support (*life*).

tollo, -ere, sustuli, sublatum (3), raise (*of shouts*); remove (chs. **14, 28**).

Tolosates, -um, *m. pl.,* the Tolosates (*Gallic tribe*).

tormentum, -i, *n.,* windlass (chs. **22, 81**); torture (ch. **4**).

tot, *indecl.,* so many.

totidem, *adv.,* so many times.

totus, -a, -um, whole.

trabs, -is, *f.,* beam, baulk.

trado, -ere, -didi, -ditum (3), hand over; introduce (ch. **39**); relate.

traduco, -ere, -duxi, -ductum (3), lead over, carry across.

traicio, -ere, -ieci, -iectum, pierce through, strike, transfix.

trans, *prep. with acc.,* across.

Transalpinus, -a, -um, Transalpine.

transcendo, -ere, -di, -sum (3), climb over, board.

transeo, -ire, -ii, -itum, cross.

transfero, -ferre, -tuli, -latum, transfer.

transfigo, -figere, -fixi, -fixum (3), pierce.

transfodio, -ere, -fodi, -fossum, transfix; impale (ch. **82**).

transgredior, -i, -gressus (*dep.*), step across.

transitus, -us, *m.,* passage, crossing.

transmitto, -ere, -misi, -missum (3), send across.

transporto (1), convey across.

Trebonius, -i, *m.,* Gaius Trebonius (*Roman general*).

trecenti, -ae, -a, three hundred.

tres, tria, three.

Treveri, -orum, *m. pl.,* the Treveri (*Gallic tribe*).

tribunus, -i, *m.,* a military tribune.

tribuo, -ere, -ui, -utum (3), assign, attribute.

triduum, -i, *n.,* space of three days.

triginta, thirty.

trini, -ae, -a, three each *or* apiece.

tripertito, *adv.,* in three divisions.

truncus, -i, *m.,* trunk.

tuba, -ae, *f.,* trumpet.

tueor (2 *dep.*), protect, defend.

Tullius, -i, *m.,* Quintus Tullius Cicero (*Roman general*).

tum, *adv.,* then; **cum ... tum,** not only ... but also.

tumultuor (1 *dep.*), make a bustle *or* disturbance.

tumultuose, *adv.,* noisily.

tumultus, -us, *m.,* tumult, confusion.

turma, -ae, *f.,* squadron (*of cavalry*).

Turoni, -orum, *m. pl.,* the Turoni (*Gallic tribe*).

turpis, -e, base, disgraceful.

turpiter, *adv.,* disgracefully.

turris, -is, *f.,* tower.

tuto, *adv.*, safely.
tutus, -a, -um, safe.

ubi, *adv.*, where, when ; **ubi primum**, as soon as.
ubicumque, *adv.*, wherever.
ubique, *adv.*, wherever.
ullus, -a, -um, any.
ulterior, -us, outer, more remote.
ultimus, -a, -um, last, most remote.
ultro, *adv.*, actually.
ululatus, -us, *m.*, howling.
umerus, -i, *m.*, shoulders.
umquam, *adv.*, ever.
una, *adv.*, together ; simultaneously (chs. **67, 87**) ; with him (ch. **38**).
undecim, eleven.
undique, *adv.*, on *or* from all sides.
universus, -a, -um, all, all together.
unus, -a, -um, one, alone ; **ad unum**, to a man.
urbanus, -a, -um, of *or* in the city (*i.e.* Rome).
urbs, **urbis**, *f.*, city.
usitatus, -a, -um, customary ; employed (ch. **22**).
usque, *adv.*, even (to), right up (to).
usus, -us, *m.*, use ; need, necessity (ch. **80**).
ut, **uti**, *conj.*, *with subj.*, in order that ; that ; *with indic.*, as, when ; inasmuch (ch. **68**).
uterque, -traque, -trumque, each (*of two*) ; both.
uti, *see* ut.
utilis, -e, useful, serviceable.
utilitas, -atis, *f.*, use, usefulness.
utor, -i, usus (3 *dep.*), *with abl.*, use ; experience.
utrimque, *adv.*, on both sides.
uxor, -oris, *f.*, wife.

vacuus, -a, -um, empty, unoccupied.
vadum, -i, *n.*, ford ; **vado transiri**, to be forded (chs. **35, 55**).
vagor (1 *dep.*), wander, patrol.
valeo (2), am strong, able ; have influence.

Valerius, -i, *m.*, Gaius Valerius Donnotaurus (*chieftain of the Helvii*).

Valetiacus, -i, *m.*, Valetiacus (*an Aeduan, brother of Cotus*).

valetudo, -inis, *f.*, health.

valles, -is, *f.*, valley.

vallum, -i, *n.*, rampart, stockade.

vallus, -i, *m.*, stake.

varietas, -atis, *f*, variety.

varius, -a, -um, various.

vehemente, *adv.*, greatly, much.

vel, *conj.*, or ; **vel . . . vel,** either . . . or ; *adv.*, even.

Veliocassi, -orum, *m. pl.*, the Veliocassi (*Gallic tribe*).

Vellaunodunum, -i, *n.*, Vellaunodunum (*town of the Senones*).

Vellavii, -orum, *m. pl.*, the Vellavii (*Gallic tribe*).

Venelli, -orum, *m. pl.*, the Venelli (*Gallic tribe*).

Veneti, -orum, *m. pl.*, the Veneti (*one of the Aremoric tribes*).

venia, -ae, *f.*, permission.

venio, -ire, veni, ventum (4), come.

Vercassivellaunus, -i, *m.*, Vercassivellaunus.

Vercingetorix, -igis, *m.*, Vercingetorix.

vereor (2 *dep.*), fear, am afraid.

vero, *adv.*, in truth, really.

versor (1 *dep.*), am occupied ; am busy (ch. **77**).

versus, *adv.*, and *prep. with acc.*, towards.

verto, -ere, -ti, -sum (3), turn ; **terga vertere,** to turn and flee.

vesper, -eri, *m.*, evening.

vester, -tra, -trum, yours, of you.

vestigium, -i, *n.*, footstep ; instant.

vestio (4), clothe.

vestis, -is, *f.*, garment, clothing.

vestitus, -us, *m.*, cloak.

veto, -are, -ui, -itum (1), forbid.

vetus, -eris, old ; long-standing.

via, -ae, *f.*, way, road.

vicis, *f.*, (*no nom.*), change, turn ; **in vicem,** in turn.

victor, -oris, victorious ; *as noun*, victor, conqueror.

victoria, -ae, *f.*, victory.

vicus, -i, *m.*, village, hamlet.

video, -ere, vidi, visum (2), see ; *in pass.*, am seen, seem.

Vienna, -ae, *f.*, Vienna (*modern Vienne*).

vigilia, -ae, *f.*, watch.

viginti, twenty.

vimen, -inis, *n.,*, twig, osier.

vinco, -ere, vici, victum (3), conquer.

vinculum, -i, *n.*, chain.

vindico (1), assert (*liberty*).

vinea, -ae, *f.*, penthouse, shed.

vir, viri, *m.*, man.

virgultum, -i, *n.*, twig ; brushwood.

Viridomarus, -i, *m.*, Viridomarus (*an Aeduan*).

viritim, *adv.*, man by man.

virtus, -utis, *f.*, valour, courage, energy.

vis, vim, vi, *pl.*, **vires, virium,** *f.*, violence, force ; *in pl.*, strength,

vita, -ae, *f.*, life.

vivus, -a, -um, alive.

vix, *adv.*, scarcely, with difficulty.

voco (1), call, summon ; invite (ch. 32).

Volcae, -arum, *m. pl.*, the Volcae Arecomici (*Gallic tribe*).

volo, velle, volui, wish.

voluntas, -atis, *f.*, will ; *in pl.*, goodwill (ch. 10).

vos, vestrum, *person. pronoun*, you.

vox, vocis, *f.*, voice.

vulgo, *adv.*, commonly.

vulgus, -i, *n.*, the people.

vulnero (1), wound.

vulnus, -eris, *n.*, wound.

CPSIA information can be obtained at www.ICGtesting.com
Printed in the USA
LVOW04s1758020715

444775LV00009B/117/P